LEVEL I SCHWESER'S SECRET

SCHWESER'S SECRET SAUCE®: 2016 LEVEL I CFA®

©2015 Kaplan, Inc. All rights reserved.

Published in 2015 by Kaplan Schweser.

Printed in the United States of America.

ISBN: 978-1-4754-3631-0

PPN: 3200-7005

FOREWORD

This book will be a valuable addition to the study tools of any CFA exam candidate. It offers a very concise and very readable explanation of the major parts of the Level I CFA curriculum. Here is the disclaimer: this book does not cover every Learning Outcome Statement (LOS) and, as you are aware, any LOS is "fair game" for the exam. We have tried to include those LOS that are key concepts in finance and accounting, have application to other LOS, are complex and difficult for candidates, require memorization of characteristics or relationships, or are a prelude to LOS at Levels II and III.

We suggest you use this book as a companion to your other, more comprehensive study materials. It is easier to carry with you and will allow you to study these key concepts, definitions, and techniques over and over, which is an important part of mastering the material. When you get to topics where the coverage here appears too brief or raises questions in your mind, this is your clue to go back to your SchweserNotes™ or the textbooks to fill in the gaps in your understanding. For the great majority of you, there is no shortcut to learning the very broad array of subjects covered by the Level I curriculum, but this volume should be a very valuable tool for learning and reviewing the material as you progress in your studies over the months leading up to exam day.

Pass rates have recently been between 35% and 45%, and returning Level I candidates make comments such as, "I was surprised at how difficult the exam was." You should not despair because of this, but you should definitely not underestimate the task at hand. Our study materials, practice exams, question bank, videos, seminars, and *Secret Sauce* are all designed to help you study as efficiently as possible, help you to grasp and retain the material, and apply it with confidence come exam day.

Best regards,

Doug Van Eaton

Dr. Doug Van Eaton, CFA
SVP of CFA Education and Level I Manager

Craig S. Prochaska

Craig S. Prochaska, CFA
Content Specialist

Kaplan Schweser

ETHICAL AND PROFESSIONAL STANDARDS

Weight on Exam	15%
SchweserNotes™ Reference	Book 1, Pages 1–52

Ethics is 15% of the Level I examination and is extremely important to your overall success (remember, you can fail a topic area and still pass the exam, but we wouldn't recommend failing Ethics). Ethics can be tricky, and small details can be important on some ethics questions. Be prepared.

In addition to starting early, study the ethics material more than once. Ethics is one of the keys to passing the exam.

STANDARDS OF PRACTICE HANDBOOK
Cross-Reference to CFA Institute Assigned Readings #1 & 2

We recommend you read the original *Standards of Practice Handbook*. Although we are very proud of our reviews of the ethics material, there are *two* reasons we recommend you read the original *Standards of Practice Handbook* (*11th Ed., 2014*). (1) You are a CFA® candidate. As such, you have pledged to abide by the CFA Institute® Standards. (2) Most of the ethics questions will likely come directly from the text and examples in the *Standards of Practice Handbook*. You will be much better off if you read both our summaries of the Standards *and* the original Handbook and all the examples presented in it.

The CFA Institute Professional Conduct Program is covered by the CFA Institute Bylaws and the Rules of Procedure for Proceedings Related to Professional Conduct. The Disciplinary Review Committee of the CFA Institute Board of Governors has overall responsibility for the Professional Conduct Program and enforcement of the Code and Standards.

CFA Institute, through the Professional Conduct staff, conducts inquiries related to professional conduct. Several circumstances can prompt such an inquiry:

- Self-disclosure by members or candidates on their annual Professional Conduct Statements of involvement in civil litigation or a criminal investigation, or that the member or candidate is the subject of a written complaint.

- Written complaints about a member or candidate's professional conduct that are received by the Professional Conduct staff.
- Evidence of misconduct by a member or candidate that the Professional Conduct staff received through public sources, such as a media article or broadcast.
- A report by a CFA exam proctor of a possible violation during the examination.
- Analysis of exam scores and materials and monitoring of websites and social media by CFA Institute.

Once an inquiry is begun, the Professional Conduct staff may request (in writing) an explanation from the subject member or candidate, and may:

- Interview the subject member or candidate.
- Interview the complainant or other third parties.
- Collect documents and records relevant to the investigation.

The Professional Conduct staff may decide:

- That no disciplinary sanctions are appropriate.
- To issue a cautionary letter.
- To discipline the member or candidate.

In a case where the Professional Conduct staff finds a violation has occurred and proposes a disciplinary sanction, the member or candidate may accept or reject the sanction. If the member or candidate chooses to reject the sanction, the matter will be referred to a panel of CFA Institute members for a hearing. Sanctions imposed may include condemnation by the member's peers or suspension of the candidate's continued participation in the CFA Program.

Code and Standards

Questions about the Code and Standards will most likely be application questions. You will be given a situation and be asked to identify whether or not a violation occurs, what the violation is, or what the appropriate course of action should be. You are not required to know the Standards by number, just by name.

One of the first Learning Outcome Statements (LOS) in the Level I curriculum is to state the six components of the Code of Ethics. Candidates should *memorize* the Code of Ethics.

Members of the CFA Institute [including Chartered Financial Analyst® (CFA®) charterholders] and candidates for the CFA designation (Members and Candidates) must:

- Act with integrity, competence, diligence, and respect and in an ethical manner with the public, clients, prospective clients, employers, employees, colleagues in the investment profession, and other participants in the global capital markets.
- Place the integrity of the investment profession and the interests of clients above their own personal interests.
- Use reasonable care and exercise independent, professional judgment when conducting investment analysis, making investment recommendations, taking investment actions, and engaging in other professional activities.
- Practice and encourage others to practice in a professional and ethical manner that will reflect credit on themselves and the profession.
- Promote the integrity and viability of the global capital markets for the ultimate benefit of society.
- Maintain and improve their professional competence and strive to maintain and improve the competence of other investment professionals.

STANDARDS OF PROFESSIONAL CONDUCT

The following is a list of the Standards of Professional Conduct. Candidates should focus on the purpose of the Standard, applications of the Standard, and proper procedures of compliance for each Standard.

The following is intended to offer a useful summary of the current Standards of Practice, but certainly does not take the place of careful reading of the Standards themselves, the guidance for implementing the Standards, and the examples in the Handbook.

1. Know the law relevant to your position.
   - Comply with the most strict law or Standard that applies to you.
   - Don't solicit gifts.
   - Don't compromise your objectivity or independence.
   - Use reasonable care.
   - Don't lie, cheat, or steal.
   - Don't continue association with others who are breaking laws, rules, or regulations.
   - Don't use others' work or ideas without attribution.
   - Don't guarantee investment results or say that past results will be certainly repeated.
   - Don't do things outside of work that reflect poorly on your integrity or professional competence.

2. Do not act or cause others to act on material nonpublic information.
   - Do not manipulate market prices or trading volume with the intent to mislead others.

3. Act solely for the benefit of your client and know to whom a fiduciary duty is owed with regard to trust accounts and retirement accounts.
   - Treat clients fairly by attempting simultaneous dissemination of investment recommendations and changes.
   - Do not personally take shares in oversubscribed IPOs.

   When in an advisory relationship:
   - Know your client.
   - Make suitable recommendations/take suitable investment action (in a total portfolio context).
   - Preserve confidential client information unless it concerns illegal activity.
   - Do not try to mislead with performance presentation.
   - Vote nontrivial proxies in clients' best interests.

4. Act for the benefit of your employer.
   - Do not harm your employer.
   - Obtain written permission to compete with your employer or to accept additional compensation from clients contingent on future performance.
   - Disclose (to employer) any gifts from clients.
   - Don't take material with you when you leave employment (you can take what is in your brain).
   - Supervisors must take action to both prevent *and* detect violations.
   - Don't take supervisory responsibility if you believe procedures are inadequate.

5. Thoroughly analyze investments.
   - Have reasonable basis.
   - Keep records.
   - Tell clients about investment process, including its risks and limitations.
   - Distinguish between facts and opinions.
   - Review the quality of third-party research and the services of external advisers.
   - In quantitative models, consider what happens when their inputs are outside the normal range.

6. Disclose potential conflicts of interest (let others judge the effects of any conflict for themselves).
   - Disclose referral arrangements.
   - Client transactions come before employer transactions which come before personal transactions.
   - Treat clients who are family members just like any client.

©2015 Kaplan, Inc.

7. Don't cheat on *any* exams (or help others to).
    *   Don't reveal CFA exam questions or disclose what topics were tested or not tested.
    *   Don't use your Society position or any CFA Institute position or responsibility to *improperly* further your personal or professional goals.
    *   Don't use the CFA designation improperly (it is *not* a noun).
    *   Don't put CFA in bold or bigger font than your name.
    *   Don't put CFA in a pseudonym that conceals your identity, such as a social media account name.
    *   Don't imply or say that holders of the CFA Charter produce better investment results.
    *   Don't claim that passing all exams on the first try makes you a better investment manager than others.
    *   Don't claim CFA candidacy unless registered for the next exam or awaiting results.
    *   There is no such thing as a CFA Level I (or II, or III).

My goodness! What *can* you do?

*   You can use information from recognized statistical sources without attribution.
*   You can be wrong (as long as you had a reasonable basis at the time).
*   You can use several pieces of nonmaterial, nonpublic information to construct your investment recommendations (mosaic theory).
*   You can do large trades that may affect market prices as long as the intent of the trade is not to mislead market participants.
*   You can say that Treasury securities are without default risk.
*   You can always seek the guidance of your supervisor, compliance officer, or outside counsel.
*   You can get rid of records after seven years.
*   You can accept gifts from clients and referral fees as long as properly disclosed.
*   You can call your biggest clients first (after fair distribution of investment recommendation or change).
*   You can accept compensation from a company to write a research report if you disclose the relationship and nature of compensation.
*   You can get drunk when not at work and commit misdemeanors that do not involve fraud, theft, or deceit.
*   You can say you have passed the Level I, II, or III CFA exam (if you really have).
*   You can accurately describe the nature of the examination process and the requirements to earn the right to use the CFA designation.

Global Investment Performance Standards (GIPS®)
Cross-Reference to CFA Institute Assigned Readings #3 & 4

Performance presentation is an area of constantly growing importance in the investment management field and an important part of the CFA curriculum. Repeated exposure is the best way to learn the material. GIPS appears to be relatively easy, but still requires a reasonable amount of time for it to sink in.

GIPS were created to provide a uniform framework for presenting historical performance results for investment management firms to serve existing and prospective clients. Compliance with GIPS is voluntary, but partial compliance cannot be referenced. There is only one acceptable statement for those firms that claim complete compliance with GIPS.

To claim compliance, a firm must present GIPS-compliant results for a minimum of five years or since firm inception. The firm must be clearly defined as the distinct business entity or subsidiary that is held out to clients in marketing materials. Performance is presented for "composites" which must include all fee-paying discretionary account portfolios with a similar investment strategy, objective, or mandate. After reporting five years of compliant data, one year of compliant data must be added each year to a minimum of ten years.

The idea of GIPS is to provide and gain global acceptance of a set of standards that will result in consistent, comparable, and accurate performance presentation information that will promote fair competition among, and complete disclosure by, investment management firms.

Verification is voluntary and is not required to be GIPS compliant. Independent verification provides assurance that GIPS have been applied correctly on a firm-wide basis. Firms that have had compliance verified are encouraged to disclose that they have done so, but must include periods for which verification was done.

There are nine major sections of the GIPS, which include:

0. Fundamentals of Compliance.

1. Input Data.

2. Calculation Methodology.

3. Composite Construction.

4. Disclosures.

5. Presentation and Reporting.

6. Real Estate.

7. Private Equity.

8. Wrap Fee/Separately Managed Account (SMA) Portfolios.

Fundamentals of Compliance

GIPS must be applied on a firm-wide basis. Total firm assets are the market value of all accounts (fee-paying or not, discretionary or not). Firm performance will include the performance of any subadvisors selected by the firm, and changes in the organization of the firm will not affect historical GIPS performance.

Firms are encouraged to use the broadest definition of the firm and include all offices marketed under the same brand name. Firms must have written documentation of all procedures to comply with GIPS.

The only permitted statement of compliance is "XYZ has prepared and presented this report in compliance with the Global Investment Performance Standards (GIPS)." There may be no claim that methodology or performance calculation of any composite or account is in compliance with GIPS (except in communication to clients about their individual accounts by a GIPS compliant firm).

The firm must provide every potential client with a compliant presentation. The firm must present a list of composites for the firm and descriptions of those composites (including composites discontinued less than five years ago) to prospective clients *upon request*. Firms are encouraged to comply with recommended portions of GIPS and must comply with updates and clarifications to GIPS.

Current recommendations that will become requirements are: (1) quarterly valuation of real estate, (2) portfolio valuation on the dates of all large cash flows (to or from the account), (3) month-end valuation of all accounts, and (4) monthly asset-weighting of portfolios within composites, not including carve-out returns in any composite for a single asset class.

QUANTITATIVE METHODS

Weight on Exam	12%
SchweserNotes™ Reference	Book 1, Pages 53–324

STUDY SESSION 2: QUANTITATIVE METHODS—BASIC CONCEPTS

THE TIME VALUE OF MONEY
Cross-Reference to CFA Institute Assigned Reading #5

Understanding time value of money (TVM) computations is essential for success not only for quantitative methods, but also other sections of the Level I exam. TVM is actually a larger portion of the exam than simply quantitative methods because of its integration with other topics. For example, any portion of the exam that requires discounting cash flows will require TVM calculations. This includes evaluating capital projects, using dividend discount models for stock valuation, valuing bonds, and valuing real estate investments. No matter where TVM shows up on the exam, the key to any TVM problem is to draw a timeline and be certain of when the cash flows will occur so you can discount those cash flows appropriately.

An interest rate can be interpreted as a required rate of return, a discount rate, or as an opportunity cost; but it is essentially the price (time value) of money for one period. When viewed as a required (equilibrium) rate of return on an investment, a nominal interest rate consists of a real risk-free rate, a premium for expected inflation, and other premiums for sources of risk specific to the investment, such as uncertainty about amounts and timing of future cash flows from the investment.

Interest rates are often stated as simple annual rates, even when compounding periods are shorter than one year. With m compounding periods per year and a stated annual rate of i, the effective annual rate is calculated by compounding the periodic rate (i/m) over m periods (the number of periods in one year).

$$\text{effective annual rate} = \left(1 + \frac{i}{m}\right)^m - 1$$

compounding periods

With a stated annual rate of 12% (0.12) and monthly compounding, the effective

$$\text{rate} = \left(1 + \frac{0.12}{12}\right)^{12} - 1 = 12.68\%$$

Future value (FV) is the amount to which an investment grows after one or more compounding periods.

- *Compounding* is the process used to determine the future value of a current amount.
- The *periodic rate* is the nominal rate (stated in annual terms) divided by the number of compounding periods (i.e., for quarterly compounding, divide the annual rate by four).
- The *number of compounding periods* is equal to the number of years multiplied by the frequency of compounding (i.e., for quarterly compounding, multiply the number of years by four).

$$\text{future value} = \text{present value} \times (1 + \text{periodic rate})^{\text{number of compounding periods}}$$

Present value (PV) is the current value of some future cash flow.

- *Discounting* is the process used to determine the present value of some future amount.
- *Discount rate* is the periodic rate used in the discounting process.

$$\text{present value} = \frac{\text{future value}}{(1 + \text{periodic rate})^{\text{number of compounding periods}}}$$

For *non-annual compounding* problems, divide the interest rate by the number of compounding periods per year, m, and multiply the number of years by the number of compounding periods per year.

An *annuity* is a stream of equal cash flows that occur at equal intervals over a given period. A corporate bond combines an annuity (the equal semiannual coupon payments) with a lump sum payment (return of principal at maturity).

- *Ordinary annuity.* Cash flows occur at the end of each compounding period.
- *Annuity due.* Cash flows occur at the beginning of each period.

Present value of an ordinary annuity. Answers the question: How much would an annuity of $X every (month, week, quarter, year) cost today if the periodic rate is *I*%?

The present value of an annuity is just the sum of the present values of all the payments. Your calculator will do this for you.

- N = number of periods.
- I/Y = interest rate per period.
- PMT = amount of each periodic payment.
- FV = 0.
- Compute (CPT) present value (PV).

In other applications, any four of these variables can be entered in order to solve for the fifth. When both present and future values are entered, they typically must be given different signs in order to calculate N, I/Y, or PMT.

Future value of an ordinary annuity. Just change to PV = 0 and CPT → FV.

If there is a mismatch between the period of the payments and the period for the interest rate, adjust the interest rate to match. Do not add or divide payment amounts. If you have a *monthly payment*, you need a *monthly interest rate*.

Present and Future Value of an Annuity Due

When using the TI calculator in END mode, the PV of an annuity is computed as of t = 0 (one period prior to the first payment date, t = 1) and the FV of an annuity is calculated as of time = N (the date of the last payment). With the TI calculator in BGN mode, the PV of an annuity is calculated as of t = 0 (which is now the date of the first payment) and the FV of an annuity is calculated as of t = N (one period after the last payment). In BGN mode the N payments are assumed to come at the beginning of each of the N periods. An annuity that makes N payments at the beginning of each of N periods, is referred to as an annuity due.

Once you have found the PV(FV) of an ordinary annuity, you can convert the discounted (compound) value to an annuity due value by multiplying by one plus the periodic rate. This effectively discounts (compounds) the ordinary annuity value by one less (more) period.

$$PV_{annuity\ due} = PV_{ordinary\ annuity} \times (1 + periodic\ rate)$$

$$FV_{annuity\ due} = FV_{ordinary\ annuity} \times (1 + periodic\ rate)$$

Perpetuities are annuities with infinite lives:

$$PV_{perpetuity} = \frac{periodic\ payment}{periodic\ interest\ rate}$$

Preferred stock is an example of a perpetuity (equal payments indefinitely).

Present (future) values of any series of cash flows is equal to the sum of the present (future) values of each cash flow. This means you can break up cash flows any way

©2015 Kaplan, Inc.

that is convenient, take the PV or FV of the pieces, and add them up to get the PV or FV of the whole series of cash flows.

DISCOUNTED CASH FLOW APPLICATIONS
Cross-Reference to CFA Institute Assigned Reading #6

Net Present Value (NPV) of an Investment Project

For a typical investment or capital project, the NPV is simply the present value of the expected future cash flows, minus the initial cost of the investment. The steps in calculating an NPV are:

- *Identify* all outflows/inflows associated with the investment.
- *Determine* discount rate appropriate for the investment.
- *Find PV* of the future cash flows. Inflows are positive and outflows are negative.
- *Compute* the sum of all the discounted future cash flows.
- *Subtract* the initial cost of the investment or capital project.

$$NPV = \frac{CF_1}{(1+r)} + \frac{CF_2}{(1+r)^2} + ... + \frac{CF_{t-1}}{(1+r)^{t-1}} + \frac{CF_t}{(1+r)^t} - NI$$

where:
CF_t = the expected net cash flow at time t
r = the discount rate = opportunity cost of capital
NI = the net (time = 0) investment in the project

With uneven cash flows, use the CF function.

Computing IRR

IRR is the discount rate that equates the PV of cash inflows with the PV of the cash outflows. This also makes IRR the discount rate that results in NPV equal to zero. In other words, the IRR is the r that, when plugged into the above NPV equation, makes the NPV equal zero.

When given a set of equal cash inflows, such as an annuity, calculate IRR by solving for I/Y.

When the cash inflows are uneven, use CF function on calculator.

Example:

Project cost is $100, CF_1 = $50, CF_2 = $50, CF_3 = $90. What is the NPV at 10%? What is the IRR of the project?

Answer:

Enter CF0 = –100, C01 = 50, F01 = 2, C02 = 90, F02 = 1.

NPV, 10, enter, ↓, CPT, display 54.395.

IRR, CPT, display 35.71 (%).

NPV vs. IRR

- *NPV decision rule*: For independent projects, adopt all projects with NPV > 0. These projects will increase the value of the firm.
- *IRR decision rule*: For independent projects, adopt all projects with IRR > required project return. These projects will also add value to the firm.

NPV and IRR rules give the same decision for independent projects.

When NPV and IRR rankings differ, rely on NPV for choosing between or among projects.

Money-Weighted vs. Time-Weighted Return Measures

Time-weighted and money-weighted return calculations are standard tools for analysis of portfolio performance.

- *Money-weighted return* is affected by cash flows into and out of an investment account. It is essentially a portfolio IRR.
- *Time-weighted return* is preferred as a manager performance measure because it is not affected by cash flows into and out of an investment account. It is calculated as the geometric mean of subperiod returns.

Various Yield Calculations

Bond-equivalent yield is two times the semiannually compounded yield. This is because U.S. bonds pay interest semiannually rather than annually.

©2015 Kaplan, Inc.

Yield to maturity (YTM) is the IRR on a bond. For a semiannual coupon bond, YTM is two times semiannual IRR. In other words, it is the discount rate that equates the present value of a bond's cash flows with its market price. We will revisit this topic again in the debt section.

Bank discount yield is the annualized percentage discount from face value:

$$\text{bank discount yield} = r_{BD} = \frac{\$\text{discount}}{\text{face value}} \times \frac{360}{\text{days}}$$

Holding period yield (HPY), also called holding period return (HPR):

$$\text{holding period yield} = \text{HPY} = \frac{P_1 - P_0 + D_1}{P_0} \text{ or } \frac{P_1 + D_1}{P_0} - 1$$

For common stocks, the cash distribution (D_1) is the dividend. For bonds, the cash distribution is the interest payment.

HPR for a given investment can be calculated for any time period (day, week, month, or year) simply by changing the end points of the time interval over which values and cash flows are measured.

Effective annual yield converts a *t*-day holding period yield to a compound annual yield based on a 365-day year:

$$\text{effective annual yield} = \text{EAY} = (1 + \text{HPY})^{365/t} - 1$$

Notice the similarity of EAY to *effective annual rate:*

$$\text{EAR} = (1 + \text{periodic rate})^m - 1$$

where *m* is the number of compounding periods per year and the periodic rate is the stated annual rate/m.

Money market yield is annualized (without compounding) based on a 360-day year:

$$\text{money market yield} = r_{MM} = \text{HPY} \times \frac{360}{t}$$

EAY and r_{MM} are two ways to annualize an HPY. Different instruments have different conventions for quoting yields. In order to compare the yields on instruments with different yield conventions, you must be able to convert the yields to a common measure. For instance, to compare a T-bill yield and a LIBOR yield, you can convert the T-bill yield from a bank discount yield to a money market yield and compare it to the LIBOR yield (which is already a money market yield). In order to compare yields on other instruments to the yield (to maturity) of a semi-annual pay bond, we simply calculate the effective semiannual yield and double it. A yield calculated in this manner is referred to as a *bond equivalent yield* (BEY).

STATISTICAL CONCEPTS AND MARKET RETURNS
Cross-Reference to CFA Institute Assigned Reading #7

The two key areas you should concentrate on in this reading are measures of central tendency and measures of dispersion. Measures of central tendency include the arithmetic mean, geometric mean, weighted mean, median, and mode. Measures of dispersion include the range, mean absolute deviation, variance, and standard deviation. When describing investments, measures of central tendency provide an indication of an investment's expected value or return. Measures of dispersion indicate the riskiness of an investment (the uncertainty about its future returns or cash flows).

Measures of Central Tendency

Arithmetic mean. A population average is called the population mean (denoted μ). The average of a sample (subset of a population) is called the sample mean (denoted $\bar{x}$). Both the population and sample means are calculated as arithmetic means (simple average). We use the sample mean as a "best guess" approximation of the population mean.

Median. Middle value of a data set, half above and half below. With an even number of observations, median is the average of the two middle observations.

Mode. Value occurring most frequently in a data set. Data set can have more than one mode (bimodal, trimodal, etc.) but only one mean and one median.

Geometric mean:

- Used to calculate compound growth rates.
- If returns are constant over time, geometric mean equals arithmetic mean.
- The greater the variability of returns over time, the greater the difference between arithmetic and geometric mean (arithmetic will always be higher).

- When calculating the geometric mean for a returns series, it is necessary to add one to each value under the radical, and then subtract one from the result.
- The geometric mean is used to calculate the time-weighted return, a performance measure.

$$\text{geometric mean return} = R_G = \sqrt[n]{(1+R_1) \times (1+R_2) \times ... \times (1+R_n)} - 1$$

Example:

A mutual fund had the following returns for the past three years: 15%, –9%, and 13%. What is the arithmetic mean return, the 3-year holding period return, and the average annual compound (geometric mean) return?

Answer:

$$\text{arithmetic mean:} \quad \frac{15\% - 9\% + 13\%}{3} = 6.333\%$$

$$\text{holding period return:} \ 1.15 \times 0.91 \times 1.13 - 1 = 0.183 = 18.3\%$$

$$\text{geometric mean:} \ R_G = \sqrt[3]{(1+0.15) \times (1-0.09) \times (1+0.13)} - 1$$
$$= \sqrt[3]{1.183} - 1 = 1.0575 - 1 = 0.0575 = 5.75\%$$

Geometric mean return is useful for finding the yield on a zero-coupon bond with a maturity of several years or for finding the average annual growth rate of a company's dividend or earnings across several years. Geometric mean returns are a compound return measure.

Weighted mean. Mean in which different observations are given different proportional influence on the mean:

$$\text{weighted mean} = \overline{X}_w = \sum_{i=1}^{n} w_i X_i = (w_1 X_1 + w_2 X_2 + ... + w_n X_n)$$
where:
$X_1, X_2, ..., X_n$ = observed values
$w_1, w_2, ..., w_n$ = corresponding weights for each observation, $\sum w_i = 1$

Weighted means are used to calculate the actual or expected return on a portfolio, given the actual or expected returns for each portfolio asset (or asset class). For portfolio returns, the weights in the formula are the percentages of the total portfolio value invested in each asset (or asset class).

Example: Portfolio return

A portfolio is 20% invested in Stock A, 30% invested in Stock B, and 50% invested in Stock C. Stocks A, B, and C experienced returns of 10%, 15%, and 3%, respectively. Calculate the portfolio return.

Answer:

$$R_p = 0.2(10\%) + 0.3(15\%) + 0.5(3\%) = 8.0\%$$

A weighted mean is also used to calculate the expected return given a probability model. In that case, the weights are simply the probabilities of each outcome.

Example: Expected portfolio return

A portfolio of stocks has a 15% probability of achieving a 35% return, a 25% chance of achieving a 15% return, and a 60% chance of achieving a 10% return. Calculate the expected portfolio return.

Answer:

$$E(R_p) = 0.15(35) + 0.25(15) + 0.60(10) = 5.25 + 3.75 + 6 = 15\%$$

Note that an arithmetic mean is a weighted mean in which all of the weights are equal to $1/n$ (where n is the number of observations).

Measures of Dispersion

Range is the difference between the largest and smallest value in a data set and is the simplest measure of dispersion. You can think of the dispersion as measuring the width of the distribution. The narrower the range, the less dispersion.

For a population, *variance* is defined as the average of the squared deviations from the mean.

Example:

Stocks A, B, and C had returns of 10%, 30%, and 20%, respectively. Calculate the population variance (denoted σ^2) and sample variance (denoted s^2).

Answer:

The process begins the same for population and sample variance.

Step 1: Calculate the mean expected return: $\dfrac{(10+30+20)}{3} = 20$

Step 2: Calculate the squared deviations from the mean and add them together:
$(10-20)^2 + (30-20)^2 + (20-20)^2 = 100 + 100 + 0 = 200$

Step 3: Divide by number of observations (n = 3) for the population variance and by the number of observations minus one for the sample variance:

$$\text{population variance} = \sigma^2 = \frac{200}{3} = 66.67$$

$$\text{sample variance} = s^2 = \frac{200}{3-1} = \frac{200}{2} = 100$$

$$\sigma^2 = \frac{\sum_{i=1}^{N}(X_i - \mu)^2}{N} \qquad\qquad s^2 = \frac{\sum_{i=1}^{n}(X_i - \overline{X})^2}{n-1}$$

Standard deviation is the square root of variance. On the exam, if the question is asking for the standard deviation, do not forget to take the square root!

Coefficient of variation expresses how much dispersion exists relative to the mean of a distribution and allows for direct comparison of the degree of dispersion across different data sets. It measures risk per unit of expected return.

$$CV = \frac{\text{standard deviation of returns}}{\text{mean return}}$$

When comparing two investments using the CV criterion, the one with the lower CV is the better choice.

The *Sharpe ratio* is widely used to evaluate investment performance and measures excess return per unit of risk. Portfolios with large Sharpe ratios are preferred to portfolios with smaller ratios because it is assumed that rational investors prefer higher excess returns (returns in excess of the risk-free rate) and dislike risk.

$$\text{Sharpe ratio} = \frac{\text{excess return}}{\text{risk}} = \frac{R_{portfolio} - R_{risk\text{-}free}}{\sigma_p}$$

If you are given the inputs for the Sharpe ratio for two portfolios and asked to select the best portfolio, calculate the Sharpe ratio, and choose the portfolio with the higher ratio.

Skewness and Kurtosis

Skewness represents the extent to which a distribution is not symmetrical.

A *right-skewed* distribution has positive skew (or skewness) and a mean that is greater than the median, which is greater than the mode.

A *left-skewed* distribution has negative skewness and a mean that is less than the median, which is less than the mode.

The attributes of normal and skewed distributions are summarized in the following illustration.

Figure 1: Skewed Distributions

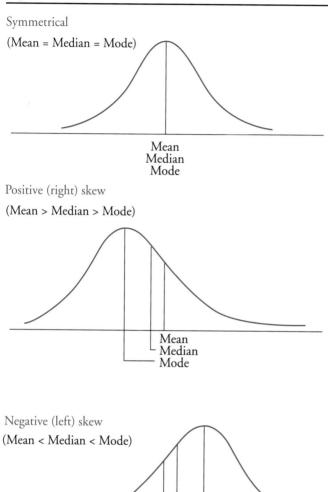

Symmetrical
(Mean = Median = Mode)

Mean
Median
Mode

Positive (right) skew
(Mean > Median > Mode)

Mean
Median
Mode

Negative (left) skew
(Mean < Median < Mode)

Mean
Median
Mode

To remember the relations, think of "pulling on the end" of a normal distribution, which is symmetrical with the mean, median, and mode equal. If you pull on the right or positive end, you get a right-skewed (positively skewed) distribution. If you can remember that adding extreme values at one end of the distribution has the greatest effect on the mean, and doesn't affect the mode or high point of the distribution, you can remember the relations illustrated in the preceding graph.

Kurtosis is a measure of the degree to which a distribution is more or less peaked than a normal distribution, which has kurtosis of 3.

Excess kurtosis is kurtosis relative to that of a normal distribution. A distribution with kurtosis of 4 has excess kurtosis of 1. It is said to have positive excess kurtosis. A distribution with positive excess kurtosis (a leptokurtic distribution) will have more returns clustered around the mean and more returns with large deviations from the mean (fatter tails). In finance, positive excess kurtosis is a significant issue in risk assessment and management, because fatter tails means an increased probability of extreme outcomes, which translates into greater risk.

An illustration of the shapes of normal and leptokurtic distribution is given in the following graph.

Figure 2: Kurtosis

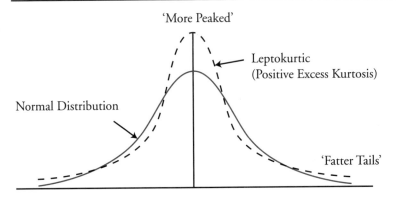

PROBABILITY CONCEPTS
Cross-Reference to CFA Institute Assigned Reading #8

The ability to apply probability rules is important for the exam. Be able to calculate and interpret widely used measures such as expected value, standard deviation, covariance, and correlation.

Important Terms

- *Random variable.* Uncertain quantity/number.
- *Outcome.* Realization of a random variable.
- *Event.* Single outcome or a set of outcomes.
- *Mutually exclusive events.* Cannot both happen at same time.
- *Exhaustive set of events.* Set that includes all possible outcomes.

The probability of any single outcome or event must not be less than zero (will not occur) and must not be greater than one (will occur with certainty). A *probability function* (for a discrete probability distribution) defines the probabilities that each outcome will occur. To have a valid probability function, it must be the case that the sum of the probabilities of any set of outcomes or events that is both mutually exclusive and exhaustive is 1 (it is certain that a random variable will take on one of its possible values). An example of a valid probability function is:

Prob (x) = x/15 for possible outcomes, x = 1, 2, 3, 4, 5

Odds For and Against

If the probability of an event is 20%, it will occur, on average, one out of five times. The "odds for" are 1-to-4 and the "odds against" are 4-to-1.

Multiplication Rule for Joint Probability

$$P(AB) = P(A \mid B) \times P(B) = P(B \mid A) \times P(A)$$

The probability that A and B will both (jointly) occur is the probability of A given that B occurs, multiplied by the (unconditional) probability that B will occur.

Addition Rule

$$P(A \text{ or } B) = P(A) + P(B) - P(AB)$$

If A and B are mutually exclusive, P(AB) is zero and $P(A \text{ or } B) = P(A) + P(B)$

Used to calculate the probability that at least one (one or both) of two events will occur.

Total Probability Rule

$$P(R) = P(R \mid I) \times P(I) + P(R \mid I^C) \times P(I^C)$$

where: I and I^C are *mutually exclusive and an exhaustive set of events* (i.e., if I occurs, then I^C cannot occur and one of the two must occur).

A tree diagram shows a variety of possible outcomes for a random variable, such as an asset price or earnings per share.

Figure 3: A Tree Diagram for an Investment Problem

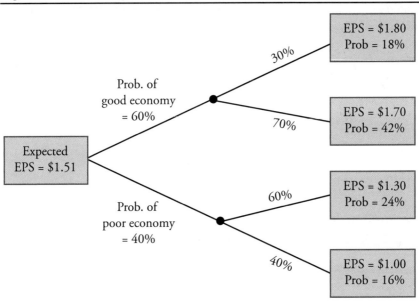

We can illustrate several probability concepts with a tree diagram. The (unconditional) expected EPS is the sum of the possible outcomes, weighted by their probabilities.

$$0.18 \times 1.80 + 0.42 \times 1.70 + 0.24 \times 1.30 + 0.16 \times 1.00 = \$1.51$$

The (conditional) expectation of EPS, given that the economy is good, is $1.73 = 0.3(1.80) + 0.7(1.70)$. Expected EPS, given that the economy is poor, is $0.6(1.30) + 0.4(1.00) = \$1.18$.

The probabilities of each of the EPS outcomes are simply the product of the two probabilities along the (branches) of the tree [e.g., $P(EPS = \$1.80) = 0.6 \times 0.3 = 18\%$].

Covariance

The *covariance* between two variables is a measure of the degree to which the two variables tend to move together. It captures the linear relationship between one random variable and another.

A *positive covariance* indicates that the variables tend to move together; a *negative covariance* indicates that the variables tend to move in opposite directions relative to their means. Covariance indicates the direction of the relationship and does not directly indicate the strength of the relationship. Therefore, if you compare the covariance measures for two sets of (paired) random variables and the second is twice the value of the first, the relationship of the second set isn't necessarily twice as strong as the first because the variance of the variables may be quite different as well.

Example:

Covariance can be calculated using a joint probability table as follows:

	$R_X = 15\%$	$R_X = 10\%$
$R_Y = 20\%$	0.30	0
$R_Y = 5\%$	0	0.70

First, find the expected returns on X and Y:

$$E(R_X) = 0.30(15) + 0.70(10) = 11.5\%$$
$$E(R_Y) = 0.30(20) + 0.70(5) = 9.5\%$$

Next calculate the covariance:

$$Cov(R_X, R_Y) = [0.3(15.0 - 11.5)(20.0 - 9.5)] + [0.7(10.0 - 11.5)(5.0 - 9.5)]$$
$$= 11.025 + 4.725 = 15.75$$

Correlation

The *correlation coefficient, r,* is a standardized measure (unlike covariances) of the strength of the linear relationship between two variables. The correlation coefficient can range from −1 to +1.

$$r = corr(R_i, R_j) = \frac{Cov(R_i, R_j)}{\sigma(R_i)\sigma(R_j)}$$

A correlation of +1 indicates a perfect positive correlation. In that case, knowing the outcome of one random variable would allow you to predict the outcome of the other with certainty.

Expected Return and Variance of a Portfolio of Two Stocks

Know how to compute the *expected return and variance for a portfolio of two assets* using the following formulas:

$$E(R_p) = w_A R_A + w_B R_B$$

$$Var_p = w_A^2 \sigma_A^2 + w_B^2 \sigma_B^2 + 2 w_A w_B \sigma_A \sigma_B \rho_{A,B}$$

$$Var_p = w_A^2 \sigma_A^2 + w_B^2 \sigma_B^2 + 2 w_A w_B Cov_{A,B}$$

Note that $\sigma_A \sigma_B \rho_{A,B} = Cov_{A,B}$ so the formula for variance can be written either way.

STUDY SESSION 3: QUANTITATIVE METHODS—APPLICATIONS

COMMON PROBABILITY DISTRIBUTIONS
Cross-Reference to CFA Institute Assigned Reading #9

Critical topics to understand include the normal distribution and areas under the normal curve, the *t*-distribution, skewness, kurtosis, and the binomial distribution. Be able to calculate confidence intervals for population means based on the normal distribution.

Discrete random variable: A limited (finite) number of possible outcomes and each has a positive probability. They can be counted (e.g., number of days without rain during a month).

Continuous random variable: An infinite number of possible outcomes. The number of inches of rain over a month can take on an infinite number of values, assuming we can measure it with infinite precision. For a continuous random variable, the probability that the random variable will take on any single one (of the infinite number) of the possible values is zero.

Probability function, p(x), specifies the probability that a random variable equals a particular value, *x*.

A *cumulative density function* (CDF), for either a discrete or continuous distribution, gives the probability that a random variable will take on a value *less than or equal to* a specific value, that is, the probability that the value will be between minus infinity and the specified value.

For the function, Prob(x) = x/15 for x = 1, 2, 3, 4, 5, the CDF is:

$$\sum_{x=1}^{X} \frac{x}{15},$$ so that F(3) or Prob (x $\leq$ 3) is 1/15 + 2/15 + 3/15 = 6/15 or 40%

This is simply the sum of the probabilities of 1, 2, and 3. Note that

Prob (x = 3, 4) can be calculated as $F(4) - F(2) = \frac{10}{15} - \frac{3}{15} = \frac{7}{15}$.

Uniform Distributions

With a uniform distribution, the probabilities of the outcomes can be thought of as equal. They are equal for all possible outcomes with a discrete uniform distribution, and equal for equal-sized ranges of a uniform continuous distribution.

For example, consider the *discrete uniform probability distribution* defined as X = {1, 2, 3, 4, 5}, p(x) = 0.2. Here, the probability for each outcome is equal to 0.2 [i.e., p(1) = p(2) = p(3) = p(4) = p(5) = 0.2]. Also, the cumulative distribution function for the *n*th outcome, $F(x_n) = np(x)$, and the probability for a range of outcomes is p(x)k, where *k* is the number of possible outcomes in the range.

A *continuous uniform distribution* over the range of 1 to 5 results in a 25% probability [1 / (5 – 1)] that the random variable will take on a value between 1 and 2, 2 and 3, 3 and 4, or 4 and 5, since 1 is one-quarter of the total range of the random variable.

The Binomial Distribution

A **binomial random variable** may be defined as the number of "successes" in a given number of trials where the outcome can be either "success" or "failure." You can recognize problems based on a binomial distribution from the fact that there are only two possible outcomes (e.g., the probability that a stock index will rise over a day's trading). The probability of success, *p*, is constant for each trial, the trials are independent, and the probability of failure (no success) is simply 1 – p. A binomial distribution is used to calculate the number of successes in *n* trials. The probability of *x* successes in *n* trials is:

$$p(x) = P(X = x) = (_nC_r)p^x(1 - p)^{n-x}$$

and the expected number of successes is *np*.

If the probability of a stock index increasing each day (*p*) is 60%, the probability (assuming independence) that the index will increase on exactly three of the next five days (and not increase on two days) is $(_5C_3)0.6^3(1 - 0.6)^2 = 0.3456$.

A binomial tree to describe possible stock price movement for n periods shows the probabilities for each possible number of successes over n periods. Additionally, assuming that the stock price over any single period will either increase by a factor U or decrease by a factor $1/U$, a binomial tree shows the possible n-period outcomes for the stock price and the probabilities that each will occur.

Normal Distribution: Properties

- Completely described by mean and variance.
- Symmetric about the mean (skewness = 0).
- Kurtosis (a measure of peakedness) = 3.
- Linear combination of jointly, normally distributed random variables is also normally distributed.

Many properties of the normal distribution are evident from examining the graph of a normal distribution's probability density function:

Figure 4: Normal Distribution Probability Density Function

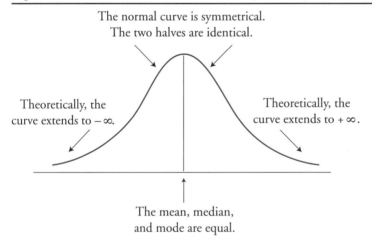

The normal curve is symmetrical.
The two halves are identical.

Theoretically, the curve extends to $-\infty$.

Theoretically, the curve extends to $+\infty$.

The mean, median, and mode are equal.

Calculating Probabilities Using the Standard Normal Distribution

The *z-value* "standardizes" an observation from a normal distribution and represents the number of standard deviations a given observation is from the population mean.

$$z = \frac{\text{observation} - \text{population mean}}{\text{standard deviation}} = \frac{x - \mu}{\sigma}$$

Confidence Intervals: Normal Distribution

A *confidence interval* is a range of values around an expected outcome within which we expect the actual outcome to occur some specified percentage of the time.

The following graph illustrates confidence intervals for a standard normal distribution, which has a mean of 0 and a standard deviation of 1. We can interpret the values on the x-axis as the number of standard deviations from the mean. Thus, for any normal distribution we can say, for example, that 68% of the outcomes will be within one standard deviation of the mean. This would be referred to as a 68% confidence interval.

Figure 5: The Standard Normal Distribution and Confidence Intervals

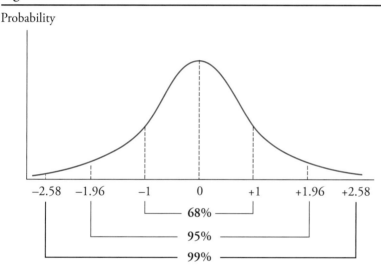

Be prepared to calculate a confidence interval on the Level I exam. Consider a normal distribution with mean μ and standard deviation σ. Each observation has an expected value of μ. If we draw a sample of size n from the distribution, the mean of the sample has an expected value of μ. The larger the sample, the closer to μ we expect the sample mean to be. The standard deviation of the means of samples of size n is simply $\sigma / \sqrt{n}$ and is called standard error of the sample mean. This allows us to construct a confidence interval for the sample mean for a sample of size n.

Example:

Calculate a 95% confidence interval for the mean of a sample of size 25 drawn from a normal distribution with a mean of 8 and a standard deviation of 4.

Answer:

The standard deviation of the means of samples of size 25 is:

$$\frac{4}{\sqrt{25}} = \frac{4}{5} = 0.8$$

A 95% confidence interval will extend 1.96 standard deviations above and below the mean, so our 95% confidence interval is:

$8 \pm 1.96 \times 0.8$, 6.432 to 9.568

We believe the mean of a sample of 25 observations will fall within this interval 95% of the time.

With a known variance, the formula for a confidence interval is:

$$\bar{x} \pm z_{\alpha/2} \frac{\sigma}{\sqrt{n}}$$

In other words, the confidence interval is equal to the mean value, plus or minus the z-score that corresponds to the given significance level multiplied by the standard error.

- Confidence intervals and z-scores are very important in hypothesis testing, a topic that will be reviewed shortly.

Shortfall Risk and Safety-First Ratio

Shortfall risk. The probability that a portfolio's return or value will be below a specified (target) return or value over a specified period.

Roy's safety-first criterion states that the optimal portfolio minimizes the probability that the return of the portfolio falls below some minimum acceptable "threshold" level.

Roy's safety-first ratio (SFRatio) is similar to the Sharpe ratio. In fact, the Sharpe ratio is a special case of Roy's ratio where the "threshold" level is the risk-free rate of return.

Under both the Sharpe and Roy criteria, the best portfolio is the one that has the largest ratio.

Roy's safety-first ratio can be calculated as:

$$\text{SFRatio} = \frac{E\left(R_p\right) - R_L}{\sigma_p}$$

With approximate normality of returns, the SFR is like a *t*-statistic. It shows how many standard deviations the expected return is above the threshold return (R_L). The greater the SFR, the lower the probability that returns will be below the threshold return (i.e., the lower the shortfall risk).

Lognormal Distribution

If *x* is normally distributed, $Y = e^x$ is lognormally distributed. Values of a lognormal distribution are always positive so it is used to model asset prices (rather than rates of return, which can be negative). The lognormal distribution is positively skewed as shown in the following figure.

Figure 6: Lognormal Distribution

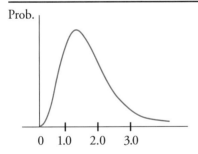

Continuously Compounded Returns

If we increase the number of compounding periods (*n*) for an annual rate of return, the limit as *n* goes toward infinity is continuous compounding. For a specific holding period return (HPR), the relation to the continuously compounded return (CCR) over the holding period is as follows:

$$CCR = \ln(1+HPR) = \ln\left(\frac{\text{ending value}}{\text{beginning value}}\right)$$

$$HPR = \frac{\text{ending value}}{\text{beginning value}} - 1 = e^{CCR} - 1$$

When the holding period is one year, so that HPR is also the effective annual return, CCR is the annual continuously compounded rate of return.

One property of continuously compounded rates is that they are additive over multiple periods. If the continuously compounded rate of return is 8%, the holding period return over a 2-year horizon is $e^{2(0.08)} - 1$, and $1,000 will grow to $1,000\ e^{2.5(0.08)}$ over two and one-half years.

Simulation

Historical simulation of outcomes (e.g., changes in portfolio values) is done by randomly selecting changes in price or risk factors from actual (historical) past changes in these factors and modeling the effects of these changes on the value of a current portfolio. The results of historical simulation have limitations since future changes may not necessarily be distributed as past changes were.

Monte Carlo simulation is performed by making assumptions about the distributions of prices or risk factors and using a large number of computer-generated random values for the relevant risk factors or prices to generate a distribution of possibly outcomes (e.g., project NPVs, portfolio values). The simulated distributions can only be as accurate as the assumptions about the distributions of and correlations between the input variables assumed in the procedure.

SAMPLING AND ESTIMATION
Cross-Reference to CFA Institute Assigned Reading #10

Know the methods of sampling, sampling biases, and the central limit theorem, which allows us to use sampling statistics to construct confidence intervals around point estimates of population means.

- *Sampling error*: Difference between the sample statistic and its corresponding population parameter:

$$\text{sampling error of the mean} = \bar{x} - \mu$$

- *Simple random sampling*: Method of selecting a sample such that each item or person in the population has the *same likelihood of being included* in the sample.
- *Stratified random sampling*: Separate the population into groups based on one or more characteristics. Take a random sample from each class based on the group size. In constructing bond index portfolios, we may first divide the bonds by maturity, rating, call feature, etc., and then pick bonds from each group of bonds in proportion to the number of index bonds in that group. This insures that our "random" sample has similar maturity, rating, and call characteristics to the index.

Sample Biases

- *Data-mining bias* occurs when research is based on the previously reported empirical evidence of others, rather than on the testable predictions of a well-developed economic theory. Data mining also occurs when analysts repeatedly use the same database to search for patterns or trading rules until one that "works" is found.
- *Sample selection bias* occurs when some data is systematically excluded from the analysis, usually because of the lack of availability.
- *Survivorship bias* is the most common form of sample selection bias. A good example of survivorship bias is given by some studies of mutual fund performance. Most mutual fund databases, like Morningstar's, only include funds currently in existence—the "survivors." Since poorly performing funds are more likely to have ceased to exist because of failure or merger, the survivorship bias in the data set tends to bias average performance upward.
- *Look-ahead bias* occurs when a study tests a relationship using sample data that was not available on the test date.
- *Time-period bias* can result if the time period over which the data is gathered is either too short or too long.

Central Limit Theorem

The *central limit theorem* of statistics states that in selecting simple random samples of size *n* from a *population* with a mean μ and a finite variance σ^2, the sampling distribution of the sample mean approaches a normal probability distribution with mean μ and a variance equal to σ^2/n as the sample size becomes large.

The central limit theorem is extremely useful because the normal distribution is relatively easy to apply to hypothesis testing and to the construction of confidence intervals.

Specific inferences about the population mean can be made from the sample mean, *regardless of the population's distribution*, as long as the sample size is sufficiently large.

Student's *t*-Distribution

- Symmetrical (bell shaped).
- Defined by single parameter, degrees of freedom (df), where df = n − 1 for hypothesis tests and confidence intervals involving a sample mean.
- Has fatter tails than a normal distribution; the lower the df, the fatter the tails and the wider the confidence interval around the sample mean for a given probability that the interval contains the true mean.
- As sample size (degrees of freedom) increases, the *t*-distribution approaches normal distribution.

Student's t-distribution is similar in concept to the normal distribution in that it is bell-shaped and symmetrical about its mean. The *t-distribution* is appropriate when working with small samples (n < 30) from populations with *unknown variance* and normal, or approximately normal, distributions. It may also be appropriate to use the *t*-distribution when the population variance is unknown and the sample size is large enough that the central limit theorem will assure the sampling distribution is approximately normal.

Figure 7: Student's *t*-Distribution and Degrees of Freedom

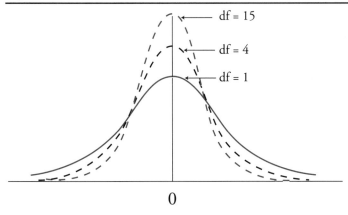

For questions on the exam, make sure you are working with the correct distribution. You should memorize the following table:

Figure 8: Criteria for Selecting Test Statistic

When sampling from a:	Test Statistic	
	Small Sample (n < 30)	*Large Sample* (n ≥ 30)
Normal distribution with *known* variance	z-statistic	z-statistic
Normal distribution with *unknown* variance	t-statistic	t-statistic*
Nonnormal distribution with *known* variance	not available	z-statistic
Nonnormal distribution with *unknown* variance	not available	t-statistic**

* The z-statistic is the standard normal, ±1 for 68% confidence, et cetera.
** The z-statistic is theoretically acceptable here, but use of the t-statistic is more conservative.

HYPOTHESIS TESTING
Cross-Reference to CFA Institute Assigned Reading #11

Hypothesis. Statement about a population parameter that is to be tested. For example, "The mean return on the S&P 500 Index is equal to zero."

Steps in Hypothesis Testing

- State the hypothesis.
- Select a test statistic.

- Specify the level of significance.
- State the decision rule for the hypothesis.
- Collect the sample and calculate statistics.
- Make a decision about the hypothesis.
- Make a decision based on the test results.

Null and Alternative Hypotheses

The *null hypothesis*, designated as H_0, is the hypothesis the researcher wants to reject. It is the hypothesis that is actually tested and is the basis for the selection of the test statistics. Thus, if you believe (seek to show that) the mean return on the S&P 500 Index is different from zero, the null hypothesis will be that the mean return on the index *equals* zero.

The *alternative hypothesis*, designated H_a, is what is concluded if there is sufficient evidence to reject the null hypothesis. It is usually the alternative hypothesis you are really trying to support. Why? Since you can never really prove anything with statistics, when the null hypothesis is rejected, the implication is that the (mutually exclusive) alternative hypothesis is valid.

Two-Tailed and One-Tailed Tests

Two-tailed test. Use this type of test when testing a parameter to see if it is different from a specified value:

$$H_0: \mu = 0 \text{ versus } H_a: \mu \neq 0$$

Figure 9: Two-Tailed Test: Significance = 5%, Confidence = 95%

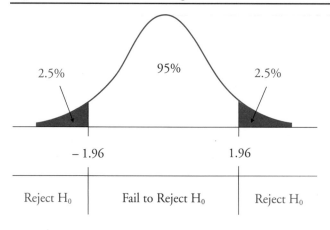

©2015 Kaplan, Inc.

One-tailed test. Use this type of test when testing a parameter to see if it is *above* or *below* a specified value:

$$H_0: \mu \leq 0 \text{ versus } H_a: \mu > 0, \text{ or}$$
$$H_0: \mu \geq 0 \text{ versus } H_a: \mu < 0$$

With respect to the first hypothesis, $\mu \leq 0$, we will reject it only if the test statistic is significantly greater than zero (in the right-hand tail of the distribution). Thus, we call it a one-tailed test.

Figure 10: One-Tailed Test: Significance = 5%, Confidence = 95%

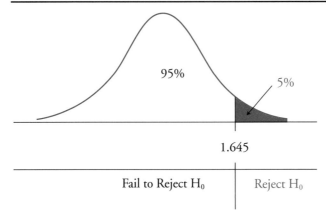

1.645

Fail to Reject H_0 Reject H_0

Test Statistic

A *test statistic* is calculated from sample data and is compared to a critical value to evaluate H_0. The most common test statistics are the z-statistic and the t-statistic. Which statistic you use to perform a hypothesis test will depend on the properties of the population and the sample size as noted above.

- Critical values come from tables and are based on the researcher's desired level of significance. As the level of significance (the α) gets smaller, the critical value gets larger and it becomes more difficult to reject the null hypothesis.
- If the test statistic exceeds the critical value (or is outside the range of critical values), the researcher rejects H_0.

Type I and Type II Errors

When testing a hypothesis, there are two possible types of errors:

- *Type I error.* Rejection of the null hypothesis when it is actually true.
- *Type II error.* Failure to reject the null hypothesis when it is actually false.

The *power of a test* is 1 − P(Type II error). The more likely that a test will reject a false null, the more powerful the test. A test that is unlikely to reject a false null hypothesis has little power.

Significance Level (α)

The *significance level* is the probability of making a Type I error (rejecting the null when it is true) and is designated by the Greek letter alpha (α). You can think of this as the probability that the test statistic will exceed or fall below the critical values by chance even though the null hypothesis is true. A significance level of 5% (a = 0.05) means there is a 5% chance of rejecting a true null hypothesis.

Figure 11: Errors in Hypothesis Testing

Type I and Type II Errors in Hypothesis Testing		
Decision	True Condition	
	H_0 is true	H_0 is false
Do not reject H_0	Correct decision	Incorrect decision Type II error
Reject H_0	Incorrect decision Type I error Significance level, α, = P(Type I error)	Correct decision Power of the test = 1 − P(Type II error)

Economically Meaningful Results

A test may indicate a significant statistical relationship (a statistically meaningful result) which is not economically significant. This is often the case when the gains from exploiting the statistical relation are small in an absolute sense so that the costs of a strategy to exploit the relation are greater than the expected gains from the strategy.

Other Hypothesis Tests

A test of the equality of the means of two independent normally distributed populations is a *t*-test based on the difference in sample means divided by a standard deviation which is calculated in one of two ways, depending on whether the variances of the two populations are assumed to be equal or not.

When random variables from two populations are dependent, the appropriate test is a *mean differences* or *paired comparisons* test. The test statistic is a *t*-statistic based on the average (mean) of the differences in the sample of the paired values of the two random variables, divided by the standard deviation of the differences between the sample pairs.

A test of whether the population variance of a normal distribution is equal to a specific value is based on the ratio of the sample variance to the hypothesized variance. The test statistic follows a Chi-square distribution and is a two-tailed test.

A test of whether the variances of two normal populations are equal is based on the ratio of the larger sample variance to the smaller sample variance. The appropriate test is an *F*-test (two-tailed), but by putting the larger sample variance in the numerator, values of the test statistic below the lower critical value are ruled out, and only the upper critical value of the *F*-statistic need be considered.

Figure 12 summarizes the test statistics used for each type of hypothesis test.

Figure 12: Types of Test Statistics

Hypothesis tests of:	Use a:
One population mean	t-statistic or Z-statistic
Two population means	t-statistic
One population variance	Chi-square statistic
Two population variances	F-statistic

Parametric and Nonparametric Tests

Parametric tests, like the *t*-test, *F*-test, and chi-square test, make assumptions regarding the distribution of the population from which samples are drawn.

Nonparametric tests either do not consider a particular population parameter or have few assumptions about the sampled population. Runs tests (which examine the pattern of successive increases or decreases in a random variable) and rank correlation tests (which examine the relation between a random variable's relative numerical rank over successive periods) are examples of nonparametric tests.

TECHNICAL ANALYSIS
Cross-Reference to CFA Institute Assigned Reading #12

This topic review presents many different technical analysis tools. Don't try to memorize them all. Focus on the basics of technical analysis and its underlying assumptions.

Assumptions of Technical Analysis

- Values, and thus prices, are determined by supply and demand.
- Supply and demand are driven by both rational and irrational behavior.
- Price and volume reflect the collective behavior of buyers and sellers.
- While the causes of changes in supply and demand are difficult to determine, the actual shifts in supply and demand can be observed in market price behavior.

Advantages of Technical Analysis

- Based on observable data (price and volume) that are not based on accounting assumptions or restatements.
- Can be used for assets that do not produce cash flows, such as commodities.
- May be more useful than fundamental analysis when financial statements contain errors or are fraudulent.

Disadvantages of Technical Analysis

- Less useful for markets that are subject to outside intervention, such as currency markets, and for markets that are illiquid.
- Short covering can create positive technical patterns for stocks of bankrupt companies.
- Cannot produce positive risk-adjusted returns over time when markets are weak-form efficient.

Types of Charts

Except for point and figure charts, all of the following chart types plot price or volume on the vertical axis and time (divided into trading periods) on the horizontal axis. Trading periods can be daily, intraday (e.g., hourly), or longer term (e.g., weekly or monthly).

Line chart: Closing prices for each trading period are connected by a line.

Bar chart: Vertical lines from the high to the low price for each trading period. A mark on the left side of the line indicates the opening price and a mark on the right side of the vertical line indicates the closing price.

Candlestick chart: Bar chart that draws a box from the opening price to the closing price on the vertical line for each trading period. The box is empty if the close is higher than the open and filled if the close is lower than the open.

Volume chart: Vertical line from zero to the number of shares (bonds, contracts) exchanged during each trading period. Often displayed below a bar or candlestick chart of the same asset over the same range of time.

Point and figure chart: Displays price trends on a grid. Price is on the vertical axis, and each unit on the horizontal axis represents a change in the direction of the price trend.

Relative strength chart: Line chart of the ratios of closing prices to a benchmark index. These charts illustrate how one asset or market is performing relative to another. Relative strength charts are useful for performing intermarket analysis and for identifying attractive asset classes and assets within each class that are outperforming others.

Trend, Support, and Resistance

A market is in an uptrend if prices are consistently reaching higher highs and retracing to higher lows. An uptrend indicates demand is increasing relative to supply. An upward sloping trendline can be drawn that connects the low points for a stock in an uptrend.

A market is in a downtrend if prices are consistently reaching lower lows and retracing to lower highs. A downtrend means supply is increasing relative to demand. A downward sloping trendline can be drawn that connects the high points in a downtrend.

Support and resistance levels are prices at which technical analysts expect supply and demand to equalize. Past highs are viewed as resistance levels, and past lows are viewed as support levels. Trendlines are also thought to indicate support and resistance levels.

The *change in polarity principle* is based on a belief that breached support levels become resistance levels, and breached resistance levels become support levels.

Figure 13: Trendlines, Support, and Resistance

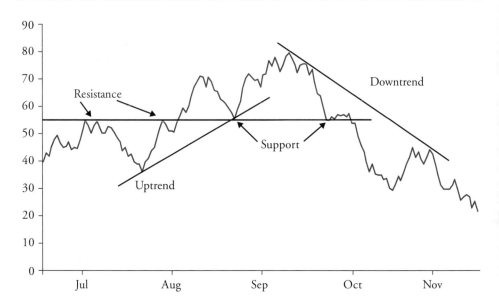

Common Chart Patterns

Reversal patterns: Head-and-shoulders; double top; triple top; inverse head-and-shoulders; double bottom; triple bottom. These price patterns are thought to indicate that the preceding trend has run its course and a new trend in the opposite direction is likely to emerge.

Continuation patterns: Triangles; rectangles; flags; pennants. These indicate temporary pauses in a trend which is expected to continue (in the same direction).

Technical analysts often use the sizes of both of these types of patterns to estimate subsequent target prices for the next move.

Price-based Indicators

Moving average lines are a frequently used method to smooth the fluctuations in a price chart. A 20-day moving average is the arithmetic mean of the last 20 closing prices. The larger number of periods chosen, the smoother the resulting moving average line will be. Moving average lines can help illustrate trends by smoothing short-term fluctuations, but when the number of periods is large, a moving average line can obscure changes in trend.

Bollinger bands are drawn a given number of standard deviations above and below a moving average line. Prices are believed to have a higher probability of falling (rising) when they are near the upper (lower) band.

Momentum oscillators include the rate of change oscillator, the Relative Strength Index (RSI), moving average convergence/divergence (MACD) lines, and stochastic oscillators.

Technical analysts use price-based indicators to identify market conditions that are overbought (prices have increased too rapidly and are likely to decrease in the near term) or oversold (prices have decreased too rapidly and are likely to increase in the near term). They also use charts of momentum oscillators to identify convergence or divergence with price trends. Convergence occurs when the oscillator shows the same pattern as prices (e.g., both reaching higher highs). Divergence occurs when the oscillator shows a different pattern than prices (e.g., failing to reach a higher high when the price does). Convergence suggests the price trend is likely to continue, while divergence indicates a potential change in trend in the near term.

Sentiment and Flow of Funds Indicators

Technical analysts also use indicators based on investors' bullish (investors expect prices to increase) or bearish (investors expect prices to decrease) sentiment. Some technical analysts interpret these indicators from a contrarian perspective. Contrarians believe markets get overbought or oversold because most investors tend to buy and sell at the wrong times, and thus it can be profitable to trade in the opposite direction from current sentiment.

Sentiment indicators include the following:

- *Put/call ratio:* Put option volume divided by call option volume.
- *Volatility index* (VIX): Measure of volatility on S&P 500 stock index options.
- *Short interest ratio:* Shares sold short divided by average daily trading volume.
- Amount of *margin debt* outstanding.
- *Opinion polls* that attempt to measure investor sentiment directly.

High levels of the put/call ratio, VIX, and short interest ratio indicate bearish market sentiment, which contrarians interpret as bullish. High levels of margin debt indicate bullish sentiment, which contrarians interpret as bearish.

Indicators of the flow of funds in the financial markets can be useful for identifying changes in the supply and demand for securities. These include the Arms index or short-term trading index (TRIN), which measures funds flowing into advancing and declining stocks; margin debt (also used as a sentiment indicator); new and secondary equity offerings; and mutual fund cash as a percentage of net assets.

Cycles and Elliott Wave Theory

Some technical analysts apply cycle theory to financial markets in an attempt to identify cycles in prices. Cycle periods favored by technical analysts include 4-year presidential cycles related to election years in the United States, decennial patterns or 10-year cycles, 18-year cycles, and 54-year cycles called Kondratieff waves.

One of the more developed cycle theories is the Elliott wave theory which is based on an interconnected set of cycles that range from a few minutes to centuries. According to Elliott wave theory, in an uptrend the upward moves in prices consist of five waves and the downward moves occur in three waves. If the prevailing trend is down, the downward moves have five waves and the upward moves have three waves. Each of these waves is composed of smaller waves that exhibit the same pattern.

The sizes of these waves are thought to correspond with ratios of Fibonacci numbers. Fibonacci numbers are found by starting with 0 and 1, then adding each of the previous two numbers to produce the next (0, 1, 1, 2, 3, 5, 8, 13, 21, and so on). Ratios of consecutive Fibonacci numbers converge to 0.618 and 1.618 as the numbers in the sequence get larger.

ECONOMICS

Weight on Exam	10%
SchweserNotes™ Reference	Book 2, Pages 1–246

STUDY SESSION 4: ECONOMICS—MICROECONOMIC ANALYSIS

DEMAND AND SUPPLY ANALYSIS: INTRODUCTION
Cross-Reference to CFA Institute Assigned Reading #13

Types of Markets

Factor markets refers to markets for factors of production, and **goods markets** refers to markets for consumer goods and services.

Capital markets refers to the markets where firms raise money for investment by selling debt (borrowing) or selling equities (claims to ownership), as well as the markets where these debt and equity claims are subsequently traded.

The Demand Function and the Demand Curve

A general form of the demand function for Good X over some period of time is:

$$Q^{Dx} = f(P_x, I, P_y...)$$

where:
Q_{Dx} = quantity demanded of Good X
P_x = price of Good X
I = some measure of individual or average income
$P_y...$ = prices of related goods

As an example, consider the weekly demand function for gasoline:

$$Q_{D\,gas} = 9 - 1.5P_{gas} + 0.02I + 0.11P_{BT} - 0.008P_{auto}$$

where income and car price are measured in thousands, and the price of bus travel (BT) is measured in average dollars per 100 miles traveled. The fact that the quantity demanded typically is negatively related to price is referred to as the **law of demand**. Note that an increase in the price of automobiles will decrease demand for gasoline (they are said to be **complements**), and an increase in the price of bus travel will increase the demand for gasoline (they are **substitutes**). The positive coefficient on income indicates that gasoline for this consumer is a **normal good**. A negative exponent on income would indicate that gasoline is an **inferior good**.

To get quantity demanded as a function of only the price of gas, insert values for all the other independent variables. Assuming that the average car price is $26,000, income is $40,000, and the price of bus travel is $25, our demand function above becomes $Q_{D \, gas} = 9 - 1.5(P_{gas}) + 0.02(40) + 0.11(25) - 0.008(26) = 12.342 - 1.5P_{gas}$, and at a price of $4 per gallon, the quantity of gas demanded per week is 6.34 gallons.

In order to find the **demand curve** that shows the price of gasoline as a function of the quantity demanded, *invert* the demand function to show price as a function of the quantity demanded. For our function, $Q_{D \, gas} = 12.342 - 1.5P_{gas}$, we get $P_{gas} = 8.228 - 0.667Q_{D \, gas}$.

The Supply Function and the Supply Curve

For a given level of technology, the quantity supplied will depend on the selling price, the price of labor (wage rate), and the price of materials. An example of a supply function for wood tables is:

$$Q_{S \, tables} = -300 + 1.5P_{tables} - 8Wage - 0.2P_{wood}$$

where the wage is in dollars per hour and the price of wood is in dollars per 100 board feet. With a wage of $12 per hour and wood priced at $150, we have $Q_{S \, tables} = -426 + 1.5P_{tables}$. In order to graph this producer's **supply curve**, invert this supply function and get $P_{tables} = 284 + 0.667Q_{S \, tables}$. The fact that a greater quantity is supplied at higher prices is referred to as the **law of supply**.

A movement along a given demand or supply curve when the equilibrium price changes represents a **change in the quantity demanded or supplied**. A change in one of the independent variables other than price will result in a shift of the curve itself, referred to as **increases or decreases in supply or demand**. For a normal good, an increase in income will increase demand, as will an increase in the price of a substitute or a decrease in the price of a complement. A decrease in the price of raw materials, a decrease in the wage rate, or advances in technology that increase productivity will all increase supply.

Aggregating Producers' Supply Curves

If there are 30 table manufacturers with the same supply function, $Q_{S\ tables} = -426 + 1.5P_{tables}$, multiply the right-hand side to get market supply: $Q_{S\ tables} = -(30 \times 426) + (30 \times 1.5) P_{tables}$, $= -12,780 + 45 P_{tables}$.

In order to get the market supply curve, invert this function to get: $P_{tables} = 0.02222 Q_{S\ tables} + 284$. Note that the slope of the supply curve is the coefficient of the quantity variable, 0.02222.

Aggregating Consumer Demand

Consider 10,000 consumers who each have the same demand function for gasoline:

$$Q_{D\ gas} = 9 - 3P_{gas} + 0.02I + 0.11P_{BT} - 0.008P_{auto}$$

When the price of bus travel is $20, income is $50,000, and the average automobile price is $30,000, $Q_{D\ gas} = 90,000 - 30,000P_{gas} + 200 \times 50 + 1,100 \times 20 - 80 \times 30$ and $Q_{D\ gas} = 119,600 - 30,000P_{gas}$.

Inverting this function, we get the market demand curve, $P_{gas} = 3.987 - 0.00003333Q_{D\ gas}$.

The slope of the demand curve is –0.00003333, or if we measure quantity of gas in thousands of gallons, we get –0.0333.

Market Equilibrium

Equilibrium market price is the price for which the quantity supplied equals the quantity demanded. We define this as the **equilibrium price** and the **equilibrium quantity**; graphically, these are identified by the point where the supply and demand curves intersect, as illustrated in Figure 1.

Figure 1: Movement Toward Equilibrium

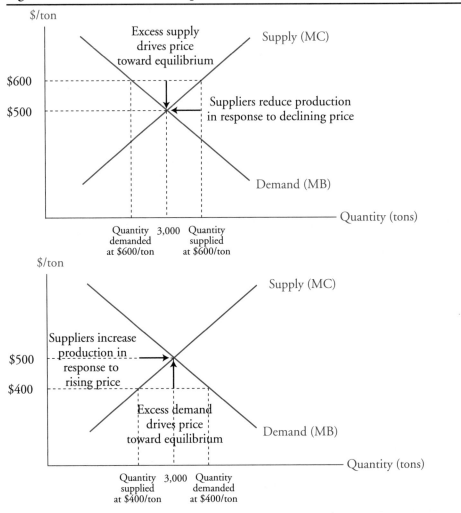

As illustrated in Figure 1, if the price is above its equilibrium level, the quantity willingly supplied exceeds the quantity consumers are willing to purchase, and we have **excess supply**. Suppliers willing to sell at lower prices will offer those prices to consumers, driving the market price down towards the equilibrium level. Conversely, if the market price is below its equilibrium level, the quantity demanded at that price exceeds the quantity supplied, and we have **excess demand**. Consumers will offer higher prices to compete for the available supply, driving the market price up towards its equilibrium level.

As long as prices higher than equilibrium result in excess supply and prices less than equilibrium result in excess demand, there are forces to drive price towards its equilibrium level and we have a **stable equilibrium**. If the supply curve is downward sloping, we can still have a stable equilibrium unless the supply curve intersects the demand curve from below, in which case the equilibrium is unstable as excess demand and excess supply conditions drive price away from its equilibrium level. Such cases are illustrated in Figure 2.

Figure 2: Stable and Unstable Equilibria

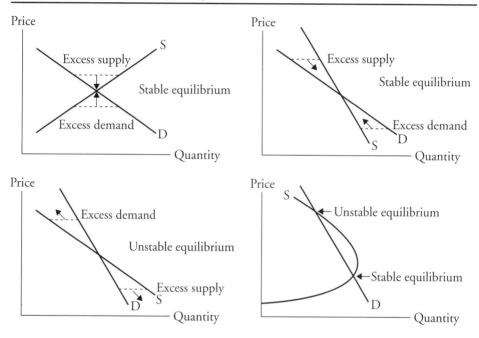

Auctions

We can distinguish between a **common value auction**, in which the value of the item (e.g., oil lease) is the same to all bidders but may not be known with certainty at the time of the auction, and a **private value auction**, in which the value of the item is specific to each bidder (e.g., artwork). In a common value auction, the **winners' curse** refers to the fact that the winning bidder is the one who most overvalues the item.

Types of auctions include:

- **Ascending price (English) auction**—highest bid wins the item, pays amount bid.
- **Sealed bid auction**—highest amount offered wins the item, pays amount bid.
- **Second price sealed bid (Vickrey) auction**—highest bid wins the item, pays the next highest bid amount. Bidders are more likely to bid their reservation price (highest amount they are willing to pay).

- **Descending price (Dutch) auction**—price is reduced until a bidder is willing to pay that price. When more units are available than the bidder takes, the price is reduced and subsequent bidders get the lower price(s).
- **Modified Dutch auction**—same as the descending price, but all bidders pay the price bid for the final units.

U.S. Treasury securities are auctioned in sealed bid modified Dutch auctions. Bidders can place *non-competitive bids*, and these are filled at the final auction price, which is the highest price (lowest yield) at which all the securities (less those going to the non-competing bidders) can be sold.

Consumer and Producer Surplus

Consumer surplus is the excess of the total value to consumers of the units they purchase above the total amount paid. **Producer surplus** is the excess of the amount producers receive for the units they sell above their total cost of production. **Total surplus** is the sum of consumer and producer surplus.

Figure 3: Consumer and Producer Surplus

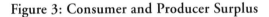

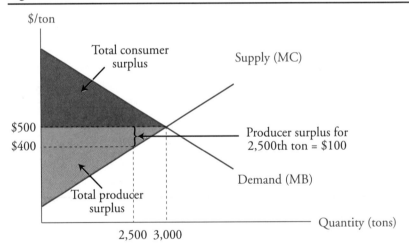

When there are no external costs or benefits associated with production and consumption of a good, demand represents marginal social benefit and supply represents marginal social cost. In this case, equilibrium quantity, where total surplus is maximized, is the amount of production when resources are allocated efficiently. Production of greater or lesser quantities results in a **deadweight loss**, either from producing units that are valued at less than their cost (overproduction) or from not producing units for which the value to consumers is greater than their cost (underproduction).

Figure 4: Deadweight Loss

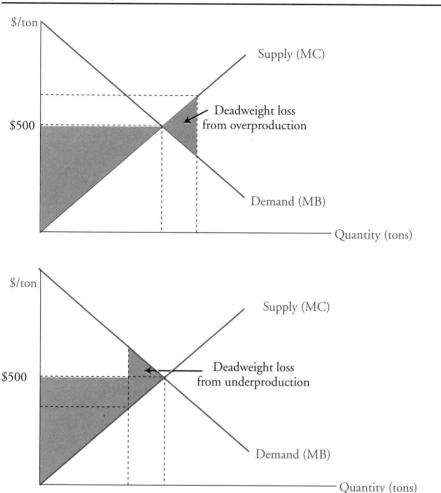

Obstacles to Efficient Allocation

Taxes, tariffs, and other **trade restrictions** reduce the equilibrium quantity below the quantity that maximizes total surplus (results in a deadweight loss).

Subsidies to the production or importation of goods increase the equilibrium quantity above the quantity that maximizes total surplus (results in a deadweight loss).

When **external costs of production** (e.g., pollution) are not borne by suppliers, there will be a deadweight loss from overproduction.

When **external benefits of consumption** are not realized by consumers, they will consume less than the efficient quantity of the good, resulting in a deadweight loss.

A **price ceiling** is a maximum legal price (e.g., rent control) that results in underproduction and excess demand, some method of non-price allocation to consumers, and deterioration of the quality of the good.

A **price floor** is a minimum legal price. In the case of a minimum wage rate, there will be an excess supply of unskilled labor (increased unemployment), non-wage worker benefits will be reduced, and producers will substitute other factors of production, including capital equipment and skilled labor, for unskilled labor.

The reduction in the equilibrium quantity from imposing a tax, and the associated deadweight loss, are the same whether the tax is levied on consumers (e.g., sales tax) or on producers (e.g., value-added tax). How the burden of the tax is shared by consumers or producers is the same in either case as well.

- A decrease (increase) in the elasticity of demand increases (decreases) the portion of the burden borne by consumers.
- A decrease (increase) in the elasticity of supply increases (decreases) the portion of the burden borne by producers.

Figure 5: Elasticity of Demand and Tax Incidence

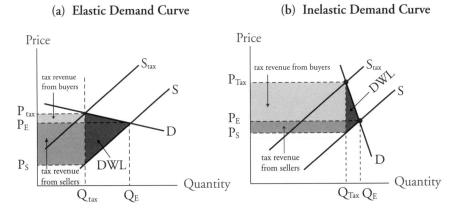

Elasticity

Price elasticity of demand is the ratio of the percent change in quantity demanded to the percent change in price.

Income elasticity of demand is the ratio of the percent change in quantity demanded to the percent change in income. For a normal good, income elasticity is positive so that an increase in income increases demand for the good. For an inferior good, income elasticity is negative so that an increase in income decreases demand for the good (e.g., bus travel).

Cross price elasticity of demand is the ratio of the percent change in quantity demanded to the percent change in the price of a related good. It is positive for a good that is a substitute in consumption (e.g., cars and bus travel) and negative for a good that is a complement in consumption (e.g., cars and gasoline).

For a demand function of the general form: $Q_D = 100 - A \times P_{good} + B \times Income + C \times P_{other\ good}$, at price and quantity P* and Q*:

- **The price elasticity of demand is A × (P*/Q*).** If A < 1, an increase (decrease) in price will increase (decrease) total revenue; if A > 1, an increase (decrease) in price will decrease (increase) total revenue.
- **The income elasticity of demand is B × (Income/Q*)** and is positive (B > 0) for normal goods and negative (B < 0) for inferior goods (an increase in income decreases quantity demanded of the good).
- **The cross price elasticity of demand is C × P_{other good}/Q*.** When C is negative the goods are complements and when C is positive the goods are substitutes.

Given two points on a demand curve, we can calculate the **arc elasticity of demand** over that range of the demand curve. When calculating the percentage changes in price and in quantity for arc elasticity, we use the midpoints of price and quantity over the range so that an increase and a decrease for either price or quantity will yield the same percentage change.

DEMAND AND SUPPLY ANALYSIS: CONSUMER DEMAND
Cross-Reference to CFA Institute Assigned Reading #14

The theory of consumer choice (utility theory) combines consumer preferences as represented by indifference curves with affordable choices as represented by a budget constraint. Indifference curves are sets of combinations (bundles) of goods among which a consumer is indifferent (i.e., all bundles of goods along an indifference curve provide the same utility).

Properties of indifference curves for two goods:

1. Indifference curves slope downward because a bundle with less of one good must have more of the other good to be equally preferred.

2. Indifference curves are convex towards the origin because successive reductions in the quantity of one good in the bundle require increasing quantities of the other good to keep utility constant. This is referred to as the diminishing **marginal rate of substitution** (MRS). The MRS is the absolute value of the slope of an indifference curve at any point. Decreasing MRS results in convexity.

3. Two indifference curves for a single consumer cannot cross. This must be the case because logically consistent preferences must be **transitive**. This means that if A is preferred to B and B is preferred to C, A must be preferred to C.

A **budget line** represents all the combinations of two goods that will just exhaust a consumer's income. A budget line bounds an area representing all affordable combinations of two goods at current prices. The y-intercept of a budget line is income/price of Good Y, and the x-intercept is income/price of Good X.

An indifference curve for an individual that is higher than (to the north-east of) another represents a set of more preferred bundles of goods. By combining an individual's indifference curves with that individual's budget constraint, we can illustrate the choice of the most preferred affordable bundle as the combination of goods along the budget line that lies on the highest attainable indifference curve. Graphically, this is the point where one of an individual's indifference curves is just tangent to his budget constraint. At this point, the absolute value of the slope of the budget line (P_X/P_Y) is equal to the marginal rate of substitution of Good Y for Good X at the indifference curve's point of tangency.

We illustrate this result in the following figure, which is consistent with an individual with an income of 200 when the price of Good Y is 20 and the price of Good X is 25.

Figure 6: A Consumer's Equilibrium Bundle of Goods

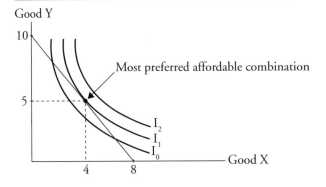

The effect of a decrease in the price of Good X is to move the x-intercept to the right (flattening the budget line), which will result in a different optimal bundle of goods. We can decompose this change into a **substitution effect**, substitution of X for Y because the relative price of Good X has decreased, and an **income effect**, approximately the effect of the income left over from consuming the original bundle of goods after the price decrease.

The income effect of the price decrease on consumption of Good X can theoretically be either positive or negative, depending on whether the good is normal or inferior over the relevant range of income.

The substitution effect is the change in consumption due to the change in relative prices and is always positive (i.e., results in increased consumption of the good that decreased in price). Graphically we show this effect as a change in consumption to a point on the consumer's original tangent indifference curve, but at the point where the slope of the curve (MRS) is equal to the slope of the new budget line after the price decrease. The three possible combinations of income and substitution effects are shown graphically in Figure 7. The three combinations, different because of the income effect, are:

1. Income effect is positive so consumption of Good X increases.

2. Income effect is negative but smaller than the positive substitution effect so that consumption of Good X increases.

3. The income effect is negative and larger than the substitution effect so that consumption of Good X decreases as a result of the decrease in its price.

Figure 7: Income and Substitution Effects

Good Y   **A: Positive Income Effect**

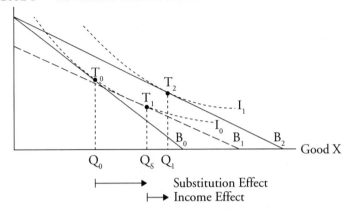

Good Y   **B: Negative Income Effect, Smaller Than Substitution Effect**

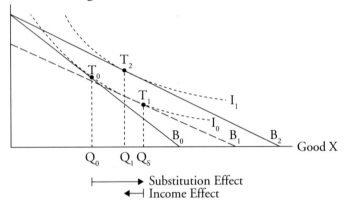

Good Y   **C: Negative Income Effect, Larger Than Substitution Effect**

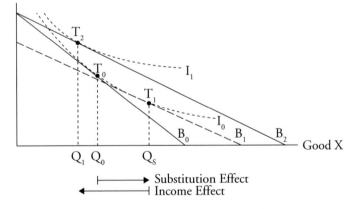

In the third panel of Figure 7, a decrease in the price of the good results in a decrease in the quantity demanded. Such a good is referred to as a **Giffen good** and is consistent with utility theory and theoretically possible.

A **Veblen good** is defined as a good for which an increase in price increases its value to some consumers, so that their quantity demanded actually increases (e.g., Gucci bag). Since such goods, if they exist, are clearly not inferior, their existence is at odds with utility theory as rational decision makers are assumed to prefer lower prices and increased consumption opportunities.

DEMAND AND SUPPLY ANALYSIS: THE FIRM
Cross-Reference to CFA Institute Assigned Reading #15

Accounting profit refers to net income on a company's financial statements. The accounting expenses that are deducted on the income statement are referred to as **explicit costs**. While interest expense on debt is an explicit cost, the return to or opportunity cost of equity capital is not reflected in net income and is referred to as an **implicit cost**. In economic analysis we use the term **economic costs** to refer to the sum of explicit and implicit costs. Economic cost as a theoretical concept includes all the explicit costs of production and sales as well as the cost of equity capital. We can summarize these relationships with the following equations:

accounting profit = total revenue – total accounting (explicit) costs

economic profit = accounting profit – implicit opportunity costs

economic profit = total revenue – total economic costs

A firm in equilibrium will have an economic profit of zero. Such a firm is covering all its costs and the required rate of return to providers of both debt and equity funding. In contrast, a firm with zero accounting profit is earning a return of zero on its equity funding. **Normal profit** is the accounting profit a firm must earn in order to satisfy equity holders and to continue to operate in the long run.

Economic rent refers to payment to a factor of production in excess of the amount necessary to retain it in its current use. That amount is the factor's **opportunity cost**, or value in its next-highest use. The payment for land is all economic rent because land is in fixed (perfectly inelastic) supply. When the supply of a factor is perfectly elastic, payment to the factor just covers its opportunity cost and the factor earns no economic rent. This difference is illustrated in Figure 8.

Figure 8: Economic Rent to Factors of Production

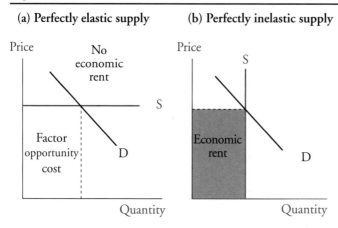

(a) Perfectly elastic supply   (b) Perfectly inelastic supply

Total revenue (TR) for any firm that charges a single price to all customers is calculated as price multiplied by quantity sold, or TR = P × Q.

Average revenue (AR) is equal to total revenue divided by the quantity sold, AR = TR / Q = P.

Marginal revenue (MR) is the increase in total revenue from selling one more unit of a good or service. A firm in a perfectly competitive market faces a horizontal (perfectly elastic) demand curve so that all units are sold at the same price regardless of quantity. In this case, average revenue and marginal revenue are both equal to the market price, AR = MR = P.

A firm that faces a downward sloping demand curve (sometimes referred to as a *price searcher*) must decrease price in order to sell a greater quantity. Assuming the firm sells all units at the same price, we still have the relationships TR = P × Q and AR = TR / Q = P. Marginal revenue will be less than price and average revenue, as shown in Figure 9.

Figure 9: Total revenue, average revenue, and marginal revenue for a price searcher

Given the demand curve for a firm's product below, we can calculate the total revenue, average revenue, and marginal revenue for the first through the eighth unit.

Quantity	1	2	3	4	5	6	7	8
Price	70	65	60	55	50	45	40	35

Quantity	Price	Average Revenue	Total Revenue	Marginal Revenue
1	70	70	70	70
2	65	65	130	60
3	60	60	180	50
4	55	55	220	40
5	50	50	250	30
6	45	45	270	20
7	40	40	280	10
8	35	35	280	0

Factors of production are the resources a firm uses to generate output. Factors of production include:

- *Land*—where the business facilities are located.
- *Labor*—includes all workers from unskilled laborers to top management.
- *Capital*—sometimes called *physical capital* or *plant and equipment* to distinguish it from financial capital. Refers to manufacturing facilities, equipment, and machinery.
- *Materials*—refers to inputs into the productive process, including raw materials and intermediate goods.

For economic analysis, we often consider only two inputs: capital and labor. The quantity of output that a firm can produce can be thought of as a function of the amounts of capital and labor employed, represented as $Q = f(K,L)$. Such a function is called a **production function**. For a given amount of capital (a firm's plant and equipment), we can examine the increase in production (the total product of labor) that will result as we increase the amount of labor employed.

The output with only one worker is considered the **marginal product** of the first unit of labor. The addition of a second worker will increase total product by the marginal product of the second worker. The typical total product curve will at first increase at increasing rates, as additional workers increase total product by greater amounts, and marginal product is increasing with additional workers. At some point, since we are holding capital constant, each additional worker adds less and less to total product, total product increases at a decreasing rate, and the marginal product of labor decreases with additional workers. At some level of labor, additional workers may actually decrease total product (think of a very crowded factory) and the marginal product of labor is negative.

When we reach the quantity of labor for which the marginal product of labor begins to decline, we have reached the point of **diminishing marginal productivity** of labor, or that labor has reached the point of **diminishing marginal returns**.

Beyond this quantity of labor, the additional output from each additional worker continues to decline. This typical assumption about the nature of labor productivity (in the short run when capital is fixed) is illustrated in Figure 10.

Figure 10: Production Function—Capital Fixed, Labor Variable

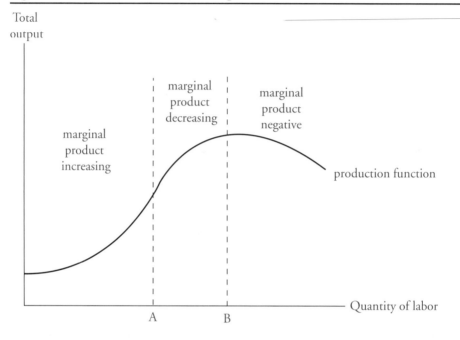

Firm Cost Curves

The relationship between output and cost may be explained in terms of three cost concepts: (1) total cost, (2) marginal cost, and (3) average cost. In examining firm costs of production, we consider two time frames: the **short run** during which some factors of production (typically capital) are assumed to be fixed, and the **long run** during which the quantities of all factors of production are assumed to be variable.

Total fixed cost (TFC) is the cost of inputs that do not vary with the quantity of output and cannot be avoided over the period of analysis. Examples of fixed costs are property, plant, and equipment; normal profit; fixed interest costs on debt financing; and wages of management and finance employees who are not directly involved in the production of the firm's product. Note that some of these costs will remain constant over some range of output but will increase if output is increased beyond some quantity (e.g., administrative salaries and utilities). These costs can be referred to as **quasi-fixed costs**. Because fixed costs must be paid (at least over the near term) even when demand for the firm's product declines, they can result in significant losses during economic downturns or when industry competition is especially aggressive.

Total variable cost (TVC) is the cost of all inputs that vary with output over the period of analysis. The largest variable costs for most firms are wages, raw materials, or both. Variable costs increase with greater output and can be reduced if a decrease in demand leads to a decrease in production.

Total cost (TC) is the sum of all costs (fixed or variable, explicit and implicit) of producing a specific level of output.

total cost = total fixed cost + total variable cost

Once we determine total costs for various levels of output, we can calculate **marginal costs** (MCs) as the addition to total cost of producing one more unit. Given output levels that are several units of output apart, dividing the difference in total cost by the number of units will provide a measure of marginal cost per unit.

marginal cost (MC) = change in total cost / change in output

average total costs (ATC) = total costs / total product

average fixed costs (AFC) = total fixed costs / total product

average variable costs (AVC) = total variable costs / total product

Figure 11 illustrates the components of total cost at various output levels. Total fixed cost is $20 per day to rent one sewing machine. Labor is the only variable cost, and the wage rate is $20 per day.

Figure 11: Total, Marginal, and Average Costs for Sam's Shirts

Output (shirts)	Labor (workers/day)	TFC ($/day)	TVC	TC	MC ($/additional shirt)	AFC ($/shirt)	AVC	ATC
0	0	20	0	20				
					-----2.50-----			
8	1	20	20	40		2.50	2.50	5.00
					----1.67-----			
20	2	20	40	60		1.00	2.00	3.00
					-----3.33-----			
26	3	20	60	80		0.77	2.31	3.08
					-----5.00-----			
30	4	20	80	100		0.67	2.67	3.33
					----10.00----			
32	5	20	100	120		0.63	3.13	3.75

TFC = Total fixed cost	cost of fixed inputs; independent of output	
TVC = Total variable cost	cost of variable inputs; changes with output	
TC = Total cost		$TC = TFC + TVC$
MC = Marginal cost	change in total cost for one unit increase in output	$MC = \Delta TC / \Delta Q$
AFC = Average fixed cost		$AFC = TFC / Q$
AVC = Average variable cost		$AVC = TVC / Q$
ATC = Average total cost		$ATC = AFC + AVC$

Using the information presented in Figure 11, we can calculate the marginal cost per shirt when output increases from 8 to 20 shirts per day. The change in TC when output increases from 8 to 20 shirts is $60 – $40 = $20. Because the change in output is 20 – 8 = 12 shirts, the marginal cost can be calculated as: MC= $20 / 12 = $1.67 per shirt.

The marginal cost (MC) and average cost curves (ATC, AVC, and AFC) for Sam's Shirts are shown in Figure 12.

Figure 12: Average and Marginal Costs

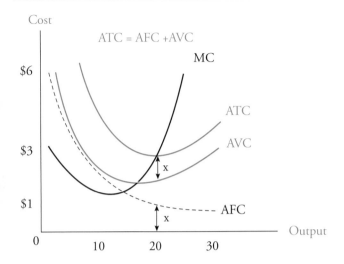

You should be familiar with the following characteristics of the cost curves in Figure 12:

- AFC slopes downward.
- The vertical distance between the ATC and AVC curves is equal to AFC.
- MC declines initially, then increases.
- MC intersects AVC and ATC at their minimum points.
- ATC and AVC are U-shaped.
- The minimum point on the ATC curve represents the lowest cost per unit.
- The MC curve above AVC is the firm's short-run supply curve (in a perfectly competitive market).

The relation between total and average output as functions of labor employed, and marginal and average cost as functions of output curves and cost curves, is illustrated in Figure 13.

Figure 13: Product and Cost Curves

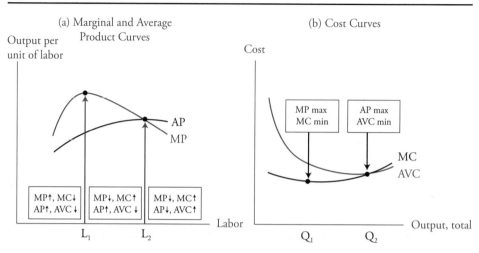

(a) Marginal and Average Product Curves

(b) Cost Curves

In the short run, a firm may be selling at less than ATC, generating an economic loss. Such a firm should continue to operate in the short run as long as price is greater than AVC. In this case, the losses from shutting down (producing zero output) in the short run would be greater (equal to TFC) than the losses from continued operation. If selling price is less than AVC, the firm will minimize its losses in the short run by ceasing operations.

In the long run, a firm should shut down if price is expected to remain less than ATC. These cases are illustrated in Figure 14. At prices below P_1 but above P_2, a profit maximizing (loss minimizing) firm should continue to operate in the short run but shut down in the long run. At prices below P_2, the firm should shut down in the short run as well. We refer to this price (minimum AVC) as the **shutdown point**.

Figure 14: Shutdown and Breakeven

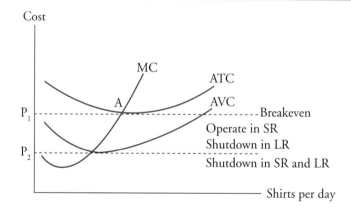

In the long run, firms can adjust their scale of operations (i.e., capital is variable). The minimum average total cost at each possible scale of operations is shown on the **long-run average total cost** (LRATC) curve.

The downward sloping segment of the long-run average total cost curve presented in Figure 15 indicates that **economies of scale** (or *increasing returns to scale*) are present. Economies of scale result from factors such as labor specialization, mass production, and investment in more efficient equipment and technology. In addition, the firm may be able to negotiate lower input prices with suppliers as firm size increases and more resources are purchased. The lowest point on the LRATC curve corresponds to the scale or plant size at which the average total cost of production is at a minimum. This scale is sometimes called the **minimum efficient scale**. At larger firm sizes, minimum average total costs begin to increase, indicating that there are **diseconomies of scale** beyond the minimum efficient scale.

Figure 15: Economies and Diseconomies of Scale

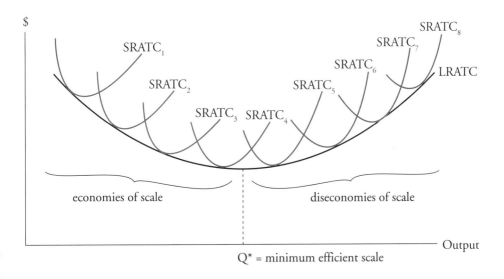

The **long-run supply curve** for an industry may slope up or down, depending on how growth of the overall industry affects production costs. It may be the case that industry growth increases the demand for productive inputs specific to the industry and increases and their market prices. The long-run supply curve for the industry is upward sloping as a result. This is referred to as an **increasing cost industry** (e.g., oil). For some industries, resource prices fall as the industry expands. In this case the industry is said to be a **decreasing cost industry**, and the long-run industry supply curve is downward sloping (e.g., flat panel TVs). For ranges of industry output over which input prices do not increase or decrease, the industry demand curve is perfectly elastic at minimum average cost. We refer to this as a **constant cost industry**.

Input Levels and Profit Maximization

For profit to be at a maximum, a firm must use the mix of inputs that minimizes the cost of producing any given quantity of output. For a firm with N productive inputs, cost minimization requires that:

$$\frac{MP_1}{P_1} = \frac{MP_2}{P_2} = ... = \frac{MP_N}{P_N}$$

This equation tells us that the additional output per dollar spent to employ one additional unit of each input must be the same. Increasing the usage of an input with higher MP/P and decreasing the usage of an input with lower MP/P will decrease costs and increase profits.

For each productive input, the additional revenue from employing one more unit is its **marginal revenue product** (MRP), which is its marginal product (additional output units) multiplied by the marginal revenue from selling the additional output units. To maximize profits, a firm will continue to increase its use of an input until its MRP is just equal to its price per unit. For profit maximization (and cost minimization) it must be the case that:

$$\frac{MRP_1}{P_1} = \frac{MRP_2}{P_2} = ... = \frac{MRP_N}{P_N} = 1.$$

THE FIRM AND MARKET STRUCTURES
Cross-Reference to CFA Institute Assigned Reading #16

We can differentiate among four types of markets based on the following characteristics:

- Number of firms and their relative sizes.
- Elasticity of the demand curves they face.
- Ways that they compete with other firms for sales.
- Ease or difficulty with which firms can enter or exit the market.

At one end of the spectrum is **perfect competition**, in which many firms produce identical products and competition forces them all to sell at the market price. At the other extreme, we have **monopoly**, where only one firm is producing the product. In between are **monopolistic competition** (many sellers and differentiated products) and **oligopoly** (few firms that compete in a variety of ways).

Characteristics of Market Structures

Markets can be differentiated by several characteristics, including number of seller firms, their market shares/industry concentration, the degree of product differentiation, the nature of competition, and barriers to entry into and exit from the industry. We can identify four primary types of market structures. An analyst, however, may be most concerned with the pricing power a particular firm has.

Perfect competition is characterized by:

- Many firms, each small relative to the market.
- Very low barriers to entry into or exit from the industry.
- Homogeneous products that are perfect substitutes.
- No advertising or branding.
- No pricing power.

Monopolistic competition is characterized by:

- Many firms.
- Low barriers to entry into or exit from the industry.
- Differentiated products, heavy advertising, and high marketing expenditure.
- Firms that have some pricing power.

Oligopoly markets are characterized by:

- Few sellers.
- High barriers to entry into or exit from the industry.
- Products that may be homogeneous or differentiated by branding and advertising.
- Firms that may have significant pricing power.

Monopoly is characterized by:

- A single firm that comprises the whole market.
- Very high barriers to enter or exit the industry.
- Advertising used to compete with substitute products.
- Significant pricing power.

Demand Characteristics

Perfect competition: Price = marginal revenue = marginal cost (in equilibrium)
Perfectly elastic firm demand curve
Zero economic profit in equilibrium

Monopolistic competition: Price > marginal revenue = marginal cost (in equilibrium)
Downward sloping firm demand curve
Zero economic profit in long-run equilibrium

Oligopoly: Price > marginal revenue = marginal cost (in equilibrium)
Downward sloping firm demand curve
May have positive economic profit in long-run equilibrium
Tends towards zero economic profit over time

Monopoly: Price > marginal revenue = marginal cost (in equilibrium)
Downward sloping firm demand curve
May have positive economic profit in long-run equilibrium
Profits may be zero because of expenditures to preserve monopoly

All firms maximize profits by producing the quantity of output for which marginal cost equals marginal revenue. Under perfect competition (perfectly elastic demand), marginal revenue also equals price. Equilibrium under perfect competition is illustrated in Figure 16.

Figure 16: Equilibrium in a Perfectly Competitive Market

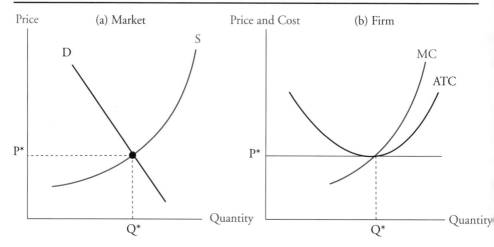

The market price, P*, is determined by the intersection of market supply and demand (Panel a). To maximize profits, each individual firm will produce the quantity for which marginal cost equals marginal revenue. This is the price when firm demand is perfectly elastic (Panel b). In long-run equilibrium, this is also the quantity for which average total cost is minimized.

An increase in market demand will result in an increase in market price, and each firm will increase output and earn economic profits in the short run. In the long run, these economic profits will attract new firms into the industry, increasing market supply and decreasing the market price until the equilibrium situation illustrated in Figure 16 is restored.

Firms in monopolistic competition or that operate in oligopoly or monopoly markets all face downward sloping demand curves. Selling price is determined from the price on the demand curve for the profit maximizing quantity of output.

An increase (decrease) in demand will increase (decrease) economic profits in the short run under all market structures. Positive economic profits result in entry of firms into the industry unless barriers to entry are high. Negative economic profits result in exit of firms from the industry unless barriers to exit are high. When firms enter (exit) an industry, market supply increases (decreases), resulting in a decrease (increase) in market price and an increase (decrease) in the equilibrium quantity traded in the market.

A **natural monopoly** refers to a situation where the average cost of production is falling over the relevant range of consumer demand. In this case, having two (or more) producers would result in a significantly higher cost of production and be detrimental to consumers.

Left unregulated, a single-price monopolist will maximize profits by producing the quantity for which MR = MC, charge the price indicated on the demand curve for that quantity, and maximize their producers' surplus. This situation is illustrated in Figure 17.

Figure 17: Monopoly Short-Run Costs and Revenues

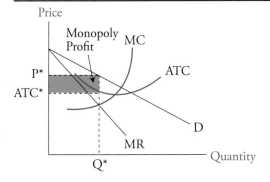

Government regulation may attempt to improve resource allocation by requiring a monopolist to institute **average cost pricing** or **marginal cost pricing** (with a subsidy to the firm if MC < ATC). Additionally, regulators often attempt to increase competition and efficiency through efforts to reduce artificial barriers to trade, such as licensing requirements, quotas, and tariffs.

Rather than estimate elasticity of demand, **concentration measures** for a market or industry are often used as an indicator of market power. One concentration measure is the **N-firm concentration ratio**, which is calculated as the sum of the percentage market shares of the largest *N* firms in a market. While this measure is simple to calculate and understand, it does not directly measure market power or elasticity of demand.

One limitation of the N-firm concentration ratio is that it may be relatively insensitive to mergers of two firms with large market shares. This problem is reduced by using an alternative measure of market concentration, the **Herfindahl-Hirschman Index** (HHI). The HHI is calculated as the sum of the squares of the market shares of the largest firms in the market.

A second limitation that applies to both concentration measures is that barriers to entry are not considered. Even a firm with high market share may not have much pricing power if barriers to entry are low and there is *potential competition* in that a competitor may enter the market if the price is high enough to produce economic profits.

There are alternative assumptions made about the nature of competition in oligopoly markets. At one extreme, competition within an oligopoly market is strong, the product undifferentiated, and the result is very much like perfect competition in the long run. At the other extreme, if oligopolistic firms successfully collude (mostly illegally), they will charge the price a monopolist would and agree to share the economic profits. Between these extremes we have the following models:

The **kinked demand curve model** is based on an assumption that a firm's competitors will not follow a price increase but will cut their prices in response to a price decrease by a competitor. Under this model, each firm faces a demand curve with a kink at the current market price – more elastic above the current price and less elastic below the current price.

The **Cournot model** assumes that the firms in a two-firm oligopoly have identical cost structures and react only to the price charged by the other firm in the prior period. Each firm will produce half the industry output and charge the same price in equilibrium. This is a special case of a **Nash equilibrium**, defined as a situation in which no firm can increase profits by changing its price/output choice. The incentive for firms to cheat on a collusive agreement that is not a Nash equilibrium is one reason that collusive agreements are difficult to maintain.

In the **dominant firm model**, one firm is assumed to have the lowest cost structure and a significant proportion of the market. In this case, the dominant firm essentially sets the price for the industry, and competitors set their output quantities taking this price as given.

Supply Curves and Market Structure

Under perfect competition, a firm's short-run supply curve is the portion of the firm's short-run marginal cost curve above average variable cost. A firm's long-run supply curve is the portion of the firm's long-run marginal cost curve above average total cost.

Firms operating under monopolistic competition, oligopoly, and monopoly do not have well-defined supply functions, so neither marginal cost curves nor average cost curves are supply curves in these cases.

To identify the type of market in which a firm operates, an analyst should focus on the number of firms in the market, their market shares, the nature of competition, the availability of substitute goods, and barriers to entry into and exit from the industry.

STUDY SESSION 5: ECONOMICS—MACROECONOMIC ANALYSIS

AGGREGATE OUTPUT, PRICES, AND ECONOMIC GROWTH
Cross-Reference to CFA Institute Assigned Reading #17

There are alternative methods of calculating gross domestic product (GDP), the market value of all final goods and services produced within a country over a specific time period, usually one year.

Using the **income approach**, GDP is calculated as the total income earned by households and businesses in the country during a time period.

Using the **expenditure approach**, GDP is calculated as the total amount spent on goods and services produced in the country during a time period.

The expenditure approach to measuring GDP can use the **sum-of-value-added method** or the **value-of-final-output method**.

- *Sum-of-value-added*: GDP is calculated by summing the additions to value created at each stage of production and distribution.
- *Value-of-final-output*: GDP is calculated by summing the values of all final goods and services produced during the period.

GDP under all these methods is the same, and estimates using different methods will differ only due to statistical discrepancies.

Nominal GDP values goods and services at their current prices. **Real GDP** measures current-year output using prices from a base year.

The GDP deflator is a price index that can be used to convert nominal GDP into real GDP by removing the effects of changes in prices. Price change estimates are based on the ratio of current-year nominal GDP to the value of the current-year output mix using base-year prices.

The four components of gross domestic product are consumption spending, business investment, government spending, and net exports. The relationship among them is:

$$GDP = C + I + G + (X - M)$$

National income is the income received by all factors of production used in the creation of final output.

Personal income is the pretax income received by households.

Personal disposable income is personal income after taxes.

Private saving and investment are related to the fiscal balance and the trade balance. A fiscal deficit must be financed by some combination of a trade deficit or an excess of private saving over private investment. We write this relation as:

$$(G - T) = (S - I) - (X - M)$$

From this relation, we can see that a government budget deficit can be offset by a trade deficit or an excess of domestic savings over domestic investment. A government budget deficit combined with a trade surplus $(X - M > 0)$ must be offset by a surplus of domestic savings over domestic investment.

The **IS curve** shows the negative relationship between the real interest rate (y-axis) and equilibrium value of aggregate income (which must equal planned expenditures) consistent with each real interest rate.

For a given level of the real money supply, the **LM curve** shows the positive relationship between the real interest rate (y-axis) and the level of aggregate income at which demand for and supply of real money balances are equal.

The points at which the IS curve intersects the LM curves for different levels of the real money supply (i.e., for different price levels, holding the nominal money supply constant) form the **aggregate demand curve**. The aggregate demand curve shows the negative relationship between GDP (real output demanded) and the price level (y-axis) when other factors are held constant.

In Panel (a) of Figure 18, we illustrate the IS curve and LM curves for different levels of the money supply (and the price level). These intersections allow us to create the aggregate demand curve in Panel (b), which shows the relation between the price level (for various levels of the money supply) and real income (real GDP).

Figure 18: Deriving the Aggregate Demand Curve

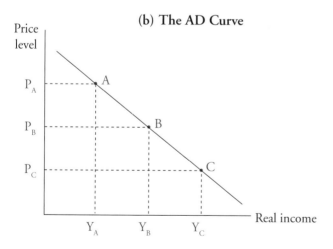

(a) The IS and LM Curves

(b) The AD Curve

The **short-run aggregate supply curve** shows the positive relationship between real GDP supplied and the price level when other factors are held constant. Because we hold some input costs fixed in the short run (e.g., wages), the SRAS curve slopes upward because higher output prices result in greater output (real wages fall).

Because all input prices are assumed to be flexible in the long run, the **long-run aggregate supply curve** is perfectly inelastic (vertical). Long-run aggregate supply represents **potential GDP**, the full-employment level of economic output.

Shifts in the aggregate demand curve are caused by changes in household wealth, business and consumer expectations, capacity utilization, fiscal policy, monetary policy, currency exchange rates, and global economic growth rates.

Shifts in the short-run aggregate supply curve are caused by changes in nominal wages or other input prices, expectations of future prices, business taxes, business subsidies, and currency exchange rates, as well as by the factors that affect long-run aggregate supply.

Shifts in the long-run aggregate supply curve are caused by changes in labor supply and quality, the supply of physical capital, the availability of natural resources, and the level of technology.

In Figure 19, we illustrate the situation in the short run when aggregate demand decreases (Panel a) and increases (Panel b). The situation in Panel a when aggregate demand has decreased is referred to as a **recessionary gap** because real GDP is less than potential real GDP (LRAS). The resulting downward pressure on input prices will result in an increase in SRAS. The SRAS curve will shift to the right as input prices fall until aggregate demand once again equals LRAS.

Figure 19: Long-Run Disequilibrium

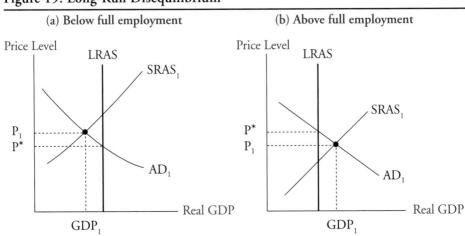

In Panel b we illustrate an increase in aggregate demand that results in an **inflationary gap**. Here real GDP is greater than potential real GDP in the short run, causing upward pressure on input prices. As input prices increase, SRAS decreases and long-run equilibrium is restored as we move along the aggregate demand curve to its intersection with LRAS.

Stagflation is simultaneous high inflation and weak economic growth, which can result from a sudden decrease in short-run aggregate supply.

Sources of economic growth include:

- Increases in the supply of labor.
- Increases in human capital.
- Increases in the supply of physical capital.
- Increases in the availability of natural resources.
- Advances in technology.

The **sustainable rate of economic growth** is determined by the rate of increase in the labor force and the rate of increase in labor productivity.

A **production function** relates economic output to the supply of labor, the supply of capital, and total factor productivity. Total factor productivity is a residual factor, which represents that part of economic growth not accounted for by increases in the supply of either labor or capital. Increases in total factor productivity can be attributed to advances in technology.

In developed countries, where a high level of capital per worker is available and capital inputs experience diminishing marginal productivity, technological advances that increase total factor productivity are the main source of sustainable economic growth.

UNDERSTANDING BUSINESS CYCLES
Cross-Reference to CFA Institute Assigned Reading #18

The business cycle has four phases: **expansion** (real GDP is increasing), **peak** (real GDP stops increasing and begins decreasing), **contraction** or **recession** (real GDP is decreasing), and **trough** (real GDP stops decreasing and begins increasing).

Figure 20: Business Cycle

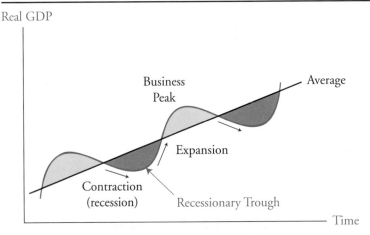

Inventory-to-sales ratios typically increase late in expansions, when sales slow unexpectedly, and decrease near the end of contractions, when sales unexpectedly begin to accelerate. As firm expectations change, firms decrease or increase production to restore their inventory-to-sales ratios to their desired levels.

Because hiring and laying off employees have high costs, firms prefer to adjust their utilization of current employees. As a result, firms are slow to lay off employees early in contractions and slow to add employees early in expansions.

Firms use their physical capital more intensively during expansions, investing in new capacity only if they believe the expansion is likely to continue. They use physical capital less intensively during contractions, but they are more likely to reduce capacity by deferring maintenance and not replacing equipment than by selling their physical capital.

Business Cycle Theories

Neoclassical economists: Business cycles are temporary and driven by changes in technology. Rapid adjustments of wages and other input prices cause the economy to move to full-employment equilibrium.

Keynesian economists: Excessive optimism or pessimism among business managers causes business cycles. Contractions can persist because wages are slow to move downward.

New Keynesians: Input prices other than wages are also slow to move downward.

Monetarists: Inappropriate changes in the rate of money supply growth cause business cycles. Money supply growth should be maintained at a moderate and predictable rate to support the growth of real GDP.

Austrian-school economists: Business cycles are initiated by government intervention that drives interest rates to artificially low levels.

Real business cycle theory: Business cycles result from utility-maximizing actions in response to real economic changes, such as external shocks and changes in technology. Policymakers should not intervene in business cycles.

Unemployment

Frictional unemployment results from the time lag necessary to match employees seeking work with employers seeking their skills and is always present as employers expand or contract their businesses and as workers move, are fired, or quit to seek other opportunities.

Structural unemployment is caused by long-run changes in the economy that eliminate some jobs while generating other jobs for which unemployed workers are not qualified, so these workers must learn new skills.

Cyclical unemployment is caused by changes in the general level of economic activity. It is positive when the economy is operating at less than full capacity and negative when an expansion leads to employment temporarily above the full employment level.

A person is considered to be **unemployed** if he is not working *and* actively searching for work. The **labor force** includes all people who are either employed or unemployed. The **unemployment rate** is the percentage of people in the labor force who are unemployed. A person who is employed part time but would prefer to work full time, or is employed at a low-paying job despite being qualified for a significantly higher-paying one, is said to be **underemployed**.

The **participation ratio** (also referred to as the *activity ratio* or *labor force participation rate*) is the percentage of the working-age population who are either employed or actively seeking employment.

Short-term fluctuations in the participation ratio can occur because of changes in the number of **discouraged workers**, those who are available for work but are neither employed nor actively seeking employment. The participation rate tends to increase when the economy expands and decrease during recessions.

The movement of discouraged workers out of and back into the labor force causes the unemployment rate to be a lagging indicator of the business cycle. Early in an expansion when hiring prospects begin to improve, the number of discouraged workers who re-enter the labor force is greater than the number hired immediately. This causes the unemployment rate to increase even though employment is expanding. To gauge the current state of the labor market, analysts should also observe other widely available indicators such as the number of employees on payrolls.

Firms' tendency to be slow to hire or lay off workers at business cycle turning points also causes the unemployment rate to lag the business cycle. The effect can also be seen in data on **productivity**, or output per hour worked. Productivity declines early in contractions as firms are slow to reduce employment and increases early in expansions as firms produce more output but are slow to hire new employees.

Inflation

Inflation is a persistent increase in the price level over time. Inflation erodes the purchasing power of a currency. Inflation favors borrowers at the expense of lenders because when the borrower returns the principal to the lender, it is worth less in terms of goods and services (in real terms) than it was worth when it was borrowed.

Inflation that accelerates out of control is referred to as **hyperinflation**, which can destroy a country's monetary system and bring about social and political upheavals.

The **inflation rate** is the percentage increase in the price level, typically compared to the prior year.

Disinflation refers to an inflation rate that is decreasing over time but remains greater than zero.

A persistently decreasing price level (i.e., a negative inflation rate) is called **deflation**. Deflation is commonly associated with deep recessions.

A **price index** measures the total cost of a specific basket of goods and services relative to its cost in a prior (base) period. The inflation rate is most often calculated as the annual percentage change in a price index. **Core inflation** is calculated by excluding food and energy prices from a price index because of their high short-term volatility.

The most widely followed price index is the **consumer price index (CPI)**, which is based on the purchasing patterns of a typical household. The **GDP deflator** (described earlier) and the **producer** or **wholesale price index** are used as measures of price inflation of goods in process and may give early indications of changes in consumer prices. Analysts can observe sub-indexes of the producer price index for different stages of processing (raw materials, intermediate goods, and finished goods) or for specific industries for indications of emerging price pressure.

A **Laspeyres price index** is based on the cost of a specific basket of goods and services that represents actual consumption in a base period. New goods, quality improvements, and consumers' substitution of lower-priced goods for higher-priced goods over time cause a Laspeyres index to be biased upward.

A **Paasche price index** uses current consumption weights for the basket of goods and services for both periods, thereby reducing substitution bias. A **Fisher price index** is the geometric mean of a Laspeyres index and a Paasche index and is termed a *chained index*.

Cost-push inflation results from a decrease in aggregate supply caused by an increase in the real price of an important factor of production, such as labor or energy. Because wages are the largest cost to businesses, analysts look to the unemployment rate as an indicator of future inflationary pressure. The **non-accelerating inflation rate of unemployment** (NAIRU) represents the unemployment rate below which upward pressure on wages is likely to develop.

Demand-pull inflation results from persistent increases in aggregate demand that increase the price level and temporarily increase economic output above its potential or full-employment level. This could result from expansionary fiscal policy when the economy is already near full employment. Monetarists focus on growth in the money supply in excess of the growth rate of real GDP as a cause of demand-pull inflation. Excessive money supply growth will create excess liquidity, reduce interest rates, and increase aggregate demand, resulting in demand-pull inflation.

Because recent inflation levels affect inflation expectations, which are reflected in input prices (commodity prices and especially wages), inflation can persist even after an economy has fallen into recession. Slow or negative economic growth together with high inflation is termed *stagflation*.

Leading, Coincident, and Lagging Indicators

Economic indicators are used by analysts to assess the current state of the economy and to provide information about future economic activity. Indicators are classified by how they rise and fall relative to the phases of the business cycle.

- *Leading indicators* have turning points that tend to precede those of the business cycle. Weekly hours in manufacturing, the S&P 500 return, private building permits, initial unemployment claims, and the real M2 money supply are examples of leading indicators.

- *Coincident indicators* have turning points that tend to coincide with those of the business cycle and are used to indicate the current phase of the business cycle. Examples are manufacturing activity, personal income, and number of non-agricultural employees.
- *Lagging indicators* have turning points that tend to occur after those of the business cycle. The bank prime lending rate, inventory-to-sales ratio, average duration of unemployment, and the change in unit labor costs are examples of lagging indicators.

A limitation of using economic indicators to predict business cycles is that their relationships with the business cycle are inexact and can vary over time.

FISCAL AND MONETARY POLICY
Cross-Reference to CFA Institute Assigned Reading #19

Fiscal policy is a government's use of taxation and spending to influence the economy.

Monetary policy deals with determining the quantity of money supplied by the central bank. Both policies aim to achieve economic growth with price level stability, although governments use fiscal policy for social and political reasons as well.

Money is defined as a **medium of exchange. Functions of money** include a medium of exchange, a store of value, and a unit of account.

In a **fractional reserve system**, new money created is a multiple of new excess reserves available for lending by banks. The potential multiplier is equal to *the reciprocal of the reserve requirement* and, therefore, is inversely related to the reserve requirement.

Three factors influence **money demand:**

1. Transaction demand, for buying goods and services.

2. Precautionary demand, to meet unforeseen future needs.

3. Speculative demand, to take advantage of investment opportunities.

The **money supply** is determined by central banks with the goal of managing inflation and other economic variables.

The **Fisher effect** states that a nominal interest rate is equal to the real interest rate plus the expected inflation rate.

Central bank roles include:

- Supplying currency, acting as banker to the government and to other banks.
- Regulating and supervising the payments system.
- Acting as a lender of last resort.
- Holding the nation's gold and foreign currency reserves.
- Conducting monetary policy.

Central banks have the objective of controlling inflation. Some central banks have additional goals such as maintaining currency stability, full employment, positive sustainable economic growth, or moderate interest rates.

Policy tools available to central banks:

- Changing the policy rate.
- Changing the reserve requirement.
- Open market operations.

The policy rate is called the *discount rate* in the United States, the *refinancing rate* by the European Central Bank, and the *two-week repo rate* in the United Kingdom. It can be thought of as the rate the central bank charges member banks to borrow reserves.

Decreasing the policy rate, decreasing reserve requirements, and making open market purchases of securities are all expansionary (tend to increase economic growth). Increasing the policy rate, increasing reserve requirements, and making open market sales of securities are all contractionary (reduce economic growth).

Effective central banks exhibit:

- *Independence*: The central bank is free from political interference.
- *Credibility*: The central bank follows through on its stated policy intentions.
- *Transparency*: The central bank makes it clear what economic indicators it uses and reports on the state of those indicators.

An increase in the growth rate of the money supply will decrease nominal and (in the short run) real interest rates, which will increase economic growth. Because lower real interest rates will decrease foreign investment and demand for the domestic currency, an increase in the growth rate of the money supply will cause the domestic currency to depreciate relative to those of the country's trading partners. The depreciation of the domestic currency will increase export demand, further increasing economic growth. In the long run, the increase in the money supply will not decrease real interest rates because inflation (and inflation expectations) will increase, offsetting the decrease in nominal interest rates. A decrease in the growth rate of the money supply will have opposite effects.

The **real trend rate** is the long-term sustainable real growth rate of an economy. The **neutral interest rate** is the sum of the real trend rate and the target inflation rate. Monetary policy is said to be contractionary when the policy rate is above the neutral rate and expansionary when the policy rate is below the neutral rate.

Reasons that monetary policy may not work as intended:

- Monetary policy changes may affect inflation expectations to such an extent that long-term interest rates move opposite to short-term interest rates.
- Individuals may be willing to hold greater cash balances without a change in short-term rates so that an expansion of the money supply does not reduce short-term rates (liquidity trap).
- Banks may be unwilling to lend greater amounts, even when they have more excess reserves as a result of an increase in the money supply.
- Short-term rates cannot be reduced below zero.
- Developing economies face unique challenges in utilizing monetary policy due to undeveloped financial markets, rapid financial innovation, and lack of credibility of the monetary authority.

Fiscal policy refers to the taxing and spending policies of the government. Objectives of fiscal policy can include:

- Influencing the level of economic activity.
- Redistributing wealth or income.
- Allocating resources among industries.

Fiscal policy is implemented by governmental changes in taxing and spending policies.

A government has a *budget surplus* when tax revenues exceed government spending and a *budget deficit* when spending exceeds tax revenue.

Fiscal policy tools include spending tools and revenue tools. Spending tools include transfer payments, current spending (goods and services used by government), and capital spending (investment projects funded by government). Revenue tools include direct and indirect taxation.

An increase (decrease) in a government budget surplus is indicative of a contractionary (expansionary) fiscal policy. Similarly, an increase (decrease) in a government budget deficit is indicative of an expansionary (contractionary) fiscal policy.

An *advantage of fiscal policy* is that indirect taxes (sales, value-added, and excise taxes) can be used to quickly implement social policies and can also be used to quickly raise revenues at a low cost.

Disadvantages of fiscal policy include time lags for implementing changes in direct taxes and time lags for capital spending changes to have an impact. Delays (lags) in realizing the effects of fiscal policy changes limit their usefulness.

Types of lags:

- **Recognition lag**: Policymakers may not immediately recognize when fiscal policy changes are needed.
- **Action lag**: Governments take time to enact needed fiscal policy changes.
- **Impact lag**: Fiscal policy changes take time to affect economic activity.

Arguments for being concerned with the size of fiscal deficit:

- Higher future taxes lead to disincentives to work, negatively affecting long-term economic growth.
- Fiscal deficits might not be financed by the market when debt levels are high.
- A *crowding-out effect* as government borrowing increases interest rates and decreases private sector investment.

Arguments against being concerned with the size of fiscal deficit:

- Debt may be financed by domestic citizens.
- Deficits for capital spending can boost the productive capacity of the economy.
- Fiscal deficits may prompt needed tax reform.
- *Ricardian equivalence* may prevail: private savings rise in anticipation of the need to repay principal on government debt.
- When the economy is operating below full employment, deficits do not crowd out private investment.

Monetary and fiscal policy will interact, and when one is expansionary and the other is contractionary, they will offset to some degree. The following table summarizes the effects for different combinations of fiscal and monetary policy.

Monetary Policy	Fiscal Policy	Interest Rates	Output	Private Sector Spending	Public Sector Spending
Tight	Tight	higher	lower	lower	lower
Easy	Easy	lower	higher	higher	higher
Tight	Easy	higher	higher	lower	higher
Easy	Tight	lower	varies	higher	lower

STUDY SESSION 6: ECONOMICS—ECONOMICS IN A GLOBAL CONTEXT

INTERNATIONAL TRADE AND CAPITAL FLOWS
Cross-Reference to CFA Institute Assigned Reading #20

Gross domestic product (GDP) is the total value of goods and services produced within a country's borders over a period. **Gross national product** (GNP) is the total value of goods and services produced by the labor and capital of a country's citizens. Income of a country's citizens working abroad is included in its GNP but not in its GDP. Income to capital in the domestic country that is owned by foreigners is included in the domestic country's GDP but not in its GNP. GDP is more closely related to economic activity within a country's borders.

A country is said to have an **absolute advantage** in the production of a good if it can produce the good at a lower cost, in terms of resources, than another country.

A country is said to have a **comparative advantage** in the production of a good if its opportunity cost, in terms of other goods that could be produced instead, is lower than that of another country. The opportunity cost of producing a unit of one good is the number of units of another good that could be produced instead.

Regardless of absolute advantage, if the opportunity costs of producing two goods are different between two countries, trading will allow each country to specialize in production of the good in which it has a comparative advantage, resulting in greater overall production of both goods and increased economic welfare. The costs of trade are primarily those imposed on workers and firms in industries that face competition from lower cost imported goods.

Assume the following labor inputs are required to produce cloth and wine in England and Portugal:

	Cloth	Wine
England	100	110
Portugal	90	80

The opportunity cost of one unit of wine in England is 110 / 100 = 1.1 units of cloth. In Portugal, the opportunity cost of one unit of wine is 80 / 90 = 0.89 units of cloth.

Portugal has an absolute advantage in producing both goods and a comparative advantage in the production of wine. England has a comparative advantage in the production of cloth (cost is 100/110 wine versus 90/80 wine for Portugal).

©2015 Kaplan, Inc.

The **Ricardian model of trade** has only one factor of production—labor. The source of comparative advantage in Ricardo's model is *differences in labor productivity* due to differences in technology.

Heckscher and Ohlin presented a model in which there are two factors of production—capital and labor. The source of comparative advantage (differences in opportunity costs) in this model is *differences in the relative amounts of each factor* the countries possess. The country that has more capital will specialize in the capital intensive good and trade for the less capital intensive good with the country that has relatively more labor and less capital. In the **Heckscher-Ohlin model**, there is a redistribution of wealth within each country between labor and the owners of capital. The price of the relatively less scarce (more available) factor of production in each country will increase so that its owners will earn more compared to what they would earn without trade.

Types of Trade Restrictions

- **Tariffs:** Taxes on imported goods collected by the government.
- **Quotas:** Limits on the amount of imports allowed over some period.
- **Export subsidies:** Government payments to firms that export goods.
- **Minimum domestic content:** Requirement that some percentage of product content must be from the domestic country.
- **Voluntary export restraint:** A country voluntarily restricts the amount of a good that can be exported, often in the hope of avoiding tariffs or quotas imposed by their trading partners.

In general, all trade restrictions make foreign producers worse off, domestic producers and industry workers better off, and domestic consumers worse off. In Figure 21, note that prior to the imposition of a quota or tariff, the total quantity demanded domestically is QD_1, and QS_1 is supplied by domestic suppliers at price P_{World}. The imposition of the tariff raises the price on imports to $P_{Protection}$, the quantity demanded decreases to QD_2, the quantity supplied by domestic producers increases to QS_2, and the quantity of imports decreases. The result is an increase in the domestic price of the good and a loss of consumer surplus equal to the blue-shaded area. The portion with vertical lines is an increase in domestic producers' surplus, the portion with horizontal lines is the total tariff revenue collected by the government, and the other two areas represent a deadweight loss.

Figure 21: Effects of Tariffs and Quotas

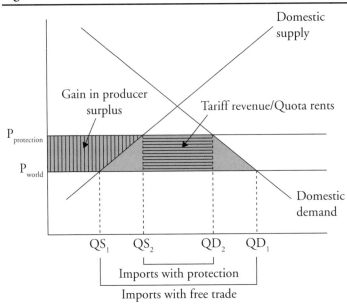

Some countries impose **capital restrictions** on the flow of financial capital across borders. Restrictions include:

- Outright prohibition of investment in the domestic country by foreigners.
- Prohibition of or taxes on the income earned on foreign investments by domestic citizens.
- Prohibition of foreign investment in certain domestic industries.
- Restrictions on repatriation of earnings of foreign entities operating in a country.

Overall, capital restrictions are thought to decrease economic welfare, but they do protect developing countries from large swings in asset prices as foreign capital moves into and out of a particular country.

Trade agreements can be categorized by the degree of economic integration among the participants. Each type of agreement in the following list includes the provisions in the previous type of agreement, so that monetary union is the most integrated and includes all the provisions listed.

- **Free trade area:** All barriers to import and export of goods and services among member countries are removed.
- **Customs union:** In addition, all member countries adopt a common set of trade restrictions with non-members.
- **Common market:** In addition, all barriers to the movement of labor and capital goods among member countries are removed.
- **Economic union:** In addition, member countries establish common institutions and economic policy.
- **Monetary union:** In addition, member countries adopt a single currency.

Balance of Payments Accounts

According to the U.S. Federal Reserve, "The BOP [**balance of payments**] includes the **current account**, which mainly measures the flows of goods and services; the **capital account**, which consists of capital transfers and the acquisition and disposal of non-produced, non-financial assets; and the **financial account**, which records investment flows."

The **current account** comprises three sub-accounts:

* Merchandise and services.
* Income receipts, including foreign income from dividends on stock holdings and interest on debt securities.
* Unilateral transfers, which are one-way transfers of assets.

The **capital account** comprises two sub-accounts:

* Capital transfers.
* Sales and purchases of non-financial assets.

The **financial account** comprises two sub-accounts:

* Government-owned assets abroad.
* Foreign-owned assets in the domestic country.

A country that has imports valued more than its exports is said to have a **current account (trade) deficit**, while countries with more exports than imports are said to have a **current account surplus**. For a country with a trade deficit, it must be balanced by a net surplus in the capital and financial accounts. As a result, investment analysts often think of all financing flows as a single "capital" account that combines items in the capital and financial accounts. Thinking in this way, any deficit in the current account must be made up by a surplus in the (combined) capital account.

In equilibrium, we have the relationship:

$$\text{exports} - \text{imports} = \text{private savings} + \text{government savings} - \text{domestic investment}$$

When total savings is less than domestic investment, imports must be greater than exports so that there is a deficit in the current account. Lower levels of private saving, larger government deficits, and high rates of domestic investment all tend to result in or increase a current account deficit. The intuition here is that low private or government savings in relation to private investment in domestic capital requires foreign investment in domestic capital.

The **International Monetary Fund** (IMF) facilitates trade by promoting international monetary cooperation and exchange rate stability, assists in setting up international payments systems, and makes resources available to member countries with balance of payments problems.

The **World Bank** provides low-interest loans, interest-free credits, and grants to developing countries for many specific purposes. It also provides resources and knowledge and helps form private/public partnerships with the overall goal of fighting poverty.

The **World Trade Organization** (WTO) has the goal of ensuring that trade flows freely and works smoothly. Their main focus is on instituting, interpreting, and enforcing a number of multilateral trade agreements, which detail global trade policies for a large majority of the world's trading nations.

CURRENCY EXCHANGE RATES
Cross-Reference to CFA Institute Assigned Reading #21

At a point in time, the **nominal exchange rate** $1.416/euro suggests that in order to purchase one euro's worth of goods and services in Euroland, the cost in U.S. dollars will be $1.416. We sometimes refer to the numerator currency as the **price currency** and the denominator currency as the **base currency**. In the case of an exchange rate quote of 1.416 USD/EUR, the U.S. dollar is the price currency (expresses the price of one euro) and the euro is the base currency (easy to remember because it is in the bottom or base of the quote).

As time passes, the **real exchange rate** tells us the dollar cost of purchasing that same unit of goods and services based on the new (current) dollar/euro exchange rate and the relative changes in the price levels of both countries. The formula for this calculation, where d/f means domestic currency per foreign currency unit, is:

$$\text{real exchange rate (d/f)} = \text{nominal exchange rate (d/f)} \times \left(\frac{\text{foreign CPI}}{\text{domestic CPI}} \right)$$

If the nominal exchange rate (d/f) increases over a period by the same percentage as the domestic price level increases relative to the foreign price level, the real exchange rate is unchanged. With the nominal exchange rate unchanged over a period, the real exchange rate will increase (decrease) if the foreign price level increases more (less) than the domestic price level.

A **spot exchange rate** is the currency exchange rate for immediate delivery.

©2015 Kaplan, Inc.

A **forward exchange rate** is a currency exchange rate for an exchange to be done in the future. Forward rates are quoted for various future dates (e.g., 30 days, 60 days, 90 days, or one year). A forward is actually an agreement to exchange a specific amount of one currency for a specific amount of another on a future date specified in the forward agreement.

The market for foreign exchange is the largest financial market in terms of the value of daily transactions and has a variety of participants, including large multinational banks (the sell side) and corporations, investment fund managers, hedge fund managers, investors, governments, and central banks (the buy side).

Participants in the foreign exchange markets are referred to as *hedgers* if they enter into transactions that decrease an existing foreign exchange risk and as *speculators* if they enter into transactions that increase their foreign exchange risk.

For a change in an exchange rate, we can calculate the **percentage appreciation or depreciation** of the *base currency*. For example, a decrease in the USD/EUR exchange rate from 1.44 to 1.42 represents a depreciation of the EUR relative to the USD of 1.39% (1.42 / 1.44 − 1 = −0.0139) because the USD price of a euro has gone down.

To calculate the appreciation or depreciation of the USD (relative to the euro), we first convert the quotes to EUR/USD (making the USD the base currency) and then proceed as above. The initial rate becomes 1/1.44 = 0.6944 EUR/USD, and the later rate becomes 1/1.42 = 0.7042 EUR/USD. The change in the exchange value of the dollar (now the base currency) is 0.7042/0.6944 − 1 = +0.0141, so the USD has appreciated 1.41% relative to the euro over the period.

Given two exchange rate quotes for three different currencies, we can calculate a **currency cross rate**. If the MXN/USD quote is 12.1 and the USD/EUR quote is 1.42, we can calculate the MXN/EUR cross rate as 12.1 × 1.42 = 17.18. That is, a euro is priced at 17.18 Mexican pesos.

Points in a foreign currency quotation are in units of the last digit of the quotation. For example, a forward quote of +25.3 when the USD/EUR spot exchange rate is 1.4158 means that the forward exchange rate is 1.4158 + 0.00253 = 1.41833 USD/EUR.

For a forward exchange rate quote given as a percentage, the percentage change in the spot rate is calculated as forward / spot − 1. A forward exchange rate quote of +1.787%, when the spot USD/EUR exchange rate is 1.4158, means that the forward exchange rate is 1.4158 (1 + 0.01787) = 1.4411 USD/EUR.

The percentage difference between the spot exchange rate and the forward exchange rate, expressed as price/base values, is approximately equal to the interest rate (i) for the base currency minus the interest rate for the price currency over the forward period. The exact relationship is:

$$\frac{\text{Forward}}{\text{Spot}} = \frac{1 + i_{\text{Price Currency}}}{1 + i_{\text{Base Currency}}} \text{ so that Forward} = \text{Spot} \times \frac{1 + i_{\text{Price Currency}}}{1 + i_{\text{Base Currency}}}$$

Exchange rate regimes for countries that do not have their own currency:

- With *formal dollarization*, a country uses the currency of another country.
- In a *monetary union*, several countries use a common currency.

Exchange rate regimes for countries that have their own currency:

- A *currency board arrangement* is an explicit commitment to exchange domestic currency for a specified foreign currency at a fixed exchange rate.
- In a *conventional fixed peg arrangement*, a country pegs its currency within margins of ±1% versus another currency.
- In a system of *pegged exchange rates within horizontal bands* or a *target zone*, the permitted fluctuations in currency value relative to another currency or basket of currencies are wider (e.g., ±2 %).
- With a *crawling peg*, the exchange rate is adjusted periodically, typically to adjust for higher inflation versus the currency used in the peg.
- With *management of exchange rates within crawling bands*, the width of the bands that identify permissible exchange rates is increased over time.
- With a system of *managed floating exchange rates*, the monetary authority attempts to influence the exchange rate in response to specific indicators, such as the balance of payments, inflation rates, or employment without any specific target exchange rate.
- When a currency is *independently floating*, the exchange rate is market-determined.

The effect of a depreciation of the domestic currency on a country's trade balance can be analyzed using either the **elasticities approach** or the **absorption approach**.

Under the *elasticities approach,* for a depreciation of the domestic currency to reduce an existing trade deficit, the elasticities (ε) of export and import demand must meet the **Marshall-Lerner condition:**

$$W_{\text{Exports}} \varepsilon_{\text{Exports}} + W_{\text{Imports}} (\varepsilon_{\text{Imports}} - 1) > 0$$

where:
ε = elasticity
W = the proportion of total trade for imports or exports

For situations where a country does not have a trade deficit or surplus, this condition simplifies to $\varepsilon_{Exports} + \varepsilon_{Imports} > 1$.

Under the *absorption approach*, national income must increase relative to national expenditure in order to decrease a trade deficit. This can also be viewed as a requirement that national saving must increase relative to domestic investment in order to decrease a trade deficit.

The **J-curve effect** refers to the fact that a depreciation of the domestic currency may increase a trade deficit in the short run (because of existing foreign-currency-priced export contracts) even though it will eventually reduce the trade deficit.

FINANCIAL REPORTING AND ANALYSIS

Study Sessions 7, 8, 9, & 10

Weight on Exam	20%
SchweserNotes™ Reference	Book 3, Pages 1–339

STUDY SESSION 7: FINANCIAL REPORTING AND ANALYSIS—AN INTRODUCTION

Study Session 7 introduces the sources of financial information on which an analyst can draw when making investment recommendations. This session outlines the basic principles of recording financial transactions and events and discusses the role of standard setting bodies in determining how transactions and events should be recorded.

FINANCIAL STATEMENT ANALYSIS: AN INTRODUCTION
Cross-Reference to CFA Institute Assigned Reading #22

The **income statement** reports on the financial performance of the firm over a period of time. The elements of the income statement include revenues, expenses, gains, and losses.

- *Revenues* are inflows from delivering or producing goods, rendering services, or other activities that constitute the entity's ongoing major or central operations.
- *Expenses* are outflows from delivering or producing goods or services that constitute the entity's ongoing major or central operations.
- *Gains and losses* are increases (decreases) in equity or net assets from peripheral or incidental transactions.

The **balance sheet** reports the firm's financial position at a point in time. The balance sheet consists of three elements:

1. *Assets* are probable current and future economic benefits obtained or controlled by a particular entity as a result of past transactions or events.

2. *Liabilities* are probable future sacrifices of economic benefits. They arise from present obligations of a particular entity to transfer assets or provide services to other entities in the future as a result of past transactions or events.

3. *Owners' equity* is the residual interest in the assets of an entity that remains after deducting its liabilities.

©2015 Kaplan, Inc.

Transactions are measured so that the fundamental accounting equation holds:

$$\text{assets} = \text{liabilities} + \text{owners' equity}$$

The **cash flow statement** reports the company's cash receipts and outflows. These cash flows are classified as follows:

- *Operating cash flows* include the cash effects of transactions that involve the normal business of the firm.
- *Investing cash flows* are those resulting from acquisition or sale of property, plant, and equipment, of a subsidiary or segment, and purchase or sale of investments in other firms.
- *Financing cash flows* are those resulting from issuance or retirement of debt and equity securities and dividends paid to stockholders.

The **statement of changes in owners' equity** reports the amounts and sources of changes in equity investors' investment in the firm.

Financial statement notes (footnotes) include disclosures that offer further detail about the information summarized in the financial statements. Footnotes allow users to improve their assessments of the amount, timing, and uncertainty of the estimates reported in the financial statements. Footnotes:

- Provide information about accounting methods and the assumptions and estimates used by management.
- Are audited, whereas other disclosures, such as supplementary schedules, are not audited.
- Provide additional information on such items as fixed assets, inventory, income taxes, pensions, debt, contingencies and commitments, marketable securities, significant customers, sales to related parties, and export sales.
- Often contain disclosures relating to contingent losses.

Supplementary schedules contain additional information. Examples of such disclosures are:

- Operating income or sales by region or business segment.
- Reserves for an oil and gas company.
- Information about hedging activities and financial instruments.

Management's commentary, or **management's discussion and analysis** (MD&A), provides an assessment of the financial performance and condition of a company from the perspective of its management. For publicly held companies in the United States, the MD&A is required to discuss:

- Trends, significant events, and uncertainties that affect the firm.
- Effects of inflation and changing prices, if material.
- Impact of off-blance-sheet and contractual obligations.

- Accounting policies that require significant judgment by management.
- Forward-looking expenditures and divestitures.

Audit Reports

An **audit** is an independent review of an entity's financial statements. Public accountants conduct audits and examine the financial reports and supporting records. The objective of an audit is to enable the auditor to provide an opinion on the fairness and reliability of the financial reports.

The independent certified public accountant employed by the board of directors is responsible for seeing that the financial statements conform to Generally Accepted Accounting Principles (GAAP). The auditor examines the company's accounting and internal control systems, confirms assets and liabilities, and generally tries to be confident that there are no material errors in the financial statements and that they conform to applicable reporting standards. The auditor's report is an important source of information.

The **standard auditor's opinion** contains three parts, stating that:

1. Whereas the financial statements are prepared by management and are its responsibility, the auditor has performed an independent review.
2. Generally accepted auditing standards were followed, thus providing *reasonable assurance* that the financial statements contain no material errors.
3. The auditor is satisfied that the statements were prepared in accordance with GAAP and that the accounting principles chosen and estimates made are reasonable. The auditor's report must also contain additional explanation when accounting methods have not been used consistently between periods.

An *unqualified opinion* indicates that the auditor believes the statements are free from material omissions and errors. If the statements make any exceptions to GAAP, the auditor may issue a *qualified opinion* and explain these exceptions in the audit report. The auditor can issue an *adverse opinion* if the statements are not presented fairly or are materially nonconforming with GAAP, or a *disclaimer of opinion* if the auditor is unable to express an opinion.

The auditor's opinion will also contain an explanatory paragraph when a material loss is probable but the amount cannot be reasonably estimated. These "uncertainties" may relate to the *going concern assumption* (financial statements assume the firm will continue to operate), the valuation or realization of assets, or to litigation. This type of disclosure may be a signal of serious problems and call for closer examination by the analyst.

Under U.S. GAAP, the auditor must state an opinion on the company's **internal controls**, the processes by which the company ensures that it presents accurate financial statements. Internal controls are the responsibility of the firm's management. Under the Sarbanes-Oxley Act, management is required to provide a report on the company's internal control system.

An analyst should examine a company's *quarterly or semiannual reports* which typically update the major financial statements and footnotes, but are not necessarily audited.

Other Information Sources

Securities and Exchange Commission filings are available from EDGAR (Electronic Data Gathering, Analysis, and Retrieval System, *www.sec.gov*). These include Form 8-K, which a company must file to report events, such as acquisitions and disposals of major assets, or changes in its management or corporate governance. Companies' annual and quarterly financial statements are also filed with the SEC (Form 10-K and Form 10-Q respectively).

Proxy statements are issued to shareholders when there are matters that require a shareholder vote. These statements, which are also filed with the SEC and available from EDGAR, are a good source of information about the election of (and qualifications of) board members, compensation, management qualifications, and the issuance of stock options.

Corporate reports and press releases are written by management and are often viewed as public relations or sales materials. Not all of the material is independently reviewed by outside auditors. Such information can often be found on the company's Web site. Management may also provide **earnings guidance** to analysts before releasing the firm's financial statements.

An analyst should review information on the economy and the company's industry and compare the company to its competitors. This information can be acquired from sources such as trade journals, statistical reporting services, and government agencies.

The **financial statement analysis framework**[1] consists of six steps:
1. State the objective and context.
2. Gather data.
3. Process the data.
4. Analyze and interpret the data.

---

1   Hennie Van Greunung and Sonja Brajovic Bratanovic, *Analyzing and Managing Banking Risk: Framework for Assessing Corporate Governance and Financial Risk,* International Bank for Reconstruction and Development, April 2003, p. 300.

5. Report the conclusions or recommendations.
6. Update the analysis.

FINANCIAL REPORTING MECHANICS
Cross-Reference to CFA Institute Assigned Reading #23

Financial statement elements are the major classifications of assets, liabilities, owners' equity, revenues, and expenses. **Accounts** are the specific records within each element where specific transactions are entered. **Contra accounts** are used for entries that offset other accounts.

Assets are the firm's economic resources. Examples of assets include the following:

*   *Cash and cash equivalents.* Risk-free securities with original maturities of 90 days or less.
*   *Accounts receivable.* Accounts receivable often have an "allowance for bad debt expense" as a contra account.
*   *Inventories.*
*   *Financial assets* such as marketable securities.
*   *Prepaid expenses.* Items that will show up on future income statements as expenses.
*   *Property, plant, and equipment.* Includes a contra-asset account for accumulated depreciation.
*   *Investment in affiliates* accounted for using the equity method.
*   *Deferred tax assets.*
*   *Intangible assets.* Economic resources of the firm that do not have a physical form, such as patents, trademarks, licenses, and goodwill.

Liabilities are claims that creditors have on the company's resources. Examples of liabilities include the following:

*   Accounts payable and trade payables.
*   Financial liabilities such as short-term notes payable.
*   Unearned revenue. Items that will show up on future income statements as revenues.
*   Income taxes payable. The taxes accrued during the past year but not yet paid.
*   Long-term debt such as bonds payable.
*   Deferred tax liabilities.

Owners' equity is the claim that the firm's owners have on its resources, which is the amount by which assets exceed liabilities. Owners' equity includes the following:

*   *Capital.* Par value of common stock.
*   *Additional paid-in capital.* Proceeds from common stock sales above par value. (Share repurchases that the company has made are represented in the contra account *Treasury stock.*)

- *Retained earnings.* Cumulative income that has not been distributed as dividends.
- *Other comprehensive income.* Changes in carrying amounts of assets and liabilities.

Revenue represents inflows of economic resources and includes the following:

- *Sales.* Revenue from the firm's day-to-day activities.
- *Gains.* Increases in assets or equity from transactions incidental to the firm's day-to-day activities.
- *Investment income* such as interest and dividend income.

Expenses are outflows of economic resources and include the following:

- *Cost of goods sold.*
- *Selling, general, and administrative expenses.* These include such expenses as advertising, salaries, rent, and utilities.
- *Depreciation* and *amortization.*
- *Tax expense.*
- *Interest expense.*
- *Losses.* Decreases in assets or equity from transactions incidental to the firm's day-to-day activities.

The Accounting Equation

The basic accounting equation (what balances in a balance sheet):

$$\text{assets} = \text{liabilities} + \text{owners' equity}$$

The expanded accounting equation shows the components of owners' equity:

$$\text{assets} = \text{liabilities} + \text{contributed capital} + \text{ending retained earnings}$$

The expanded accounting equation can also be stated as:

$$
\begin{aligned}
\text{assets} \quad = \quad &\text{liabilities} \\
&+ \text{contributed capital} \\
&+ \text{beginning retained earnings} \\
&+ \text{revenue} \\
&- \text{expenses} \\
&- \text{dividends}
\end{aligned}
$$

Keeping the accounting equation in balance requires **double-entry accounting**, in which a transaction has to be recorded in at least two accounts. An increase in an asset account, for example, must be balanced by a decrease in another asset account or by an increase in a liability or owners' equity account.

Accruals and Adjustments

Revenues and expenses are not always recorded at the same time cash changes hands. The principle of **accrual accounting** requires that revenue is recorded when the firm earns it, and expenses are recorded when the firm incurs them, regardless of whether cash has actually been paid. Accruals fall into four categories:

1. *Unearned revenue:* Cash increases and a liability for the goods or services the firm must provide in the future is recorded in the same amount.
2. *Accrued revenue:* Revenue is recorded for credit sales, accounts receivable increases, and inventory decreases.
3. *Prepaid expenses:* Cash decreases and an asset (prepaid expenses) increases. The asset decreases and expenses increase when the expense is actually incurred.
4. *Accrued expenses:* The firm owes cash for expenses it has incurred but has not paid. A liability for accrued expenses, such as wages payable, increases.

With unearned revenue and prepaid expenses, cash changes hands first and the revenue or expense is recorded later. With accrued revenue and accrued expenses, the revenue or expense is recorded first. In all these cases, the effect of accrual accounting is to recognize revenues or expenses in the appropriate period.

Most assets are recorded on the financial statements at their historical cost. In some cases, however, accounting standards require balance sheet values of certain assets to reflect their current market values. Accounting entries that update these assets' values are called **valuation adjustments**. To keep the accounting equation in balance, changes in asset values are also changes in owners' equity, through gains or losses on the income statement or in other comprehensive income.

Information flows through an accounting system in four steps:

1. *Journal entries* record every transaction, showing which accounts are changed by what amounts.
2. The *general ledger* sorts the journal entries by account.
3. At the end of the accounting period, an *initial trial balance* is prepared that shows the balances in each account. If any adjusting entries are needed, they will be recorded and reflected in an *adjusted trial balance*.
4. The account balances from the adjusted trial balance are presented in the financial statements.

An analyst doesn't have access to the detailed information that flows through a company's accounting system, but only sees the financial statements. The analyst needs to understand the various accruals, adjustments, and management assumptions that went into the financial statements. These are often explained in the footnotes to the statements and in Management's Discussion and Analysis.

Because these adjustments and assumptions are to some extent at the discretion of management, the possibility exists that management may manipulate or misrepresent the company's financial performance and/or condition.

FINANCIAL REPORTING STANDARDS
Cross-Reference to CFA Institute Assigned Reading #24

Given the variety and complexity of possible transactions, and the estimates and assumptions a firm must make when presenting its performance, financial statements could potentially take any form if reporting standards didn't exist. Reporting standards ensure that the information is useful to a wide range of users, including security analysts, the firm's creditors, and current and potential investors, by making financial statements comparable to one another and narrowing the range within which management's estimates can be seen as reasonable.

Standard-setting bodies are professional organizations of accountants and auditors that establish financial reporting standards. **Regulatory authorities** are government agencies that have the legal authority to enforce compliance with financial reporting standards.

The two primary standard-setting bodies are the *Financial Accounting Standards Board* (FASB) and the *International Accounting Standards Board* (IASB). In the United States, the FASB sets forth Generally Accepted Accounting Principles (U.S. GAAP). Outside the United States, the IASB establishes International Financial Reporting Standards (IFRS). Many national standard-setting bodies, including the FASB, are working toward convergence with IFRS.

Desirable attributes of standard-setters:

- Observe high professional standards.
- Have adequate authority, resources, and competencies to accomplish its mission.
- Have clear and consistent standard-setting processes.
- Guided by a well-articulated framework.
- Operate independently while still seeking input from stakeholders.
- Should not be compromised by special interests.
- Decisions are made in the public interest.

Regulatory authorities, such as the *Securities and Exchange Commission* (SEC) in the United States and the *Financial Services Authority* (FSA) in the United Kingdom, are established by national governments to enforce accounting standards.

Most national authorities belong to the *International Organization of Securities Commissions* (IOSCO). Because of the increasing globalization of securities markets, IOSCO is seeking to attain uniform financial regulations across countries.

Barriers to Developing a Single Set of Standards

One barrier to developing one universally accepted set of accounting standards (referred to as convergence) is simply that different standard-setting bodies and the regulatory authorities of different countries disagree on what the best treatment of the item or issue is. Other barriers result from the political pressures that regulatory bodies face from business groups and others that will be affected by changes in their reporting standards.

The ideas on which the IASB bases its standards are expressed in its "Framework for the Preparation and Presentation of Financial Statements." The IASB framework details the objective of financial statements, defines the qualitative characteristics they should have, and specifies the reporting elements that are required. The framework also notes certain constraints and assumptions that are involved in financial statement preparation.

The objective of financial reporting according to the IASB framework is "to provide financial information about the reporting entity that is useful to existing and potential investors, lenders, and other creditors in making decisions about providing resources to the entity." Stated another way, the objective of financial statements is the fair presentation of a company's financial performance.

Qualitative Characteristics

The two fundamental characteristics that make financial information useful are **relevance** and **faithful representation**.[2]

- Financial statements are relevant if they contain information that can influence economic decisions or affect evaluations of past events or forecasts of future events.
- Information that is faithfully representative is complete, neutral (absence of bias), and free from error.

Four characteristics enhance relevance and faithful representation: comparability, verifiability, timeliness, and understandability.

- *Comparability*. Financial statement presentation should be consistent among firms and across time periods.

---

2. *Conceptual Framework for Financial Reporting (2010).* paragraphs QC5-18.

- *Verifiability.* Independent observers, using the same methods, obtain similar results.
- *Timeliness.* Information is available to decision makers before the information is stale.
- *Understandability.* Users with basic business knowledge should be able to understand the statements.

Constraints and Assumptions

One of the constraints on financial statement preparation is the need to balance reliability, in the sense of being free of error, with the timeliness that makes the information relevant. Cost is also a constraint; the benefit that users gain from the information should be greater than the cost of presenting it. A third constraint is the fact that intangible and non-quantifiable information cannot be captured directly in financial statements.

The two primary assumptions that underlie financial statements are the accrual basis and the going concern assumption. The accrual basis requires that revenue be recognized when earned and expenses recognized when incurred, regardless of when cash is actually paid. The going concern assumption presumes that the company will continue to operate for the foreseeable future.

Required Financial Statements

The *required financial statements* are as follows:

- Balance sheet.
- Statement of comprehensive income.
- Cash flow statement.
- Statement of changes in owners' equity.
- Explanatory notes, including a summary of accounting policies.

The general **features for preparing financial statements** are stated in IAS No. 1:

- *Fair presentation,* faithfully representing the effects of the entity's transactions and events.
- *Going concern basis,* assuming that the firm will continue to exist unless its management intends to (or must) liquidate it.
- *Accrual basis* of accounting is used to prepare the financial statements other than the statement of cash flows.
- *Consistency* between periods in how items are presented and classified.
- *Materiality,* meaning the financial statements should be free of misstatements or significant omissions.
- *Aggregation* of similar items and separation of dissimilar items.
- *No offsetting* of assets against liabilities or income against expenses unless a specific standard permits or requires it.

- *Reporting frequency* must be at least annually.
- *Comparative information* for prior periods should be included unless a specific standard states otherwise.

IAS No. 1 also states that most entities should present a *classified balance sheet* showing current and noncurrent assets and liabilities and describes the minimum information that is required on the face of each financial statement and in the notes.

IFRS vs. U.S. GAAP

U.S. GAAP consists of standards issued by the FASB along with numerous other pronouncements and interpretations. Both the IASB and the FASB have frameworks for preparing and presenting financial statements. The two organizations are working toward a common framework, but the two frameworks differ in several aspects at present.

Until these frameworks converge, analysts will need to interpret financial statements that are prepared under different standards. In many cases, however, a company will present a **reconciliation statement** showing what their financial results would have been under an alternative reporting system.

Even when a unified framework emerges, special reporting standards that apply to particular industries (e.g., insurance, banking) will continue to exist.

A *coherent financial reporting framework* is one that fits together logically. Such a framework should be transparent, comprehensive, and consistent.

- *Transparency*—full disclosure and fair presentation reveal the underlying economics of the company to the financial statement user.
- *Comprehensiveness*—all types of transactions that have financial implications should be included, including new kinds that emerge.
- *Consistency*—similar transactions should be accounted for in similar ways across companies, geographic areas, and time periods.

Barriers to creating a coherent financial reporting framework include issues related to valuation, standard setting, and measurement.

- *Valuation*—The different measurement bases for valuation involve a trade-off between relevance and reliability. Bases that require little judgment, such as historical cost, tend to be more reliable, but may be less relevant than a base like fair value that requires more judgment.

- *Standard setting*—Three approaches to standard setting are a "principles-based" approach that relies on a broad framework, a "rules-based" approach that gives specific guidance about how to classify transactions, and an "objectives-oriented" approach that blends the other two approaches. IFRS is largely a principles-based approach. U.S. GAAP has traditionally been more rules-based, but FASB is moving toward an objectives-oriented approach.
- *Measurement*—Another trade-off in financial reporting is between properly valuing the elements at one point in time (as on the balance sheet) and properly valuing the changes between points in time (as on the income statement). An "asset/liability" approach, which standard setters have largely used, focuses on balance sheet valuation. A "revenue/expense" approach would tend to focus on the income statement.

As financial reporting standards continue to evolve, analysts need to monitor how these developments will affect the financial statements they use. An analyst should be aware of new products and innovations in the financial markets that generate new types of transactions. These might not fall neatly into the existing financial reporting standards.

To keep up to date on the evolving standards, an analyst can monitor professional journals and other sources, such as the IASB (*www.iasb.org*) and FASB (*www.fasb.org*) Web sites. CFA Institute produces position papers on financial reporting issues through the CFA Centre for Financial Market Integrity (*www.cfainstitute.org/cfacentre*).

An analyst should use the disclosures about financial standards in the footnotes and MD&A to evaluate what policies are discussed, whether they cover all the relevant data in the financial statements, which policies required management to make estimates, and whether the disclosures have changed since the prior period. In disclosing the likely impact of implementing recently issued accounting standards, management can discuss the impact of adopting the standard, conclude that the standard does not apply or will not affect the financial statements materially, or state that they are still evaluating the effects of the new standards.

STUDY SESSION 8: FINANCIAL REPORTING AND ANALYSIS—INCOME STATEMENTS, BALANCE SHEETS, AND CASH FLOW STATEMENTS

UNDERSTANDING INCOME STATEMENTS
Cross-Reference to CFA Institute Assigned Reading #25

The income statement reports the revenues and expenses of the firm for a period of time. The income statement is sometimes referred to as the "statement of operations," the "statement of earnings," or the "profit and loss statement (P&L)."

The income statement equation is:

$$revenues - expenses = net\ income$$

Revenues are the amounts reported from the sale of goods and services in the normal course of business. **Expenses** are the amounts incurred to generate revenue, such as cost of goods sold, operating expenses, interest, and taxes. Expenses are grouped together by their nature or function.

The income statement also includes **gains and losses**, which result from incidental transactions outside the firm's normal business activities.

Presentation Formats

A firm can present its income statement using a single-step or multi-step format. In a single-step statement, all revenues are grouped together and all expenses are grouped together. A multi-step format includes subtotals such as gross profit and operating profit.

Gross profit is the amount that remains once the cost of a product or service is subtracted from revenue. Subtracting operating expenses, such as selling, general and administrative expenses, from gross profit results in another subtotal known as **operating profit** or operating income.

For *nonfinancial firms*, operating profit is the amount that remains before financing costs and income taxes are considered. Subtracting interest expense and income taxes from operating profit results in the firm's **net income**, sometimes referred to as "earnings" or the "bottom line." For *financial firms*, interest expense is usually considered an operating expense.

If a firm has a controlling interest in a subsidiary and consolidates the subsidiary's results with its own, the pro-rata share of the subsidiary's income for the portion of the subsidiary that the firm does not own is reported in the firm's income statement as **noncontrolling interest** or **minority owners' interest**.

General Principles of Revenue Recognition

Under the accrual method of accounting, revenue is recognized when earned, and expenses to produce that revenue are recognized when incurred. Accrual accounting does not necessarily coincide with the receipt or payment of cash, so firms can manipulate net income through their choices about revenue and expense recognition.

According to the International Accounting Standards Board (IASB), revenue is recognized from the sale of goods when:[3]

1. The risk and reward of ownership is transferred.
2. There is no continuing control or management over the goods sold.
3. Revenue can be reliably measured.
4. There is a probable flow of economic benefits.
5. The cost can be reliably measured.

For services rendered, revenue is recognized when:[4]

1. The amount of revenue can be reliably measured.
2. There is a probable flow of economic benefits.
3. The stage of completion can be measured.
4. The cost incurred and cost of completion can be reliably measured.

The Securities and Exchange Commission (SEC) lists four criteria to determine whether revenue should be recognized.[5]

1. There is evidence of an arrangement between the buyer and seller.
2. The product has been delivered or the service has been rendered.
3. The price is determined or determinable.
4. The seller is reasonably sure of collecting money.

Revenue is usually recognized at delivery, but revenue may be recognized before delivery occurs or after delivery takes place in some circumstances.

Long-Term Contracts

Specific revenue recognition methods are used for contracts (often related to construction projects) that extend beyond one accounting period. In certain cases involving service contracts or licensing agreements, the firm may simply recognize revenue equally over the term of the contract or agreement.

The *percentage-of-completion method* is appropriate when the outcome of the project can be reliably estimated. Revenue, expense, and profit are recognized in proportion to the total cost incurred to date, divided by the total expected cost of the project.

---

3. IAS No. 18, *Revenue*, paragraph 14.
4. IAS No. 18, *Revenue*, paragraph 20.
5. SEC Staff Accounting Bulletin 101.

Under International Financial Reporting Standards (IFRS), if the firm cannot reliably measure the outcome of the project, revenue is recognized to the extent of contract costs, costs are expensed when incurred, and profit is recognized at completion.

Under U.S. GAAP, the *completed-contract method* is used when the outcome of a project cannot be reliably measured or the project is short-term. Revenue, expense, and profit are only recognized when the contract is complete.

As compared to the completed contract method, the percentage-of-completion method is considered more aggressive because revenue is reported sooner. The percentage-of-completion method provides smoother earnings and results in better matching of revenues and expenses. Cash flow is the same under both methods.

An **installment sale** occurs when a firm finances a sale and payments are expected to be received over an extended period. If collectability is certain, revenue is recognized at the time of sale. If collectability cannot be reasonably estimated, the **installment method** is used, and if collectability is highly uncertain, the **cost recovery method is used**.

Under the *installment method*, profit recognized is the proportion of cash collected multiplied by the total expected profit. The installment method is used in limited circumstances, usually involving the sale of real estate. Under the *cost recovery method*, profit is recognized only when, and to the extent that, cash collections exceed estimated total costs.

In a **barter transaction**, two parties exchange goods or services without any cash payment. According to U.S. GAAP, revenue can be recognized at fair value only if the firm has historically received cash payments for such services and can use this historical experience to determine fair value.[6] Under IFRS, revenue from barter transactions must be measured based on the fair value of revenue from similar non-barter transactions with unrelated parties.[7]

Gross vs. Net Revenue Reporting

Under **gross revenue reporting**, the selling firm reports sales revenue and cost of goods sold separately. Under **net revenue reporting**, only the difference between sales and cost is reported. While profit is the same, reported sales are higher using

---

6. Emerging Issues Task Force EITF 99–17, "Accounting for Advertising Barter Transactions."
7. IASB, SIC Interpretation 31, Revenue – Barter Transactions Involving Advertising Services, paragraph 5.

gross revenue reporting. Firms disclose their revenue recognition policies in the financial statement footnotes.

Users of financial information must consider two points when analyzing a firm's revenue: (1) how conservative the firm's revenue recognition policies are (recognizing revenue sooner rather than later is more aggressive), and (2) to what extent the firm's policies rely on estimates and judgments.

IFRS-U.S. GAAP Convergence

In May 2014, IASB and FASB issued principles-based standards for revenue recognition that are scheduled go into effect December 15, 2016, for U.S. GAAP reporting firms and January 1, 2017, for IFRS reporting firms. The central principle is that a firm should recognize revenue when it has transferred a good or service to a customer.

The converged standards identify a five-step process for recognizing revenue:

1. Identify the contract(s) with a customer.

2. Identify the performance obligations in the contract.

3. Determine the transaction price.

4. Allocate the transaction price to the performance obligations in the contract.

5. Recognize revenue when (or as) the entity satisfies a performance obligation.

A **performance obligation** is a promise to deliver a distinct good or service. A **transaction price** is the amount a firm expects to receive from a customer in exchange for transferring a good or service

Recognition of Expense

Under the accrual method of accounting, expense recognition is based on the *matching principle,* whereby expenses for producing goods and services are recognized in the period in which the revenue for the goods and services is recognized. Expenses that are not tied directly to generating revenue, such as administrative costs, are called *period costs* and are expensed in the period incurred.

The cost of long-lived assets must also be matched with revenues. The allocation of cost over an asset's useful life is known as **depreciation** or **amortization** expense.

If a firm sells goods or services on credit or provides a warranty to the customer, the matching principle requires the firm to estimate bad-debt expense and/or warranty expense. Since estimates are involved, it is possible for firms to delay the recognition of expense. Delayed expense recognition increases net income and is, therefore, more aggressive.

Depreciation

Most firms use the **straight-line depreciation** method for financial reporting purposes. However, most assets generate proportionally more benefits in their early years and an **accelerated depreciation** method is more appropriate for matching revenues and expenses. In the early years of an asset's life, the straight-line method will result in lower depreciation expense and higher net income than accelerated methods.

Straight-line depreciation (SL) allocates an equal amount of depreciation each year over the asset's useful life as follows:

$$\text{SL depreciation expense} = \frac{\text{cost} - \text{residual value}}{\text{useful life}}$$

The most common *accelerated method* of depreciation is the **double-declining balance method** (DDB), which uses 200% of the straight-line rate, applied against the declining balance (value net of depreciation). If an asset's life is 10 years, the straight-line rate is 1/10 or 10%. The DDB rate for this asset is 2/10 or 20%.

$$\text{DDB depreciation} = \left(\frac{2}{\text{useful life}}\right)(\text{asset cost} - \text{accumulated depreciation})$$

DDB does not use the residual value in the calculations, but depreciation stops once residual value has been reached.

Inventory

Under the **first-in, first-out** (FIFO) method, the first item purchased is the first item sold. FIFO is appropriate for inventory that has a limited shelf life. Under the **last-in, first-out** (LIFO) method, the last item purchased is the first item sold. LIFO is appropriate for inventory that does not deteriorate with age. For example, a coal mining company will sell coal off the top of the pile. The **average cost** method, which allocates the average cost of all inventory to each unit sold, is popular because of its ease of use.

In the United States, LIFO is popular because of the income tax benefits. LIFO results in higher cost of goods sold in an inflationary environment. Higher cost of goods sold results in lower taxable income, and thus lower income taxes. LIFO inventory accounting is not permitted under IFRS.

Intangible Assets

Amortization expense of intangible assets with limited lives is similar to depreciation; the expense should match the benefits/value used over the period. Most firms, however, use the straight-line method. Goodwill and other intangible assets with *indefinite lives* are not amortized. However, they must be tested for impairment at least annually. If the asset is impaired, an expense is recognized in the income statement.

Operating and Nonoperating Components of the Income Statement

Operating and *nonoperating transactions* are usually reported separately in the income statement. For a nonfinancial firm, nonoperating transactions may result from investment income and financing expenses (interest). The income from and the gains and losses on the sale of these securities are not a part of the firm's normal business operations. For a financial firm, such income, gains, and losses may be considered operating income.

Discontinued Operations

A *discontinued operation* (must be physically and operationally distinct from the rest of the firm) is one that management has decided to dispose of, but either has not yet done so, or disposed of in the current period after the operation had generated income or losses. Income and losses from discontinued operations are reported separately in the income statement, net of tax, after income from continuing operations. While discontinued operations do not affect net income from continuing operations, the analyst must decide their effect on firm earnings and cash flows in the future.

Unusual or infrequent items are recorded for events that are either unusual in nature *or* infrequent in occurrence, but *not* both. Unusual or infrequent items are included in income from continuing operations. Examples include:

- Gains or losses from the sale of assets or part of a business (that do not qualify as discontinued operations).
- Impairments, write-offs, write-downs, and restructuring costs.

An analyst must review these to determine their effect, if any, on future income.

Extraordinary Items

Under U.S. GAAP, an *extraordinary item* is both unusual and infrequent in occurrence (e.g., losses from an expropriation of assets or uninsured losses from natural disasters). Extraordinary items are reported separately in the income statement, net of tax, after income from continuing operations. IFRS does not allow extraordinary treatment in the income statement.

Although extraordinary items do not affect income from continuing operations, an analyst may want to review them to determine whether some portion should be included when forecasting future income (i.e., they may not be *that* extraordinary).

Accounting Changes

A **change in accounting principle** refers to the change from one GAAP or IFRS method to another method and requires retrospective application so all of the prior period financial statements currently presented are restated to reflect the change.

Generally, a **change in accounting estimate** is the result of a change in management's judgment, usually due to new information. For example, management may change the estimated useful life of an asset because new information indicates the asset has a longer life than originally expected. A change in estimate is applied prospectively and does not require the restatement of prior financial statements. Accounting changes typically do not affect cash flow. An analyst should review accounting principle changes and changes in accounting estimates to determine the impact on future operating results.

A change from an incorrect accounting method to one that is acceptable under GAAP or IFRS, or the correction of an accounting error, is reported as a **prior-period adjustment**. Prior-period adjustments are made by restating results for all prior period statements presented in the current financial statements. Disclosure of the nature of the adjustment and of its effect on net income is also required.

Prior-period adjustments usually involve errors or new accounting standards and typically do not affect cash flow unless tax accounting is also affected. Analysts should review adjustments carefully because errors may indicate weaknesses in the firm's internal control system.

Earnings Per Share

The following basic definitions are essential.

Potentially dilutive securities. These securities include stock options, warrants, convertible debt, and convertible preferred stock.

Dilutive securities. Those securities that would *decrease EPS* if exercised and converted to common stock.

Antidilutive securities. Those securities that would *increase EPS* if exercised and converted to common stock.

Simple capital structure. A capital structure that contains *no potentially dilutive securities.* This structure contains only common stock, nonconvertible debt, and nonconvertible preferred stock.

Complex capital structures. Complex structures contain *potentially dilutive securities* such as options, warrants, or convertible securities.

Weighted average number of shares outstanding. Each share issue is weighted by the portion of the year it was outstanding. Stock splits and stock dividends are applied retroactively to the beginning of the year, so "old" shares are converted to "new" shares for consistency.

Basic EPS

The basic EPS calculation *does not* consider the effects of any dilutive securities in the computation of EPS. It is the only EPS presented for firms with simple capital structures and is one of the two EPS calculations presented for firms with complex capital structures.

$$\text{basic EPS} = \frac{\text{net income} - \text{preferred dividends}}{\text{weighted average number of common shares outstanding}}$$

Diluted EPS

If a firm has a complex capital structure (contains potentially dilutive securities), both basic and diluted EPS must be reported. To calculate diluted EPS, treat any *dilutive* securities as if they were converted to common stock from the first of the year (or when issued if issued during the current year).

Each potentially dilutive security must be considered separately to determine whether or not it is actually dilutive for the current reporting period. Only income from continuing operations (excluding discontinued operations, extraordinary items, and accounting changes) is considered in determining diluted EPS.

To determine whether a convertible security is dilutive, calculate:

$$\frac{\text{convertible pfd. dividends}}{\#\text{ shares from conversion of pfd.}} \quad \text{or} \quad \frac{\text{convertible debt interest }(1-\text{tax rate})}{\#\text{ shares from conversion of debt}}$$

If the calculated amount is less than basic EPS, the security is dilutive.

When considering dilutive securities, the denominator is the basic EPS denominator adjusted for the equivalent number of common shares created by the conversion of all outstanding dilutive securities (convertible bonds, convertible preferred shares, plus options and warrants).

$$\text{diluted EPS} = \frac{\text{adjusted income available for common shares}}{\substack{\text{weighted-average common and} \\ \text{potential common shares outstanding}}}$$

where adjusted income available for common shares is:
earnings available for common shares
+ dividends on dilutive convertible preferred stock
+ after-tax interest on dilutive convertible debt

Therefore, diluted EPS is:

$$\text{diluted EPS} = \frac{\left[\text{net income}-\substack{\text{preferred}\\\text{dividends}}\right] + \left(\substack{\text{convertible}\\\text{preferred}\\\text{dividends}}\right) + \left(\substack{\text{convertible}\\\text{debt}\\\text{interest}}\right)(1-t)}{\left(\substack{\text{weighted}\\\text{average}\\\text{shares}}\right) + \left(\substack{\text{shares from}\\\text{conversion of}\\\text{conv. pfd. shares}}\right) + \left(\substack{\text{shares from}\\\text{conversion of}\\\text{conv. debt}}\right) + \left(\substack{\text{shares}\\\text{issuable from}\\\text{stock options}}\right)}$$

With respect to convertible bonds, remember that what you are looking for is a reduction in EPS. The denominator is rising due to the increased number of shares, and the numerator is rising due to the after-tax interest cost savings. When the denominator is rising faster than the numerator, conversion is dilutive.

Treasury Stock Method

The *treasury stock method* assumes that the hypothetical funds received by the company from the exercise of options or warrants are used to purchase shares of the company's common stock at the average market price over the reporting period.

Options and warrants are dilutive whenever the exercise price is less than the average stock price over the reporting period.

$$\text{new shares (treasury stock method)} = \frac{\text{avg. mkt. price} - \text{exercise price}}{\text{average market price}} \times \text{\# of shares covered by options/warrants}$$

Financial Ratios Based on the Income Statement

A vertical **common-size income statement** expresses all income statement items as a percentage of sales. This format is useful for time-series and cross-sectional analysis and facilitates the comparison of firms of different sizes.

It is usually more meaningful to present income tax expense as an effective rate, equal to income tax expense divided by pre-tax income, than as a percentage of sales.

Profitability ratios examine how well management has done at generating profits from sales. The different ratios are designed to isolate specific costs. Generally, higher margin ratios are desirable.

Gross profit margin is the ratio of gross profit (sales less cost of goods sold) to sales:

$$\text{gross profit margin} = \frac{\text{gross profit}}{\text{revenue}}$$

Gross profit margin can be increased by raising sales prices or lowering per-unit cost.

Net profit margin is the ratio of net income to sales:

$$\text{net profit margin} = \frac{\text{net income}}{\text{revenue}}$$

Net profit margin can be increased by raising sales prices or cutting costs.

Any subtotal presented in the income statement can be expressed in terms of a margin ratio (to revenues). For example, *operating profit margin* is equal to operating income divided by revenue. *Pretax margin* is equal to pre-tax earnings divided by revenue.

Items Excluded from the Income Statement that Affect Owners' Equity

Transactions with owners:

1. Issuing or reacquiring stock.
2. Dividends paid.

Transactions included in other comprehensive income:

1. Foreign currency translation gains and losses.
2. Adjustments for minimum pension liability.
3. Unrealized gains and losses from *cash flow hedging* derivatives.
4. Unrealized gains and losses from *available-for-sale* securities.

Comprehensive income is a measure that includes all changes to equity other than owner contributions and distributions.

UNDERSTANDING BALANCE SHEETS
Cross-Reference to CFA Institute Assigned Reading #26

The balance sheet shows the values of the assets and liabilities of the firm at a point in time. Values may be historical values, fair market values, or historical values adjusted for amortization of premiums or discounts. Balance sheet items can be divided into assets, liabilities, and equity.

$$\text{assets} = \text{liabilities} + \text{owners' equity}$$

A **classified balance sheet** groups together similar items (current assets, current liabilities, current liabilities, noncurrent liabilities) to arrive at significant subtotals. Under IFRS, a **liquidity-based presentation** may be used if it is more relevant and reliable, as for a financial institution.

Accrual Process

The accrual method of accounting creates assets and liabilities.

- Cash received in advance of recognizing revenue results in an increase in assets (cash) and an increase in liabilities (unearned revenue).
- Recognizing revenue before cash is received results in an increase in assets (accounts receivable) and an increase in equity (retained earnings). Cash paid in advance of recognizing expense results in a decrease in one asset (cash) and an increase in another asset (prepaid expenses) by the same amount.
- Recognizing an expense before cash is paid results in an increase in liabilities (accrued expenses) and a decrease in equity (retained earnings).

Current and Noncurrent Assets and Liabilities

Current assets include cash and other assets that will be converted into cash or used up within one year or operating cycle, whichever is greater.

Current liabilities are obligations that will be satisfied within one year or operating cycle, whichever is greater. More specifically, a liability that meets any of the following criteria is considered current:

- Settlement is expected during the normal operating cycle.
- It is held for trading purposes.
- Settlement is expected within one year.
- There is no unconditional right to defer settlement for at least one year.

Current assets minus current liabilities equals **working capital**.

Noncurrent assets do not meet the definition of current assets; that is, they will not be converted into cash or used up within one year or operating cycle.

Noncurrent liabilities do not meet the criteria of current liabilities.

If a firm includes (consolidates) balance sheet accounts of a subsidiary that is not 100% owned, the firm reports a **noncontrolling interest** or **minority interest** in its consolidated balance sheet. The noncontrolling interest is the pro-rata share of the subsidiary's net assets (equity) not owned by the parent company. Noncontrolling interest is reported in the equity section of the consolidated balance sheet.

Measurement Bases of Assets and Liabilities

Balance sheet assets and liabilities are valued using both **historical cost** and **fair value**.

- *Historical cost* is the value that was exchanged at the acquisition date. Historical cost is objective (highly reliable), but its relevance to an analyst declines as values change.
- *Fair value* is the amount at which an asset could be bought or sold, or a liability can be incurred or settled, between knowledgeable, willing parties in an arm's length transaction.

Some of the more common **current assets** are:

- **Cash, and cash equivalents**—cash equivalents typically mature in 90 days or less (e.g., 90-day T-bills).
- **Accounts receivable (trade receivables)**—receivables are reported net of any allowance for bad debt.
- **Inventories**—items held for sale or used in the manufacture of goods to be sold. Firms that use the **retail method** measure inventory at retail prices and subtract an expected gross margin to reflect cost.
- **Marketable securities**—debt or equity securities that are traded in a public market.
- **Other current assets**—includes prepaid expenses.

Some examples of **current liabilities** are:

- **Accounts payable (trade payables)**—amounts owed to suppliers.
- **Notes payable**—obligations in the form of promissory notes due to creditors within one year or operating cycle, whichever is greater.
- **Current portion of long-term debt**—the principal portion of debt due within one year or operating cycle, whichever is greater.
- **Taxes payable**—current taxes that have been recognized in the income statement but have not yet been paid.
- **Accrued liabilities (accrued expenses)**—expenses that have been recognized in the income statement but are not yet contractually due.
- **Unearned revenue (income)**—cash collected in advance of providing goods and services. The related liability is to provide those goods and services.

Tangible Assets

Long-term assets with physical substance are known as *tangible assets*. Tangible assets, such as plant, equipment, and natural resources, are reported on the balance sheet at historical cost less accumulated depreciation or depletion.

Land is also a tangible asset that is reported at historical cost and is not depreciated.

Under IFRS, tangible assets held for capital appreciation or to earn rental income are classified as **investment property**.

Intangible Assets

Intangible assets are long-term assets that lack physical substance. The cost of an identifiable intangible asset is amortized over its useful life. Examples of identifiable intangible assets include patents, trademarks, and copyrights.

An intangible asset that is *unidentifiable* cannot be purchased separately and may have an infinite life. The best example of an unidentifiable intangible asset is goodwill.

Goodwill is created when a business is purchased for more than the fair value of its assets net of liabilities. Goodwill is not amortized, but must be tested for impairment (a decrease in its fair value) at least annually. Since goodwill is not amortized, firms can manipulate net income upward by allocating more of the acquisition price to goodwill and less to the identifiable assets. The result is less depreciation and amortization expense and thus higher net income.

When computing ratios, analysts should eliminate goodwill from the balance sheet and goodwill impairment charges from the income statement for comparability. Also, analysts should evaluate future acquisitions in terms of the price paid relative to the earning power of the acquired firm.

Intangible assets that are purchased are reported on the balance sheet at historical cost less accumulated amortization. Except for certain legal costs, intangible assets that are created internally, including research and development costs, are expensed as incurred under U.S. GAAP and are not shown on the balance sheet.

Under IFRS, a firm must identify the research stage and the development stage. Accordingly, the firm must expense costs during the research stage but *may* capitalize costs incurred during the development stage.

All of the following should be expensed as incurred, and do not create balance sheet assets:

- Start-up and training costs.
- Administrative overhead.
- Advertising and promotion costs.
- Relocation and reorganization costs.
- Termination costs.

Some analysts completely eliminate intangible assets, particularly unidentifiable intangibles, for analytical purposes. This is inadvisable. Analysts should consider the economic value of each intangible asset before making an adjustment.

Accounting Treatments for Financial Instruments

Marketable investment securities are classified as one of the following:

- **Held-to-maturity securities.** Debt securities acquired with the intent to be held to maturity are reported on the balance sheet at amortized cost. Amortized cost is equal to the face (par) value less any unamortized discount or plus any unamortized premium, as it is with debt issued by the firm.
- **Trading securities.** Debt and equity securities acquired with the intent to profit from near-term price fluctuations are reported on the balance sheet at fair value. Unrealized gains and losses are recognized in the income statement. **Derivatives** are treated as trading securities.
- **Available-for-sale securities.** Debt and equity securities that are not expected to be held to maturity or traded in the near term are reported on the balance sheet at fair value. Unrealized gains and losses are not recognized in the income statement, but are reported in other comprehensive income as a part of stockholders' equity.

Dividend and interest income, and realized gains and losses (actual gains or losses when the securities are sold), are recognized in the income statement for all three classifications of securities.

Figure 1: Summary of Investment Security Classifications

	Trading	*Available-for-sale*	*Held-to-maturity*
Balance sheet	Fair value	Fair value	Amortized cost
Income statement	• Dividends • Interest • Realized G/L • Unrealized G/L	• Dividends • Interest • Realized G/L	• Interest • Realized G/L

Components of Owners' Equity

Owners' equity is the residual interest in assets that remains after subtracting an entity's liabilities. The owners' equity section of the balance sheet includes:

- **Contributed capital**—the total amount received from the issuance of common and preferred stock.
- **Noncontrolling interest** (minority interest)—the minority shareholders' pro-rata share of the net assets (equity) of a consolidated subsidiary that is partially owned by the parent.
- **Retained earnings**—the cumulative net income of the firm since inception that has not been paid out as dividends.

- **Treasury stock**—stock that has been reacquired by the issuing firm but not yet retired. Treasury stock has no voting rights and does not receive dividends.
- **Accumulated other comprehensive income**—includes all changes in stockholders' equity not recognized in the income statement or from issuing stock, reacquiring stock, and paying dividends.

Under U.S. GAAP, the firm can report comprehensive income in the income statement (below net income), in a separate statement of comprehensive income, or in the statement of changes in stockholders' equity. Under IFRS, a firm can include all revenue and expense items in the statement of comprehensive income, or may present a separate income statement and a statement of comprehensive income.

The **statement of changes in stockholders' equity** summarizes all transactions that increase or decrease the equity accounts for the period.

Analysis of the Balance Sheet

A vertical **common-size balance sheet** expresses all balance sheet accounts as a percentage of total assets and allows the analyst to evaluate the balance sheet changes over time (*time-series analysis*) as well as to compare the balance sheets with other firms, industry, and sector data (*cross-sectional analysis*). Several commercial services provide data for comparison.

Liquidity ratios measure the firm's ability to satisfy short-term obligations when due.

- The **current ratio** is the best-known measure of liquidity.

$$\text{current ratio} = \frac{\text{current assets}}{\text{current liabilities}}$$

A current ratio of less than one means the firm has negative working capital and may be facing a liquidity crisis. Working capital is equal to current assets minus current liabilities.

- The **quick ratio** (acid test ratio) is a more conservative measure of liquidity because it excludes inventories and less liquid current assets from the numerator.

$$\text{quick ratio} = \frac{\text{cash} + \text{marketable securities} + \text{receivables}}{\text{current liabilities}}$$

- The **cash ratio** is the most conservative measure of liquidity.

$$\text{cash ratio} = \frac{\text{cash} + \text{marketable securities}}{\text{current liabilities}}$$

The higher its liquidity ratios, the more likely the firm will be able to pay its short-term bills when due. The ratios differ only in the assumed liquidity of the current assets.

Solvency ratios measure a firm's financial risk and measure the firm's ability to satisfy long-term obligations (its solvency). The higher the ratio, the greater the financial leverage and the greater the financial risk.

- The **long-term debt-to-equity ratio** measures long-term financing sources relative to the equity base.

$$\text{long-term debt-to-equity} = \frac{\text{total long-term debt}}{\text{total equity}}$$

- The **debt-to-equity ratio** measures total debt relative to the equity base.

$$\text{debt-to-equity} = \frac{\text{total debt}}{\text{total equity}}$$

- The **total debt ratio** measures the extent to which assets are financed by creditors.

$$\text{total debt ratio} = \frac{\text{total debt}}{\text{total assets}}$$

- The **financial leverage ratio** is a variation of the debt-to-equity ratio that is used as a component of the DuPont model.

$$\text{financial leverage ratio} = \frac{\text{total assets}}{\text{total equity}}$$

©2015 Kaplan, Inc.

UNDERSTANDING CASH FLOW STATEMENTS
Cross-Reference to CFA Institute Assigned Reading #27

The **cash flow statement** provides information beyond that available from net income and other financial data. The cash flow statement provides information about a firm's liquidity, solvency, and financial flexibility. The cash flow statement reconciles the beginning and ending balances of cash over an accounting period. The change in cash is a result of the firm's operating, investing, and financing activities as follows:

	Operating activities
+	Investing activities
+	Financing activities
=	Change in cash balance
+	Beginning cash balance
=	Ending cash balance

Figure 2: U.S. GAAP Cash Flow Classifications

Operating Activities

Inflows	*Outflows*
Cash collected from customers	Cash paid to employees and suppliers
Interest and dividends received	Cash paid for other expenses
Sale proceeds from trading securities	Acquisition of trading securities
	Interest paid
	Taxes paid

Investing Activities

Inflows	*Outflows*
Sale proceeds from fixed assets	Acquisition of fixed assets
Sale proceeds from debt & equity investments	Acquisition of debt & equity investments
Principal received from loans made to others	Loans made to others

Financing Activities

Inflows	*Outflows*
Principal amounts borrowed from others	Principal paid on amounts from others
Proceeds from issuing stock	Payments to reacquire stock
	Dividends paid to shareholders

Noncash investing and financing activities are not reported in the cash flow statement but must be disclosed in either a footnote or a supplemental schedule to the cash flow statement.

Differences Between U.S. GAAP and IFRS

Under IFRS:

- Interest and dividends received may be classified as either CFO or CFI.
- Dividends paid to shareholders and interest paid on debt may be classified as either CFO or CFF.
- Income taxes are reported as operating activities unless the expense can be tied to an investing or financing transaction.

Direct Method and Indirect Methods Calculating CFO

Two different methods of presenting the cash flow statement are permitted under U.S. GAAP and IFRS: the direct method and the indirect method. The use of the direct method is encouraged by both standard setters. The difference in the two methods relates to the presentation of cash flow from operating activities. Total cash flow from operating activities is exactly the same under both methods, and the presentation of cash flow from investing activities and from financing activities is exactly the same under both methods.

The direct method provides more information than the indirect method. The main advantage of the indirect method is that it focuses on the differences between net income and operating cash flow.

Direct Method

The direct method presents operating cash flow by taking each item from the income statement and converting it to its cash equivalent by adding or subtracting the changes in the corresponding balance sheet accounts. The following are examples of operating cash flow components:

- Cash collected from sales is the main component of CFO. Cash collections are calculated by adjusting sales for the changes in accounts receivable and unearned (deferred) revenue.
- Cash used in the production of goods and services (cash inputs) is calculated by adjusting cost of goods sold (COGS) for the changes in inventory and accounts payable.

©2015 Kaplan, Inc.

Indirect Method

Using the indirect method, operating cash flow is calculated in four steps:

Step 1: Begin with net income.

Step 2: Subtract gains or add losses that resulted from financing or investing cash flows (such as gains from sale of land).

Step 3: Add back all noncash charges to income (such as depreciation and amortization) and subtract all noncash components of revenue.

Step 4: Add or subtract changes to related balance sheet operating accounts as follows:

- Increases in the operating asset accounts (uses of cash) are subtracted, while decreases (sources of cash) are added.
- Increases in the operating liability accounts (sources of cash) are added, while decreases (uses of cash) are subtracted.

Most firms present the cash flow statement using the indirect method. For analytical purposes, it may be beneficial to *convert the cash flow statement to the direct method.* Examples of such conversion for two items are:

Cash collections from customers:
1. Begin with net sales from the income statement.
2. Subtract (add) any increase (decrease) in the accounts receivable balance as reported in the indirect method.
3. Add (subtract) an increase (decrease) in unearned revenue.

Cash payments to suppliers:
1. Begin with cost of goods sold (COGS) as reported in the income statement.
2. If depreciation and/or amortization have been included in COGS (they increase COGS), they must be eliminated when computing the cash paid to suppliers.
3. Subtract (add) any increase (decrease) in the accounts payable balance as reported in the indirect method.
4. Add (subtract) any increase (decrease) in the inventory balance as disclosed in the indirect method.
5. Subtract any inventory write-off that occurred during the period.

Disclosure Requirements

Under U.S. GAAP, a direct method presentation must also disclose the adjustments necessary to reconcile net income to cash flow from operating activities. The reconciliation is not required under IFRS.

Under IFRS, payments for interest and taxes must be disclosed separately in the cash flow statement under either method (direct or indirect). Under U.S. GAAP, payments for interest and taxes can be reported in the cash flow statement or disclosed in the footnotes.

Investing and Financing Cash Flows

Investing cash flows (CFI) are calculated by subtracting expenditures on new assets from the proceeds of asset sales.

When calculating the cash from an asset that has been sold, it is necessary to consider any gain or loss from the sale using the following formula:

cash from asset sold = book value of the asset + gain (or − loss) on sale

Financing cash flows (CFF) are determined by measuring the cash flows occurring between the firm and its suppliers of capital. Cash flows between the firm and creditors result from new borrowings and debt repayments. Note that interest paid is technically a cash flow to the creditors, but it is already included in CFO under U.S. GAAP. Cash flows between the firm and the shareholders occur when equity is issued, shares are repurchased, and dividends are paid. CFF is the sum of these two measures:

net cash flows from creditors = new borrowings − principal repaid

net cash flows from shareholders = new equity issued − share repurchases − cash dividends

Analysis of the Cash Flow Statement

1. Operating Cash Flow

The analyst should identify the major determinants of operating cash flow, primarily the firm's earning-related activities and changes in noncash working capital.

Equality of operating cash flow and net income is an indication of high quality earnings but can be affected by the stage of business cycle and of the firm's life cycle. Earnings that exceed operating cash flow may be an indication of premature recognition of revenues or delayed recognition of expenses.

©2015 Kaplan, Inc.

2. Investing Cash Flow

Increasing capital expenditures, a use of cash, is usually an indication of growth. Conversely, a firm may reduce capital expenditures or even sell capital assets in order to conserve or generate cash. This may result in higher cash outflows in the future as older assets are replaced or growth resumes.

3. Financing Cash Flow

The financing activities section of the cash flow statement reveals information about whether the firm is generating cash by issuing debt or equity. It also provides information about whether the firm is using cash to repay debt, reacquire stock, or pay dividends.

The cash flow statement can be converted to **common-size format** by expressing each line item as a percentage of revenue. Alternatively, each inflow of cash can be expressed as a percentage of total cash inflows and each outflow of cash can be expressed as a percentage of total cash outflows.

Free cash flow is a measure of cash that is available for discretionary purposes; that is, the cash flow that is available once the firm has covered its obligations and capital expenditures.

Free cash flow to the firm (FCFF) is the cash available to all investors, including stockholders and debt holders. FCFF can be calculated using net income or operating cash flow as a starting point.

FCFF is calculated from net income as:

$$\text{FCFF} = \text{NI} + \text{non-cash charges} + [\text{interest expense} \times (1 - \text{tax rate})] - \text{net capital investment} - \text{working capital investment}$$

FCFF is calculated from operating cash flow as:

$$\text{FCFF} = \text{CFO} + [\text{interest expense} \times (1 - \text{tax rate})] - \text{net capital expenditure}$$

Free cash flow to equity (FCFE) is the cash flow that is available for distribution to the common shareholders; that is, after all obligations have been paid. FCFE can be calculated as follows:

$$\text{FCFE} = \text{CFO} - \text{net capital expenditure} + \text{net borrowing}$$

Cash Flow Ratios That Measure Performance

- The **cash flow-to-revenue ratio** measures the amount of operating cash flow generated for each dollar of revenue.

$$\text{cash flow-to-revenue} = \frac{\text{CFO}}{\text{net revenue}}$$

- The **cash return-on-assets ratio** measures the return of operating cash flow attributed to all providers of capital.

$$\text{cash return-on-assets} = \frac{\text{CFO}}{\text{average total assets}}$$

Cash Flow Ratios That Measure Coverage

- The **debt coverage ratio** measures financial risk and leverage.

$$\text{debt coverage} = \frac{\text{CFO}}{\text{total debt}}$$

- The **interest coverage ratio** measures the firm's ability to meet its interest obligations.

$$\text{interest coverage} = \frac{\text{CFO} + \text{interest paid} + \text{taxes paid}}{\text{interest paid}}$$

FINANCIAL ANALYSIS TECHNIQUES
Cross-Reference to CFA Institute Assigned Reading #28

With respect to analysis of financial statements, there are a number of key ratios that should simply be memorized including:

- Current, quick, and cash ratios.
- All the ratios in the cash conversion cycle (the turnover ratios are more important, like receivables, inventory, and payables turnover).
- Turnover ratios use sales in the numerator, except for payables and inventory turnover ratios, which use purchases and COGS, respectively.
- Gross profit margin, net profit margin, and operating profit margin are readily available from a common-size income statement.

©2015 Kaplan, Inc.

- Return on equity (ROE) is critical. Definitely know the three- and five-component DuPont ROE decompositions.
- Debt-to-equity, total debt, interest coverage, and fixed financial coverage ratios (remember to add lease interest expense to numerator and denominator).
- The retention ratio and growth rate are important concepts that also appear in Corporate Finance and Equity Investments.

Usefulness and Limitations of Ratio Analysis

Financial ratios provide useful information to analysts, including:

- Insights into the financial relationships that are useful in forecasting future earnings and cash flows.
- Information about the financial flexibility of the firm.
- A means of evaluating management's performance.

Financial ratios have limitations:

- Ratios are not useful when viewed in isolation. Ratios should be interpreted relative to industry averages, economy-wide firm averages, and the company's own historical performance.
- Comparisons with other companies are made more difficult because of different accounting methods. Some of the more common differences include inventory methods (FIFO and LIFO), depreciation methods (accelerated and straight-line), and lease accounting (capital and operating).
- There may be difficulty in locating comparable ratios when analyzing companies that operate in multiple industries.
- Conclusions cannot be made from viewing one set of ratios. Ratios must be viewed relative to one another.
- Judgment is required. Determining the target or comparison value for a ratio is difficult and may require some range of acceptable values.

Common-size balance sheets and income statements. These statements normalize balance sheets and income statements and allow the analyst to make easier comparisons of different-sized firms. A vertical common-size balance sheet expresses each balance sheet account as a *percentage of total assets*. A horizontal common-size balance sheet expresses each account as a ratio to the first-year value (e.g., 1.1 indicates an increase of 10% above the first-year value). A vertical common-sized income statement expresses each income statement item as a *percentage of sales*.

Measures of liquidity:

$$\text{current ratio} = \frac{\text{current assets}}{\text{current liabilities}}$$

$$\text{quick ratio} = \frac{\text{cash} + \text{marketable securities} + \text{receivables}}{\text{current liabilities}}$$

Measures of operating performance—turnover ratios and the cash conversion cycle:

$$\text{receivables turnover} = \frac{\text{annual sales}}{\text{average receivables}}$$

$$\text{inventory turnover} = \frac{\text{cost of goods sold}}{\text{average inventory}}$$

$$\text{payables turnover ratio} = \frac{\text{purchases}}{\text{average trade payables}}$$

$$\text{days of sales outstanding} = \frac{365}{\text{receivables turnover}}$$

$$\text{days of inventory on hand} = \frac{365}{\text{inventory turnover}}$$

$$\text{number of days of payables} = \frac{365}{\text{payables turnover ratio}}$$

$$\begin{array}{c} \text{cash} \\ \text{conversion} \\ \text{cycle} \end{array} = \left(\begin{array}{c} \text{days of sales} \\ \text{outstanding} \end{array} \right) + \left(\begin{array}{c} \text{days of inventory} \\ \text{on hand} \end{array} \right) - \left(\begin{array}{c} \text{number of} \\ \text{days of} \\ \text{payables} \end{array} \right)$$

Measures of operating performance—operating efficiency ratios:

$$\text{total asset turnover} = \frac{\text{revenue}}{\text{average total assets}}$$

$$\text{fixed asset turnover} = \frac{\text{revenue}}{\text{average net fixed assets}}$$

$$\text{working capital turnover} = \frac{\text{revenue}}{\text{average working capital}}$$

Measures of operating performance—operating profitability:

$$\text{gross profit margin} = \frac{\text{gross profit}}{\text{revenue}}$$

$$\text{operating profit margin} = \frac{\text{operating income}}{\text{revenue}} = \frac{\text{EBIT}}{\text{revenue}}$$

$$\text{net profit margin} = \frac{\text{net income}}{\text{revenue}}$$

Return on total capital (ROTC):

$$\text{return on total capital} = \frac{\text{EBIT}}{\text{average total capital}}$$

Total capital includes debt capital, so interest is added back to net income.

Return on equity (ROE):

$$\text{return on total equity} = \frac{\text{net income}}{\text{average total equity}}$$

$$\text{return on common equity} = \frac{\text{net income} - \text{preferred dividends}}{\text{average common equity}}$$

Measures of solvency:

$$\text{debt-to-equity ratio} = \frac{\text{total debt}}{\text{total shareholders' equity}}$$

$$\text{debt-to-capital} = \frac{\text{total debt}}{\text{total debt} + \text{total shareholders' equity}}$$

$$\text{debt-to-assets} = \frac{\text{total debt}}{\text{total assets}}$$

$$\text{financial leverage} = \frac{\text{average total assets}}{\text{average total equity}}$$

Measures of interest coverage:

$$\text{interest coverage} = \frac{\text{EBIT}}{\text{interest payments}}$$

$$\text{fixed charge coverage} = \frac{\text{EBIT} + \text{lease payments}}{\text{interest payments} + \text{lease payments}}$$

Growth analysis:

$$g = \text{retention rate} \times \text{ROE}$$

$$\text{retention rate} = 1 - \frac{\text{dividends declared}}{\text{net income available to common}}$$

DuPont analysis. The DuPont method decomposes the ROE to better analyze firm performance. An analyst can see the impact of leverage, profit margin, and turnover on ROE. There are two variants of the DuPont system: the traditional approach and the extended system.

Both approaches begin with:

$$\text{return on equity} = \left(\frac{\text{net income}}{\text{equity}} \right)$$

The *traditional DuPont equation* is:

$$\text{return on equity} = \left(\frac{\text{net income}}{\text{sales}}\right)\left(\frac{\text{sales}}{\text{assets}}\right)\left(\frac{\text{assets}}{\text{equity}}\right)$$

You may also see it presented as:

$$\text{return on equity} = \left(\begin{array}{c}\text{net profit}\\\text{margin}\end{array}\right)\left(\begin{array}{c}\text{asset}\\\text{turnover}\end{array}\right)\left(\begin{array}{c}\text{leverage}\\\text{ratio}\end{array}\right)$$

The traditional DuPont equation is arguably the most important equation in ratio analysis since it breaks down a very important ratio (ROE) into three key components. If ROE is low, it must be that at least one of the following is true: the company has a poor profit margin; the company has poor asset turnover; or the firm is under-leveraged.

The *extended DuPont equation* takes the net profit margin and breaks it down further. The extended DuPont equation can be written as:

$$\text{ROE} = \left(\frac{\text{net income}}{\text{EBT}}\right)\left(\frac{\text{EBT}}{\text{EBIT}}\right)\left(\frac{\text{EBIT}}{\text{revenue}}\right)\left(\frac{\text{revenue}}{\text{total assets}}\right)\left(\frac{\text{total assets}}{\text{total equity}}\right)$$

You may also see it presented as:

$$\text{ROE} = \left(\begin{array}{c}\text{tax}\\\text{burden}\end{array}\right)\left(\begin{array}{c}\text{interest}\\\text{burden}\end{array}\right)\left(\begin{array}{c}\text{EBIT}\\\text{margin}\end{array}\right)\left(\begin{array}{c}\text{asset}\\\text{turnover}\end{array}\right)\left(\begin{array}{c}\text{financial}\\\text{leverage}\end{array}\right)$$

Pro Forma Financial Statements

Both common-size financial statements and ratio analysis can be used in preparing pro forma financial statements. A forecast of financial results that begins with an estimate of a firm's next-period revenues might use the most recent COGS from a common-size income statement. Similarly, the analyst may believe that certain ratios will remain the same or change in one direction or the other for the next period. In the absence of any information indicating a change, an analyst may choose to incorporate the operating profit margin and other ratios from the prior period into a pro forma income statement for the next period. Beginning with an estimate of next-period sales, the estimated operating profit margin can be used to forecast operating profits for the next period.

Following are three methods of examining the variability of financial outcomes around point estimates:

1. **Sensitivity analysis** is based on "what if" questions, such as: What will be the effect on net income if sales increase by 3% rather than the estimated 5%?

2. **Scenario analysis** is based on specific scenarios (a specific set of outcomes for key variables) and will also yield a range of values for financial statement items.

3. **Simulation** is a technique in which probability distributions for key variables are selected and a computer generates a distribution of outcomes based on repeated random selection of values for the key variables.

STUDY SESSION 9: FINANCIAL REPORTING AND ANALYSIS— INVENTORIES, LONG-LIVED ASSETS, INCOME TAXES, AND NON-CURRENT LIABILITIES

INVENTORIES
Cross-Reference to CFA Institute Assigned Reading #29

For a manufacturing firm, raw materials, goods in process, and finished goods are recorded on the balance sheet as a current asset called inventory.

Costs included in inventory on the balance sheet include:

- Purchase cost.
- Conversion cost.
- Allocation of fixed production overhead based on normal capacity levels.
- Other costs necessary to bring the inventory to its present location and condition.

All of these costs for inventory acquired or produced in the current period are added to beginning inventory value and then allocated either to cost of goods sold for the period or to ending inventory.

Period costs, such as unallocated overhead, abnormal waste, most storage costs, administrative costs, and selling costs, are expensed.

Inventory Cost Allocation Methods

First-in, first-out (FIFO) assumes costs incurred for items that are purchased or manufactured first are the first costs to enter the cost of goods sold (COGS) computation. The balance of ending inventory is made up of those costs most recently incurred.

Last-in, first-out (LIFO) assumes costs incurred for items that are purchased or manufactured most recently are the first costs to enter the COGS computation. The balance of ending inventory is made up of costs that were incurred for items purchased or manufactured at the earliest time. Note that in the United States, companies using LIFO for tax purposes must also use LIFO in their financial statements, and that LIFO is not permitted under IFRS.

Weighted average costing calculates an average cost per unit by dividing cost of goods available by total units available. This average cost is used to determine both COGS and ending inventory.

With the *specific identification* method, individual items in inventory, such as a car dealer's cars in inventory, are carried at their individual costs and added to COGS as they are sold.

All of these methods are permitted under U.S. GAAP, but IFRS do not permit LIFO inventory accounting.

Inventory Values on the Balance Sheet

Under IFRS, inventories are valued at the lower of cost or net realizable value, which is estimated sales proceeds net of direct selling costs. Inventory "write-up" is allowed, but only to the extent that a previous write-down to net realizable value was recorded.

Under U.S. GAAP, inventories are valued at the lower of cost or market. "Market" is usually equal to replacement cost but cannot exceed net realizable value or be less than net realizable value minus a normal profit margin. No subsequent "write-up" is allowed.

Periodic and Perpetual Inventory Systems

Firms account for changes in inventory using either a periodic or perpetual system. In a **periodic inventory system**, inventory values and COGS are determined at the end of the accounting period. No detailed records of inventory are maintained;

rather, inventory acquired during the period is reported in a Purchases account. At the end of the period, purchases are added to beginning inventory to arrive at cost of goods available for sale. To calculate COGS, ending inventory is subtracted from goods available for sale.

In a **perpetual inventory system**, inventory values and COGS are updated continuously. Inventory purchased and sold is recorded directly in inventory when the transactions occur. Thus, a Purchases account is not necessary.

For the FIFO and specific identification methods, ending inventory values and COGS are the same whether a periodic or perpetual system is used. However, periodic and perpetual inventory systems can produce different values for inventory and COGS under the LIFO and weighted average cost methods.

LIFO vs. FIFO

In periods of rising prices and stable or increasing inventory quantities:

LIFO results in:	*FIFO results in:*
Higher COGS	Lower COGS
Lower gross profit	Higher gross profit
Lower inventory balances	Higher inventory balances

In periods of falling prices:

LIFO results in:	*FIFO results in:*
Lower COGS	Higher COGS
Higher gross profit	Lower gross profit
Higher inventory balances	Lower inventory balances

For a firm using the (weighted) average cost inventory method, all of these values will be between those for the LIFO and FIFO methods.

LIFO Reserve

Firms that report under LIFO must report a **LIFO reserve**, the amount by which LIFO inventory is less than FIFO inventory. To make financial statements prepared under LIFO comparable to those of FIFO firms, an analyst must:

1. Add the LIFO reserve to LIFO inventory.

2. Increase retained earnings by the LIFO reserve.

When prices are increasing, a LIFO firm will pay less in taxes than it would pay under FIFO. For this reason, analysts often decrease a LIFO firm's cash by the tax rate times the LIFO reserve and increase retained earnings by the LIFO reserve net of tax, instead of the full LIFO reserve.

The difference between LIFO COGS and FIFO COGS is equal to the change in the LIFO reserve for the period. To convert COGS from LIFO to FIFO, simply subtract the change in the LIFO reserve.

LIFO Liquidation

A **LIFO liquidation** occurs when a LIFO firm's inventory quantities decline. In a rising price environment, COGS are based on older, lower unit costs, which makes COGS artificially low. The reduction in COGS from a LIFO liquidation increases gross and net profits and margins, but these increases are not sustainable. A decrease in the LIFO reserve (disclosed in footnotes for LIFO companies) can alert analysts that a LIFO liquidation may be responsible for an increase in current-period profits and profit margins.

Ratios for Evaluating Inventory Management

Ratios that are directly affected by the choice of inventory accounting method include inventory turnover, days of inventory, and gross profit margin.

High inventory turnover relative to other firms in an industry may indicate too little inventory and low turnover may indicate inventory that is too great. Comparing the firm's revenue growth to that of the industry can provide information on whether inventories are too large (slow moving or obsolete) or too small (so that sales are lost to a significant degree).

Ratios and Inventory Method

Profitability. As compared to FIFO, LIFO produces higher COGS in the income statement and will result in lower earnings. Any profitability measure that includes COGS will be lower under LIFO. For example, higher COGS will result in lower gross, operating, and net profit margins as compared to FIFO.

Liquidity. Compared to FIFO, LIFO results in a lower inventory value on the balance sheet. Because inventory (a current asset) is lower under LIFO, the current ratio, a popular measure of liquidity, is also lower under LIFO than under FIFO. Working capital is lower under LIFO as well, because current assets are lower. The quick ratio is unaffected by the firm's inventory cost flow method because inventory is excluded from its numerator.

Activity. Inventory turnover (COGS / average inventory) is higher for firms that use LIFO compared to firms that use FIFO. Under LIFO, COGS is valued at more recent, higher costs (higher numerator), while inventory is valued at older, lower costs (lower denominator). Higher turnover under LIFO will result in lower days of inventory on hand (365 / inventory turnover).

Solvency. LIFO results in lower total assets compared to FIFO because LIFO inventory is lower. Lower total assets under LIFO result in lower stockholders' equity (assets – liabilities). Because total assets and stockholders' equity are lower under LIFO, the debt ratio and the debt-to-equity ratio are higher under LIFO compared to FIFO.

LONG-LIVED ASSETS
Cross-Reference to CFA Institute Assigned Reading #30

The purchase cost of assets that will provide economic benefits to the firm over more than one year is typically not taken as an expense in the year of acquisition, but is capitalized (creating an asset on the balance sheet) and spread over an asset's useful economic life by recording depreciation of the asset's value.

Compared to taking the acquisition cost as an expense in the period of acquisition, capitalization decreases expenses (which increases net income), increases assets and equity (which decreases reported leverage), reduces income variability, and increases operating cash flow and decreases investing cash flow in the same amounts, since the cost of a capitalized assets is treated as an investing cash flow rather than an operating cash flow.

The following table summarizes the financial implications of capitalizing versus expensing:

	Capitalizing	*Expensing*
Income variability	Lower	Higher
Profitability—first year (ROA & ROE) and Net Income	Higher	Lower
Profitability—later years (ROA & ROE) and Net Income	Lower	Higher
Total cash flows (assuming no tax effects)	Same	Same
Cash flow from operations	Higher	Lower
Cash flow from investing	Lower	Higher
Leverage ratios (debt/equity & debt/assets)	Lower	Higher

Capitalization of interest. Interest costs incurred when constructing assets over multiple periods for firm use or for sale must be capitalized under both U.S. GAAP and IFRS, either to the balance sheet asset value or to inventory, respectively. The expense is recognized over time as either asset depreciation or in COGS when a constructed asset is sold.

Capitalization of construction interest reduces interest expense in the period of capitalization and increases either depreciation or COGS. Capitalized interest expense is treated as an investing, rather than operating, cash outflow and an analyst should take account of this difference. To better measure interest coverage, an analyst should add capitalized interest to interest expense and increase EBIT by adding depreciation expense from previously capitalized interest.

Internally Created Intangible Assets

For internally generated intangible assets, firms reporting under IFRS must expense research costs as incurred but may capitalize development costs (costs incurred after technological feasibility and the intent to use or sell the completed asset have been established).

Under U.S. GAAP, generally both research and development expenditures related to internally created intangible assets must be expensed as incurred. An exception is the creation of software for internal use or sale to others. After specific criteria are met, costs to develop software must be capitalized under U.S. GAAP.

Depreciation

The historical cost of capitalized physical assets is allocated over their economic (useful) lives by recording depreciation expense. Depreciation methods include straight-line (an equal amount each period), accelerated (greater in the early years of an asset's life), and units-of-production (proportional to asset use).

Straight-line depreciation:

$$\text{depreciation expense} = \frac{\text{original cost} - \text{salvage value}}{\text{depreciable life}}$$

Double-declining balance (an accelerated method):

$$\text{DDB depreciation in year } x = \frac{2}{\text{asset life in years}} \times \text{book value at beginning of year } x$$

Note that the salvage value is not used to compute annual depreciation under the double-declining balance method. The end-of-period book (carrying) value of an asset, however, is not allowed to go below its estimated salvage value.

Units of production and service hours depreciation. Under this method, an asset's depreciable basis is divided by estimated units of production or total service hours. Each period, depreciation is calculated as cost-per-unit (hour) times the number of units produced (hours of service).

Financial Statement Effects of Depreciation Methods

Compared to straight-line depreciation, an accelerated depreciation method will result in greater depreciation expense in the early years of an asset's life. This will reduce EBIT, net income, assets, and equity, and decrease ROA and ROE, compared to straight-line depreciation. When an accelerated method is used for tax reporting, taxable income is less in the early years of an asset's life, reducing taxes and increasing reported cash flows.

Over an asset's useful life, total depreciation and income are the same under all methods; only the timing of expense and income is affected.

Note that increasing (decreasing) the estimated salvage value or estimated asset life will decrease (increase) periodic depreciation expense, increasing reported income.

Useful Lives and Salvage Values

Calculating depreciation expense requires estimating an asset's useful life and its salvage (residual) value. Firms can manipulate depreciation expense, and therefore net income, by increasing or decreasing either of these estimates.

A longer estimated useful life decreases annual depreciation and increases reported net income, while a shorter estimated useful life will have the opposite effect. A higher estimate of the salvage value will also decrease depreciation and increase net income, while a lower estimate of the salvage value will increase depreciation and decrease net income.

A change in an accounting estimate, such as useful life or salvage value, is put into effect in the current period and prospectively. That is, the change in estimate is applied to the asset's carrying (book) value and depreciation is calculated going forward using the new estimate. The previous periods are not affected by the change.

Intangible Assets

Purchased assets that do not have physical substance but have finite lives (e.g., patents and franchises) are reported on the balance sheet at their fair values, which are reduced over their economic lives by amortization (like depreciation of a physical asset).

Internally developed intangible assets are not reported on the balance sheet. Values of intangible assets that do not have finite lives (e.g., goodwill) and of those that can be renewed at minimal cost (e.g., trademarks) are not amortized, but must be checked periodically for impairment.

Derecognition of Long-Lived Assets

Long-lived assets are *derecognized* and removed from the balance sheet when they are sold, exchanged, or abandoned.

When a long-lived asset is sold, the asset is removed from the balance sheet and the difference between the sale proceeds and the carrying value of the asset is reported as a gain or loss in the income statement. The carrying value is equal to original cost minus accumulated depreciation and any impairment charges.

The gain or loss is usually reported in the income statement as a part of other gains and losses, or reported separately if material. Also, if the firm presents its cash flow statement using the indirect method, the gain or loss is removed from net income to compute cash flow from operations because the proceeds from selling a long-lived asset are an investing cash inflow.

If a long-lived asset is abandoned, the treatment is similar to a sale, except there are no proceeds. In this case, the carrying value of the asset is removed from the balance sheet and a loss of that amount is recognized in the income statement.

If a long-lived asset is exchanged for another asset, a gain or loss is computed by comparing the carrying value of the old asset with fair value of the old asset (or the fair value of the new asset if that value is clearly more evident). The carrying value of the old asset is removed from the balance sheet and the new asset is recorded at its fair value.

Impairments

Under IFRS, the firm must annually assess whether events or circumstances indicate an **impairment** of an asset's value has occurred. For example, there may have been a significant decline in the market value of the asset or a significant change in the asset's physical condition. If so, the asset's value must be tested for impairment.

An asset is impaired when its carrying value (original cost less accumulated depreciation) exceeds the **recoverable amount.** The recoverable amount is the greater of its fair value less any selling costs and its **value in use.** The value in use is the present value of its future cash flow stream from continued use.

If impaired, the asset's value must be written down on the balance sheet to the recoverable amount. An impairment loss, equal to the excess of carrying value over the recoverable amount, is recognized in the income statement.

Under IFRS, the loss can be reversed if the value of the impaired asset recovers in the future. However, the loss reversal is limited to the original impairment loss. Thus, the carrying value of the asset after reversal cannot exceed the carrying value before the impairment loss was recognized.

Under U.S. GAAP, an asset is tested for impairment only when events and circumstances indicate the firm may not be able to recover the carrying value through future use.

Determining an impairment and calculating the loss potentially involves two steps. In the first step, the asset is tested for impairment by applying a **recoverability test.** If the asset is impaired, the second step involves measuring the loss.

Recoverability. An asset is considered impaired if the carrying value (original cost less accumulated depreciation) is greater than the asset's future *undiscounted* cash flow stream. Because the recoverability test is based on estimates of future undiscounted cash flows, tests for impairment involve considerable management discretion.

Loss measurement. If impaired, the asset's value is written down to fair value on the balance sheet and a loss, equal to the excess of carrying value over the fair value of the asset (or the *discounted* value of its future cash flows if the fair value is not known), is recognized in the income statement.

Under U.S. GAAP, loss recoveries are not permitted.

Asset Revaluations

Under U.S. GAAP, long-lived assets cannot be revalued upward, except that held-for-sale assets can be revalued upward to the extent of previous impairment writedowns.

Under IFRS, assets may be revalued upward to fair value. Gains reversing previous writedowns are reported on the income statement, and any excess gains are taken as an adjustment to equity in an account called **revaluation surplus**.

The initial effects of upward asset revaluations are to increase assets and stockholders' equity, and net income where gains are taken into income. If a depreciable asset is revalued upward, depreciation will be greater, and income less, in subsequent periods.

Analysis of Long-Lived Assets

An analyst can use financial statement disclosures to estimate the **average age** and **useful life** of a firm's long-lived assets. Older, less-efficient assets may make a firm less competitive. The average age of assets is useful in estimating the timing of major capital expenditures and a firm's future financing requirements. These estimates are most accurate for a firm that uses straight-line depreciation.

$$\text{average age} = \frac{\text{accumulated depreciation}}{\text{annual depreciation expense}}$$

$$\text{total useful life} = \frac{\text{gross PP \& E}}{\text{annual depreciation expense}}$$

$$\text{remaining useful life} = \frac{\text{net PP\&E}}{\text{annual depreciation expense}}$$

Investment Property

Under IFRS (but not U.S. GAAP), property a firm holds for capital appreciation or to collect rental income is classified as *investment property*. Firms can value investment property using either a cost model or a fair value model. Under the fair value model, increases in value above historical cost are recognized as gains on the income statement. This differs from the revaluation model for property, plant, and equipment, where increases above historical cost are recognized in equity as revaluation surplus.

Asset Purchases vs. Leases

Firms may lease long-lived assets rather than purchasing them. Leases are classified as either finance leases or operating leases.

An **operating lease** is essentially a rental arrangement. No asset or liability is recorded on the balance sheet by the lessee, and the periodic lease payments are simply recognized as rental expense in the income statement.

A **finance lease** is, in substance, a purchase of an asset that is financed with debt and must be capitalized. At the inception of a finance lease, the lessee adds a lease asset and an equal lease liability to the balance sheet. Over the term of the lease, the lessee recognizes both depreciation expense on the asset and interest expense on the liability. This treatment is the same as if the asset were purchased with only borrowed funds.

Do not confuse capitalizing a lease with capitalizing a purchased asset. When a firm capitalizes a purchase, it recognizes an asset on the balance sheet. When it capitalizes a lease, it recognizes both an asset and a liability.

INCOME TAXES
Cross-Reference to CFA Institute Assigned Reading #31

Definitely know this terminology. From the tax return we have:

- *Taxable income:* Income subject to tax as reported on the tax return.
- *Taxes payable:* The tax liability based on taxable income, as shown on the tax return.
- *Income tax paid:* The actual cash outflow for taxes paid during the current period.
- *Tax loss carryforwards:* Losses that could not be deducted on the tax return in the current period but may be used to reduce taxable income and taxes payable in future periods.

On the financial statements, we find *pretax income*, which is income before income tax expense. Pretax income on the income statement is used to calculate:

- *Income tax expense:* A noncash income statement item that includes cash tax expense plus any increase (minus any decrease) in the deferred tax liability minus any increase (plus any decrease) in the deferred tax asset.

- *Deferred income tax expense:* The excess of income tax expense over taxes payable.
- *Valuation allowance:* A contra account that reduces a deferred tax asset for the probability that it will not be realized (U.S. GAAP).

Deferred Tax Liabilities

Deferred tax liabilities are balance sheet amounts that result from an excess of income tax expense over taxes payable and are expected to result in future cash outflows.

The most common reason for creation of a deferred tax liability is that depreciation expense on the income statement (straight-line) is less than depreciation expense on the tax return (accelerated). Pretax income is therefore greater than taxable income, and income tax expense is greater than income tax payable. The taxes that are "deferred" by using accelerated depreciation on the tax return are carried as a deferred tax liability on the balance sheet.

Deferred Tax Assets

Deferred tax assets are balance sheet amounts that result when taxes payable are greater than income tax expense. This results when revenues are recognized for tax prior to their recording on the financial statements, or when expenses for financial reporting are recorded prior to recognizing them as deductible expenses for tax. Prior losses in excess of those that can be used to offset previous income represent a tax-loss carryforward, which is an asset as it will reduce future taxes.

An example of an expense item that can give rise to a deferred tax asset is warranty expense. On the income statement, estimated warranty expense is deductible; on the tax return, only warranty expense actually incurred is deductible. Early on, this leads to taxes payable being greater than income tax expense, which gives rise to a deferred tax asset. In future periods, taxes payable will be less than income tax expense, and the "benefit" of the asset will be realized.

Calculating deferred tax liabilities and assets. Under the liability method, all temporary differences between taxable income and pretax income are multiplied by the expected future tax rate (typically the current rate) to calculate deferred tax assets and liabilities. They are not netted; deferred tax assets and liabilities can be on the balance sheet simultaneously and separately.

Financial analysis. If a company's assets are growing, it may be the case that a deferred tax liability is not expected to reverse in the foreseeable future; an analyst should treat this "liability" as additional equity (decrease the DTL and increase equity). If the liability is expected to reverse, the liability should be adjusted to

---

present value terms to the extent practicable. Decide which is more appropriate on a case-by-case basis.

Tax basis. Gains or losses can result when an asset is sold or a liability is paid when there is a difference between the proceeds or payment and the tax basis of the asset or liability. The tax basis for a long-lived asset is its historical cost minus accumulated tax depreciation. The tax basis for debt is historical proceeds adjusted for the amortization of any original discount or premium to par.

Change in tax rates. A change in tax rates will be reflected by an adjustment to both deferred tax asset and liability accounts. A decrease (increase) in the tax rate will decrease (increase) both deferred tax assets and liabilities; the net change is reflected in income tax expense for the current period.

DTL and DTA Calculations

Consider a firm with a 40% tax rate that has $1,000 in financial statement depreciation and $3,000 of tax return depreciation, as well as $500 of warranty expense that cannot be deducted in the current period for taxes.

The firm will report a DTL of $(3,000 - 1,000)(0.40) = \$800$ and a DTA of $(500 - 0)(0.40) = \$200$. Reported income tax expense is greater than taxes payable by $800 - 200 = \$600$.

A change in the firm's expected tax rate from 40% to 30% would reduce the DTL to $600 and the DTA to $150. The reduction of $200 in the DTL and the decrease in the DTA of $50 net to a $150 decrease in liabilities, which will reduce reported income tax expense (taxes payable – net deferred tax liability) by $150. Net income/profitability is increased, equity is increased, and leverage is decreased by the change.

Permanent vs. Temporary Differences

So far, our examples have been temporary differences between taxable income and pretax income that will potentially reverse over time. In the case of interest income on tax-exempt bonds, for example, pretax income is greater than taxable income, and this will not reverse. There is no deferred asset or liability created, and the difference is reflected in a difference between the effective tax rate (income tax expense/pretax income) and the statutory rate on the tax return.

Valuation Allowance

A firm's management must report a valuation allowance, under U.S. GAAP, if it is probable that part or all of a DTA will not be realized because of the firm's inability to generate taxable income in the future. An increase (decrease) in the valuation allowance decreases (increases) the net DTA and reported income. The analyst should examine the reasons for the change as management can manipulate earnings by changing the valuation allowance.

Firms report the details of DTL and DTA changes over the period, as well as a reconciliation of the differences between their effective tax rate (financial statements) and the statutory tax rate (tax return). These details can help an analyst understand the implications of the events that give rise to changes in deferred tax items and better predict future tax rates by considering the factors that caused a difference between the statutory and effective rates.

Some differences in reporting result from the fact that under IFRS upward asset revaluations give rise to DTAs, DTLs and DTAs are netted for reporting purposes, and, rather than reporting a valuation allowance, DTAs are adjusted directly for any probability that they will not be realized (reversed).

Non-current (Long-term) Liabilities
Cross-Reference to CFA Institute Assigned Reading #32

Bonds issued at par:

- *Balance sheet impact.* The value carried on books throughout a bond's life will be equal to face value.
- *Interest expense.* This is always equal to the book value of bonds at the beginning of the period multiplied by the market rate of interest at issuance. With bonds issued at par value, this is the same as the bond's coupon rate.
- *Cash flow.* Cash flow from operations includes a deduction for cash interest expense. Interest expense is equal to the coupon payment. Cash flow from financing is increased by the amount received at issuance and decreased by the payment made when the bonds are redeemed.

Bonds issued at a premium or discount:

- *Balance sheet impact.* Bonds that were originally sold at a premium will always be shown at a premium on the balance sheet. This premium will be amortized toward zero over the life of the bond. Bonds that were originally sold at a discount will always be recorded on the balance sheet at a discount. This discount will be amortized toward zero over the life of the bond. Hence, the book value of both premium and discount bonds will converge to the bond's par or face value at their maturity dates.

- *Interest expense.* In the case of bonds issued at a premium, recorded interest expense will be lower than the coupon payment. Amortization of the bond's premium will serve to reduce the interest expense shown on the income statement. In general, interest expense will equal the coupon payment less the premium amortization. In the case of discount bonds, the interest expense will be higher than the coupon payment. Here, amortization of the bond's discount will serve to increase the interest expense reported on the income statement. In general, interest expense will equal the coupon payment plus the discount amortization.

- *Cash flow.* For premium bonds, the cash coupon is higher than interest expense. Consequently, CFO is lower and CFF is higher, relative to a company that does not have premium bonds in its capital structure. For discount bonds, the cash coupon is lower than interest expense. Consequently, CFO is higher and CFF is lower, relative to a company that does not have discount bonds.

Debt covenants contained in the bond indenture place restrictions on the firm that protect bondholders and thereby increase the value of the firm's bonds. Typically, such covenants include restrictions on paying common dividends if bond interest is not paid; on the values of specific financial ratios; and on additional debt issuance, acquisitions, mergers, and asset sales.

An analyst can find additional information about a firm's financing liabilities in the footnotes. Typically, disclosures will include the nature of the liabilities, maturity dates, call and conversion provisions, restrictions, collateral pledged as security, and the amount of debt maturing in each of the next five years.

Under both U.S. GAAP and IFRS, recent changes allow firms to report more financial liabilities at fair value. An increase (decrease) in market rates decreases (increases) the present value of the future liability. For analysis, the fair value of liabilities may be more appropriate than amortized historical proceeds as a firm with lower-rate debt is in better financial shape than one that differs only by having higher-rate debt. A downward (upward) adjustment in the value of a firm's liabilities will increase (decrease) its equity and decrease (increase) its leverage ratios.

Derecognition of Debt

When bonds mature, no gain or loss is recognized by the issuer. At maturity, any original discount or premium has been fully amortized; thus, the book value of a bond liability and its face value are the same. The cash outflow to repay a bond is reported in the cash flow statement as a financing cash flow.

A firm may choose to **redeem** bonds before maturity because interest rates have fallen, because the firm has generated surplus cash through operations, or because funds from the issuance of equity make it possible (and desirable).

When bonds are redeemed before maturity, a gain or loss is recognized by subtracting the redemption price from the book value of the bond liability at the reacquisition date. For example, consider a firm that reacquires $1 million face amount of bonds at 102% of par when the carrying value of the bond liability is $995,000. The firm will recognize a loss of $25,000 ($995,000 carrying value – $1,020,000 redemption price). Had the carrying value been greater than the redemption price, the firm would have recognized a gain.

Under U.S. GAAP, any remaining unamortized bond issuance costs must be written off and included in the gain or loss calculation. Writing off the cost of issuing the bond will reduce a gain or increase a loss. No write-off is necessary under IFRS because the issuance costs are already accounted for in the book value of the bond liability.

Any gain or loss from redeeming debt is reported in the income statement, usually as a part of continuing operations, and additional information is disclosed separately. Redeeming debt is usually not a part of the firm's day-to-day operations; thus, analysts often eliminate the gain or loss from the income statement for analysis and forecasting.

When presenting the cash flow statement using the indirect method, any gain (loss) is subtracted from (added to) net income in calculating cash flow from operations. The redemption price is reported as an outflow from financing activities.

Leases

A firm may choose to lease, rather than purchase, assets:

- To conserve cash.
- Because of attractive financing (lower interest costs).
- To avoid risk of asset obsolescence.

- To avoid reporting a balance sheet liability (with an operating lease) and improve leverage ratios.
- Flexibility to design custom lease liability.
- Tax advantage (U.S.) if an off-balance-sheet lease can be treated as ownership for tax (deduct depreciation and interest expense).

Lease Classification

Under U.S. GAAP, a lease must be classified by the lessee as a *finance (capital) lease* if any one of the following four criteria is met:

- The title is transferred to the lessee at the end of the lease period.
- A bargain purchase option exists.
- The lease period is at least 75% of the asset's life.
- The present value of the lease payments is at least 90% of the fair value of the asset.

If none of the criteria hold, the lease will be classified as an *operating lease*. Lease classification under IFRS is similar (without specific quantitative tests) and a lease must be classified as a finance lease if substantially all of the risks and rewards of ownership are transferred to the lessee.

Financial Statement Effects of Leases

When a lease is reported as a finance lease, the firm adds a lease asset and a lease liability to its balance sheet in equal amounts. Over time, the firm recognizes interest expense on the lease liability and depreciation expense on the lease asset. The liability decreases each period by the excess of the lease payment over the interest expense.

When a lease is classified as an operating lease, no balance sheet entries are made, and the lease payment is reported as an expense each period.

Because of these differences, compared to a firm reporting a lease as an operating lease, a firm reporting the same lease as a finance lease will report: higher assets, higher liabilities, higher operating cash flow and lower financing cash flow (portion of lease payment that reduces the lease liability is considered a financing cash flow) over the life of the lease. Since the sum of interest expense and depreciation is greater than the lease payment in the early years of a finance lease, reporting a lease as a finance lease will decrease net income and profitability ratios compared to reporting the lease as an operating lease.

The following tables summarize the effects of capital leases compared to operating leases on financial statement items and ratios.

Figure 3: Effects of Lease Classification (Financial Statement Totals)

Financial Statement Totals	Finance Lease	Operating Lease
Assets	Higher	Lower
Liabilities	Higher	Lower
Net income (in the early years)	Lower	Higher
Cash flow from operations	Higher	Lower
Cash flow from financing	Lower	Higher
Total cash flow	Same	Same

Figure 4: Effects of Lease Classification (Ratios)

Ratios	Finance Lease	Operating Lease
Current ratio (CA/CL)	Lower	Higher
Working capital (CA – CL)	Lower	Higher
Asset turnover (Sales/TA)	Lower	Higher
Return on assets (EAT/TA)	Lower	Higher
Return on equity (EAT/E)	Lower	Higher
Debt/equity	Higher	Lower

With a finance lease, the next lease payment is recognized as a current liability, reducing the current ratio and net working capital. Operating income (EBIT) is higher for a finance lease because the interest expense is not subtracted in its calculation. Total net income will be the same over the entire lease term regardless of classification, but net income will be lower in the early years for a finance lease because interest costs are higher in the early years (the sum of depreciation and interest expense exceeds the lease payment).

Lessor Treatment of Lease Transactions

If the conditions for a finance lease are not met, a lessor reports a lease as an operating lease. A lessor reports the lease payments as income and depreciates the leased asset on its balance sheet.

If the conditions for a finance lease are met, a lessor reports the lease as either a **sales-type lease** or a **direct financing lease**. From a lessor's perspective, when the carrying value of the leased asset is less than the present value of the lease payments, as is the case when the lessor is the manufacturer of the leased asset, the lease is treated as a sales-type lease. In this case, the lessor reports the transaction as if the asset were sold at the lease value (recognizing profit at lease initiation) and as if a loan was provided to the lessee. A lease receivable (asset) is added to the lessor's balance sheet. Interest income and a reduction in the value of the lease receivable asset (future lease payments) are reported as lease payments are received. The interest income is treated as operating cash inflow and the reduction in the asset value is treated as an investing cash inflow.

If the lessor's book value for the leased asset is the same as the present value of the lease, the lease is reported as a direct financing lease. An example would be a leasing company that leases cars to customers, first purchasing the automobiles from various manufacturers. The lessor records interest income over the life of the lease (as if it were purely a loan transaction) and no profit at the inception of the lease. Interest income is reported as an operating cash inflow and reduction in the value of the lease asset is reported as an investing cash inflow, just as with a sales-type lease.

With a sales-type finance lease, recognizing profit at the inception of the lease increases the lessor's net income, retained earnings, and assets compared to an operating lease or direct financing lease. The lessor reports higher net income in the early years for a direct financing lease compared to an operating lease. This pattern results because interest income from the direct financing lease decreases over time, while the payment on the operating lease is level. Over the life of the lease, lessor net income is the same whether a lease is treated as an operating lease or as a direct financing lease.

Pension Plans

A **defined contribution plan** is a retirement plan in which the firm contributes a sum each period to the employee's retirement account. The firm makes no promise to the employee regarding the future value of the plan assets. The investment decisions are left to the employee, who assumes all of the investment risk. On the income statement, pension expense is simply equal to the employer's contribution. There is no future liability to report on the balance sheet.

In a **defined benefit plan**, the firm promises to make periodic payments to employees after retirement. The benefit is usually based on the employee's years of service and the employee's compensation at, or near, retirement. For example, an employee might earn a retirement benefit of 2% of her final salary for each year of service. Because the employee's future benefit is defined, the employer assumes the investment risk.

Financial reporting for a defined benefit plan is much more complicated than for a defined contribution plan because the employer must estimate the value of the future obligation to its employees. The obligation involves forecasting a number of variables, such as future compensation levels, employee turnover, retirement age, mortality rates, and an appropriate discount rate.

For defined benefit plans, if the fair value of the plan's assets is greater than the estimated pension liability, the plan is said to be **overfunded** and the sponsoring firm records a **net pension asset** on its balance sheet. If the fair value of the plan's assets is less than the estimated pension liability, the plan is **underfunded** and the firm records a **net pension liability** on its balance sheet.

The change in the net pension asset or liability is reported each year. Some components of the change are included in net income while others are included in other comprehensive income. Figure 5 illustrates the treatments under IFRS and U.S. GAAP.

Figure 5: Components of the Change in a Net Pension Asset or Liability

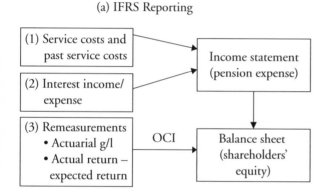

(a) IFRS Reporting

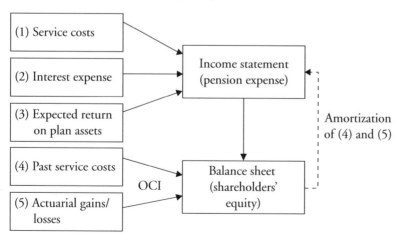

(b) U.S. GAAP Reporting

Under IFRS, the change in net pension asset or liability has three components: service costs, net interest expense or income, and remeasurements. Pension expense on the income statement is the sum of service costs (present value of additional benefits earned over the year) and net interest expense or income (beginning value of net pension liability or asset multiplied by the discount rate used to determine the present value of plan assets).

Remeasurements are recognized as other comprehensive income. These include actuarial gains or losses and the difference between the actual return on plan assets and the return included in net interest expense or income. Under IFRS, remeasurements are not amortized to the income statement over time.

Under U.S. GAAP, the change in net pension asset or liability has five components. Pension expense in the current period has three components: service costs, net interest expense, and the expected return on plan assets (a positive expected return decreases pension expense).

Past service costs (retroactive benefits awarded to employees when a plan is initiated or amended) and actuarial gains or losses are recognized as other comprehensive income. These are amortized to pension expense over time.

STUDY SESSION 10: FINANCIAL REPORTING AND ANALYSIS— FINANCIAL REPORTING QUALITY AND FINANCIAL STATEMENT ANALYSIS

FINANCIAL REPORTING QUALITY
Cross-Reference to CFA Institute Assigned Reading #33

When discussing the quality of a firm's financial statements, we must distinguish between the quality of its financial reporting and the quality of its reported results.

Financial reporting quality refers to the characteristics of a firm's financial statements, primarily with respect to how well they follow generally accepted accounting principles (GAAP). However, given that GAAP allow choices among methods, estimates, and specific treatments, compliance with GAAP by itself does not necessarily produce financial reporting of the highest quality.

High quality financial reporting must be *decision-useful*. Two characteristics of decision-useful financial reporting are *relevance* and *faithful representation*. Financial statements are relevant when the information presented is useful in making decisions and likely to affect these decisions. Faithful representation encompasses the qualities of completeness, neutrality, and the absence of errors.

The **quality of earnings** is a separate issue. The quality of reported earnings (not the quality of earnings reports) is high if earnings represent an adequate return on equity and are sustainable; that is, they are expected to recur in future periods. A firm can have high financial reporting quality but low earnings quality (inadequate returns/unsustainable), but if a firm has low-quality financial reporting, we might not be able to determine the quality of its earnings.

Quality of financial reports may be ranked from best to worst, based on the quality of earnings and financial reporting:

1. Reporting is compliant with GAAP and decision-useful; earnings are sustainable and adequate.

2. Reporting is compliant with GAAP and decision-useful, but earnings are not sustainable or not adequate.

3. Reporting is compliant with GAAP, but earnings quality is low and reporting choices and estimates are biased.

4. Reporting is compliant with GAAP, but the amount of earnings is actively managed to increase, decrease, or smooth reported earnings.

5. Reporting is not compliant with GAAP, although the numbers presented are based on the company's actual economic activities.

6. Reporting is not compliant and includes numbers that are fictitious or fraudulent.

Neutral Accounting vs. Conservative or Aggressive Accounting

Financial statements should be neutral (unbiased) to be most valuable to users. Biased reporting can be conservative or aggressive. Choices made within GAAP are considered **conservative** if they tend to decrease the company's reported earnings and financial position for the current period and considered **aggressive** if they increase reported earnings or improve the financial position for the current period. Aggressive accounting often results in decreased earnings in future periods, while conservative accounting will tend to increase future period earnings.

Both these types of bias are used by management to **smooth earnings**. During periods of higher-than-expected (or higher than a specific benchmark) earnings, management may employ a conservative bias (e.g., by adjusting an accrued liability upward to reduce reported earnings for that period). This effectively defers the recognition of these earnings to a future period. If, in a future period, earnings are less than expected, a more aggressive earnings choice (e.g., decreasing the accrued liability) can increase reported earnings. The initial increase in the accrued liability is sometimes referred to as putting earnings in the "cookie jar" (so that they may be enjoyed later).

Conservatism in financial reporting is not necessarily "good." Either type of bias is a deviation from neutral reporting or faithful representation. Sometimes GAAP themselves can introduce conservatism by imposing higher standards of verification for revenue and profit than for expenses and accrual of liabilities. While conservative bias is not ideal for users of financial statements, it may be beneficial in reducing the probability of future litigation from users claiming they were misled, in reducing current period tax liability, and in protecting the interests of those who have less complete information than management, such as buyers of the company's debt.

Some examples of conservative versus aggressive financial reporting choices are shown in Figure 6.

Figure 6: Aggressive and Conservative Accounting

Aggressive	*Conservative*
Capitalize current period costs	Expense current period costs
Longer estimates of the lives of depreciable assets	Shorter estimates of the lives of depreciable assets
Higher estimated salvage values	Lower estimated salvage values
Straight-line depreciation	Accelerated depreciation
Delayed recognition of impairments	Early recognition of impairments
Smaller reserve for bad debt	Greater reserve for bad debt
Smaller valuation allowances on deferred tax assets	Larger valuation allowances on deferred tax assets

Motivations and Conditions for Low-Quality Financial Reporting

Three factors that typically exist in cases where management provides low-quality financial reporting are *motivation, opportunity,* and *rationalization* of the behavior.

One important motivation for aggressive accounting choices is to meet or exceed benchmark or expected earnings per share growth. The manager's motivation may be to enhance her reputation and improve future career opportunities or to simply increase incentive compensation. Other possible motivations are to gain credibility with equity market investors or improve the way the company is viewed by its customers and suppliers. For companies that are highly leveraged and unprofitable, aggressive accounting may be motivated by a desire to avoid violating debt covenants.

Circumstances that provide opportunity for low-quality, or even fraudulent, financial reporting include weak internal controls, inadequate oversight by the board of directors, the large range of acceptable accounting treatments, or inconsequential penalties in the case of accounting fraud.

The third likely factor in low-quality financial reporting is rationalization by management for less-than-ethical actions. Whether the story is "I'll fix it next period" or "I have to do it to get my bonus and pay for my parents' care," the resulting behavior is the same.

Requiring audited financial statements is one mechanism to discipline financial reporting quality. However, an unqualified or "clean" audit opinion does not guarantee that no fraud has occurred; it only offers reasonable assurance that the financial statements (prepared the under the direction of management) have been "fairly reported" with respect to the applicable GAAP. The auditor is selected and paid by the firm being audited.

Non-GAAP Measures

Firms will sometimes report accounting measures that are not defined or required under GAAP. Such measures typically exclude some items in order to make the firm's performance look better. Management may exclude items because they are one-time or nonoperating costs that will not affect operating earnings going forward, because the items are non-cash charges, or to "improve comparability with companies that use different accounting methods" for depreciation or restructuring charges.

In the United States, companies that report non-GAAP measures in their financial statements are required to:

- Display the most comparable GAAP measure with equal prominence.
- Provide an explanation by management as to why the non-GAAP measure is thought to be useful.
- Reconcile the difference between the non-GAAP measure and the most comparable GAAP measure.
- Disclose other purposes for which the firm uses the non-GAAP measure.
- Include, in any non-GAAP measure, any items that are likely to recur in the future, even those treated as nonrecurring, unusual, or infrequent in the financial statements.

IFRS require that firms using non-IFRS measures in financial reports must:

- Define and explain the relevance of such non-IFRS measures.
- Reconcile the differences between the non-IFRS measure and the most comparable IFRS measure.

Accounting Methods, Choices and Estimates, and Warning Signs

Revenue recognition. Firms can choose where in the shipping process the customer takes title to the goods: free-on-board (FOB) at the shipping point or FOB at the destination. Choosing terms of FOB at the shipping point will mean that revenue is recognized earlier compared to FOB at the destination.

Firms can also manage the timing of revenue recognition by accelerating or delaying shipments. If additional revenue is required to meet targets, firms can offer discounts or special financing terms to increase orders in the current period or ship goods to distributors without receiving an order. Overloading a distribution channel with more goods than would normally be sold during a period is referred to as **channel stuffing**. In periods when high earnings are expected, management may wish to delay recognition of revenue to the next period and hold or delay customer shipments to achieve this.

In a **bill-and-hold transaction**, the customer buys the goods and receives an invoice but requests that the firm keep the goods at their location for a period of time. The use of fictitious bill-and-hold transactions can increase earnings in the current period by recognizing revenue for goods that are actually still in inventory. Revenue for future periods will be decreased as real customer orders for these bill-and-hold items are filled but not recognized in revenue, offsetting the previous overstatement of revenue.

Accounting warning signs related to revenue recognition may include:

- Changes in revenue recognition methods.
- Use of barter transactions.
- Use of rebate programs that require estimation of the impact of rebates on net revenue.
- Lack of transparency with regard to how the various components of a customer order are recorded as revenue.
- Revenue growth out of line with peer companies.
- Receivables turnover is decreasing over multiple periods.
- Decreases in total asset turnover, especially when a company is growing through acquisition of other companies.
- Inclusion of nonoperating items or significant one-time sales in revenue.

Estimates of credit losses. On the balance sheet, the reserve for uncollectible debt is an offset to accounts receivable. If management determines the probability that accounts receivable will be uncollectible is lower than their current estimate, a decrease in the reserve for uncollectible debt will increase net receivables and increase net income. An increase in the estimate of credit losses would have the opposite effect.

A firm that simply underestimates the percentage of receivables that will be uncollectible will report higher receivables and higher net income as a result. At some point, when actual uncollectible accounts exceed the low estimate, the firm will report an additional expense that will reduce net income and net receivables.

Other reserves, such as a reserve for warranty expense, can also be changed to manage reported earnings. A decrease in the estimated warranty expense as a percentage of sales will increase earnings, while an increase in the reserve for warranty expense will decrease earnings.

Valuation allowance. Recall that, under U.S. GAAP, a valuation allowance reduces the carrying value of a deferred tax asset based on managers' estimates of the probability it will not be realized. Similar to the effects of an allowance for bad debt, increasing a valuation allowance will decrease the net deferred tax asset on the balance sheet and reduce net income for the period, while a decrease in the valuation allowance will increase the net deferred tax asset and increase net income for the period. The valuation allowance can be understated to show higher asset values, and it can be adjusted over time to smooth earnings. Under IFRS, while no explicit valuation allowance is reported, deferred tax assets (and liabilities) are adjusted to the expected recoverable amount.

Depreciation methods and estimates. Compared to straight-line depreciation, an accelerated depreciation method increases expenses and decreases net income in the early years of an asset's life. In the later years of an asset's life, this will reverse; expenses will be lower, and net income will be higher.

Estimates of useful life and salvage value can also affect depreciation expense and, thereby, net income and the carrying value of an asset. An increase in salvage value will decrease depreciation expense, increase operating income, and result in a greater carrying value for the asset. A smaller salvage value will have the opposite effects. If the salvage value of an asset is set higher than the actual sale price at the end of the asset's life, a loss on the sale of the asset will decrease net income in the period in which the asset is disposed of. Using a longer estimated useful life decreases periodic depreciation expense and increases net income in the early years of an asset's life compared to using a shorter estimated useful life.

Depreciation methods, estimated asset lives, or estimates of salvage values that are out of line with those of peer companies in the industry are an accounting warning sign.

Amortization and impairment. Management choices and estimates regarding amortization of purchased intangible assets are similar to those for depreciation of tangible assets. The intangible asset goodwill is not amortized but is subject to an impairment test. By ignoring or delaying recognition of an impairment charge for goodwill, management can increase earnings in the current period.

Inventory method. During periods of rising prices, cost of goods sold (COGS) under the FIFO method will be less than COGS under the weighted-average costing method. Gross profit, gross margin, and earnings will all be greater under the FIFO method than under the weighted-average method as a result. Balance sheet inventory value will be greater under FIFO than under the weighted-average method. During periods of decreasing prices, the opposite is true.

FIFO results in more accurate balance sheet inventory values because inventory value is closer to current replacement cost than under the weighted-average cost or LIFO method. Conversely, COGS are closer to current (replacement) cost under the LIFO and weighted-average cost method so that gross and net margins better reflect economic reality under those methods.

Accounting warning signs related to inventories may include a declining inventory turnover ratio or, for a firm using LIFO under U.S. GAAP, drawing down inventory levels so that COGS reflects the lower costs of items acquired in past periods, which increases current period earnings.

Related-party transactions. If a public firm does business with a supplier that is private and controlled by management, adjusting the price of goods supplied can shift profits either to or from the private company to manage the earnings reported by the public company.

Capitalizing expenses. Any expense that can be capitalized creates an asset on the balance sheet, and the impact of the expense on net income can be spread over many years. Capitalization also affects cash flow classifications. If an expense is capitalized, the entire amount is classified as an investing cash outflow so that operating cash flow is increased by that amount. Analysts should take notice if a firm capitalizes costs that are not typically capitalized by firms in their industry.

Capitalizing interest expense will decrease cash flow from investing and increase cash flow from operations, along with its effects on the pattern of earnings from depreciating the interest expense over time rather than expensing it all in the current period. The ability under IFRS to classify interest paid, interest received, and dividends received as either operating or financing cash flows gives management some ability to manage reported operating cash flow.

Stretching payables. Delaying payments that would normally be made near the end of a reporting period until the beginning of the next accounting period will increase operating cash flow in the current period and reduce it in some subsequent period. There is no effect on reported earnings in the current period from stretching payables.

Other accounting warning signs:

- The ratio of operating cash flow to net income is persistently less than one or declining over time.
- Fourth-quarter earnings show a pattern (either high or low) compared to the seasonality of earnings in the industry or seasonality of revenue for the firm.
- Certain expenses are classified as nonrecurring but appear regularly in financial reports.
- Gross or operating profit margins are noticeably higher than are typical for the industry and peer companies.
- Management typically provides only minimal financial reporting information and disclosure.
- Management typically emphasizes non-GAAP earnings measures and uses special or nonrecurring designations aggressively for charges.
- Growth by purchasing a large number of businesses can provide many opportunities to manipulate asset values and future depreciation and amortization and make comparisons to prior period earnings problematic.

FINANCIAL STATEMENT ANALYSIS: APPLICATIONS
Cross-Reference to CFA Institute Assigned Reading #34

This topic covers the use of common-size financial statements and other ratio analysis to evaluate past performance, prepare projections of future earnings, assess credit quality, and screen for equity investments; and adjusting financial statements to facilitate comparison between companies.

Analysis Based on Ratios

Trends in financial ratios and differences between a firm's financial ratios and those of its competitors or industry averages can indicate important aspects of a firm's business strategy and whether a strategy is succeeding. Some examples of interpreting ratios are:

- Premium and custom products are usually sold at higher gross margins than less differentiated commodity-like products, so we should expect cost of goods sold to be a higher proportion of sales for the latter.

- We might also expect a company with products that have cutting-edge features and high quality to spend a higher proportion of sales on research and development. This proportion may be quite low for a firm purchasing components from suppliers rather than developing new features and capabilities in-house.
- The ratio of gross profits to operating profits will be larger for a firm that has relatively high research and development and/or advertising expenditures.
- If a firm claims it will improve earnings per share by cutting costs, examination of operating ratios and gross margins over time will reveal whether the firm has actually been able to implement such a strategy.

Forecasting Financial Performance for a Firm

A forecast of future net income and cash flow often begins with a forecast of future sales based on the top-down approach (especially for shorter horizons).

- Begin with a forecast of GDP growth, often supplied by outside research or an in-house economics group.
- Use historical relationships to estimate the relationship between GDP growth and the growth of industry sales.
- Determine the firm's expected market share for the forecast period, and multiply by industry sales to forecast firm sales.
- In a simple forecasting model, some historical average or trend-adjusted measure of profitability (operating margin, EBT margin, or net margin) can be used to forecast earnings.
- In complex forecasting models, each item on an income statement and balance sheet can be estimated based on separate assumptions about its growth in relation to revenue growth.
- For multi-period forecasts, the analyst typically employs a single estimate of sales growth at some point that is expected to continue indefinitely.
- To estimate cash flows, the analyst must make assumptions about future sources and uses of cash, especially as regards changes in working capital, capital expenditures on new fixed assets, issuance or repayments of debt, and issuance or repurchase of stock.
- A typical assumption is that noncash working capital as a percentage of sales remains constant.
- A first-pass model might indicate a need for cash in future periods, and these cash requirements can then be met by projecting necessary borrowing in future periods. For consistency, interest expense in future periods must also be adjusted for any increase in debt and reflected in the income statement, which must be reconciled with the pro forma balance sheet by successive iterations.

Role of Financial Statement Analysis in Assessing Credit Quality

The three Cs of credit analysis are:
1. **Character:** *Character* refers to firm management's professional reputation and the firm's history of debt repayment.
2. **Collateral:** The ability to pledge specific *collateral* reduces lender risk.
3. **Capacity:** The *capacity* to repay requires close examination of a firm's financial statements and ratios. Since some debt is for periods of 30 years or longer, the credit analyst must take a very long-term view of the firm's prospects.

Credit rating agencies, such as Moody's and Standard and Poor's, use items to assess firm creditworthiness that can be separated into four general categories:

1. *Scale and diversification.* Larger companies and those with more different product lines and greater geographic diversification are better credit risks.
2. *Operational efficiency.* Such items as operating ROA, operating margins, and EBITDA margins fall into this category. Along with greater vertical diversification, high operating efficiency is associated with better debt ratings.
3. *Margin stability.* Stability of the relevant profitability margins indicates a higher probability of repayment (leads to a better debt rating and a lower interest rate). Highly variable operating results make lenders nervous.
4. *Leverage.* Ratios of operating earnings, EBITDA, or some measure of free cash flow to interest expense or total debt make up the most important part of the credit rating formula. Firms with greater earnings in relation to their debt and in relation to their interest expense are better credit risks.

Screening for Potential Equity Investments

In many cases, an analyst must select portfolio stocks from the large universe of potential equity investments. Accounting items and ratios can be used to identify a manageable subset of available stocks for further analysis.

Criteria commonly used to screen for attractive equity investments include low P/E, P/CF or P/S; high ROE, ROA, or growth rates of sales and earnings; and low leverage. Multiple criteria are often used because a screen based on a single factor can include firms with other undesirable characteristics.

Analysts should be aware that their equity screens will likely include and exclude many or all of the firms in particular industries.

Financial Statement Adjustments to Facilitate Comparisons

Differences in accounting methods chosen by firms subject to the same standards, as well as differences in accounting methods due to differences in applicable accounting standards, can make comparisons between companies problematic.

An analyst must be prepared to adjust the financial statements of one company to make them comparable to those of another company or group of companies.

Common adjustments required include adjustment for:

- Differences in depreciation methods and assumptions.
- Differences in inventory cost flow assumptions/methods.
- Differences in the treatment of the effect of exchange rate changes.
- Differences in classifications of investment securities.
- Operating leases.
- Capitalization decisions.
- Goodwill.

CORPORATE FINANCE

Study Session 11

Weight on Exam	7%
SchweserNotes™ Reference	Book 4, Pages 1–113

For only 7% of the total exam, there is a lot of material to cover. Don't become too immersed in detail.

CAPITAL BUDGETING
Cross-Reference to CFA Institute Assigned Reading #35

Capital budgeting is identifying and evaluating projects for which the cash flows extend over a period longer than a year. The process has four steps:

1. Generating ideas.
2. Analyzing project proposals.
3. Creating the firm's capital budget.
4. Monitoring decisions and conducting a post-audit.

Categories of capital budgeting projects include:

- Replacement projects to maintain the business.
- Replacement projects to reduce costs.
- Expansion projects to increase capacity.
- New product or market development.
- Mandatory projects, such as meeting safety or environmental regulations.
- Other projects, including high-risk research and development or management pet projects, are not easily analyzed through the capital budgeting process.

Five Key Principles of Capital Budgeting

1. Decisions are based on *incremental cash flows*. Sunk costs are not considered. Externalities, including *cannibalization* of sales of the firm's current products, should be included in the analysis.

2. Cash flows are based on *opportunity costs*, which are the cash flows the firm will lose by undertaking the project.

3. *Timing* of the cash flows is important.

4. Cash flows are analyzed on an *after-tax basis*.

5. *Financing costs* are reflected in the required rate of return on the project, *not* in the incremental cash flows.

Projects can be *independent* and evaluated separately, or *mutually exclusive*, which means the projects compete with each other and the firm can accept only one of them. In some cases, *project sequencing* requires projects to be undertaken in a certain order, with the accept/reject decision on the second project depending on the profitability of the first project.

A firm with *unlimited funds* can accept all profitable projects. However, when *capital rationing* is necessary, the firm must select the most valuable group of projects that can be funded with the limited capital resources available.

Capital Budgeting Methods

The *payback period* is the number of years it takes to recover the initial cost of the project. You must be given a maximum acceptable payback period for a project. This criterion ignores the time value of money and any cash flows beyond the payback period.

The *discounted payback period* is the number of years it takes to recover the initial investment in present value terms. The discount rate used is the project's cost of capital. This method incorporates the time value of money but ignores any cash flows beyond the discounted payback period.

The *profitability index* is the present value of a project's future cash flows divided by the initial cash outlay. The decision rule is to accept a project if its profitability index is greater than one, which is the same as the IRR > cost of capital rule and the NPV > 0 rule (since PI = 1 + NPV/Initial Outlay).

Net present value for a normal project is the present value of all the expected future cash flows minus the initial cost of the project, using the project's cost of capital. A project that has a positive net present value should be accepted because it is expected to increase the value of the firm (shareholder wealth).

The *internal rate of return* is the discount rate that makes the present value of the expected future cash flows equal to the initial cost of the project. If the IRR is greater than the project's cost of capital, it should be accepted because it is expected to increase firm value. If the IRR is equal to the project's cost of capital, the NPV is zero.

IRR > Cost of Capital ⟹ Accept the project
IRR = Cost of Capital ⟹ NPV = 0

©2015 Kaplan, Inc.

For an independent project, the criteria for acceptance (NPV > 0 and IRR > project cost of capital) are equivalent and always lead to the same decision.

For mutually exclusive projects, the NPV and IRR decision rules can lead to different rankings because of differences in project size and/or differences in the timing of cash flows. The NPV criterion is theoretically preferred, as it directly estimates the effect of project acceptance on firm value.

Be certain you can calculate all of these measures quickly and accurately with your calculator.

Since inflation is reflected in the WACC (or project cost of capital) calculation, future cash flows must be adjusted upward to reflect positive expected inflation, or some wealth-increasing (positive NPV) projects will be rejected.

Larger firms, public companies, and firms where management has a higher level of education tend to use NPV and IRR analysis. Private companies and European firms tend to rely more on the payback period in capital budgeting decisions.

In theory, a positive NPV project should increase the company's stock price by the project's NPV per share. In reality, stock prices reflect investor expectations about a firm's ability to identify and execute positive NPV projects in the future.

COST OF CAPITAL
Cross-Reference to CFA Institute Assigned Reading #36

Knowing how to calculate the *weighted average cost of capital* (WACC) and all of its components is critical.

$$WACC = (w_d)[k_d(1-t)] + (w_{ps})(k_{ps}) + (w_{ce})(k_{cd})$$

Here, the *w*s are the proportions of each type of capital, the *k*s are the current costs of each type of capital (debt, preferred stock, and common stock), and *t* is the firm's *marginal* tax rate.

The proportions used for the three types of capital are target proportions and are calculated using market values. An analyst can use the WACC to compare the after-tax cost of raising capital to the expected after-tax returns on capital investments.

Cost of equity capital. There are three methods. You will likely know which to use by the information given in the problem.

1. CAPM approach: $k_{ce} = RFR + \beta(R_{market} - RFR)$.

2. Discounted cash flow approach: $k_{ce} = (D_1 / P_0) + g$.

3. Bond yield plus risk premium approach: k_{ce} = current market yield on the firm's long-term debt + risk premium.

Cost of preferred stock is always calculated as follows:

$$k_{ps} = \frac{D_{ps}}{P}$$

Cost of debt is the average market yield on the firm's outstanding debt issues. Since interest is tax deductible, k_d is multiplied by $(1 - t)$.

Firm decisions about which projects to undertake are independent of the decision of how to finance firm assets at minimum cost. The firm will have long-run target weights for the percentages of common equity, preferred stock, and debt used to fund the firm. Investment decisions are based on a WACC that reflects each source of capital at its target weight, regardless of how a particular project will be financed or which capital source was most recently employed.

An analyst calculating a firm's WACC should use the firm's target capital structure if known, or use the firm's current capital structure based on market values as the best indicator of its target capital structure. The analyst can incorporate trends in the company's capital structure into his estimate of the target structure. An alternative would be to apply the industry average capital structure to the firm.

A firm's WACC can increase as it raises larger amounts of capital, which means the firm has an upward sloping *marginal cost of capital curve*. If the firm ranks its potential projects in descending IRR order, the result is a downward sloping *investment opportunity schedule*. The amount of the capital investment required to fund all projects for which the IRR is greater than the marginal cost of capital is the firm's *optimal capital budget*.

A **project beta** can be used to determine the appropriate cost of equity capital for evaluating a project. Using the "pure-play method," the project beta is estimated based on the equity beta of a firm purely engaged in the same business as the project. The pure-play firm's beta must be adjusted for any difference between the capital structure (leverage) of the pure-play firm and the capital structure of the company evaluating the project.

For a developing market, the **country risk premium** (CRP) is calculated as:

$$CRP = [\text{sovereign bond yield} - \text{T-bond yield}] \times \left(\frac{\text{std. dev. of developing country index}}{\text{std. dev. of sovereign bonds in U.S. currency}} \right)$$

The required return on equity securities is then:

$$k_{CE} = RFR + \beta\,[E(R_{MKT}) - RFR + CRP]$$

A **break-point** refers to a level of total investment beyond which the WACC increases because the cost of one component of the capital structure increases. It is calculated by dividing the amount of funding at which the component cost of capital increases by the target capital structure weight for that source of capital.

When new equity is issued, the **flotation costs** (underwriting costs) should be included as an addition to the initial outlay for the project when calculating NPV or IRR.

MEASURES OF LEVERAGE
Cross-Reference to CFA Institute Assigned Reading #37

Business Risk vs. Financial Risk

Business risk refers to the risk associated with a firm's operating income and is the result of:

- Sales risk (variability of demand).
- Operating risk (proportion of total costs that are fixed costs).

Financial risk. Additional risk common stockholders have to bear because the firm uses fixed cost sources of financing.

Degree of operating leverage (DOL) is defined as:

$$DOL = \frac{\%\ \text{change in EBIT}}{\%\ \text{change in sales}}$$

The DOL at a particular level of sales, Q, is calculated as:

$$DOL = \frac{Q(P-V)}{Q(P-V)-F}$$

$$= \frac{S-TVC}{S-TVC-F}$$

One way to help remember this formula is to know that if fixed costs are zero, there is no operating leverage (i.e., DOL = 1).

Degree of financial leverage (DFL) is defined as:

$$DFL = \frac{\% \text{ change in EPS}}{\% \text{ change in EBIT}}$$

The DFL at a particular level of sales is calculated as:

$$DFL = \frac{EBIT}{EBIT - \text{interest expense}}$$

One way to help remember this formula is to know that if interest costs are zero (no fixed-cost financing), there is no financial leverage (i.e., DFL = 1). In this context, we treat preferred dividends as interest.

Degree of total leverage (DTL) is the product of DOL and DFL:

$$DTL = DOL \times DFL$$

$$= \frac{\% \text{ change in EBIT}}{\% \text{ change in sales}} \times \frac{\% \text{ change in EPS}}{\% \text{ change in EBIT}} = \frac{\% \text{ change in EPS}}{\% \text{ change in sales}}$$

$$= \frac{Q(P-V)}{Q(P-V)-F-I} = \frac{S-TVC}{S-TVC-F-I}$$

Breakeven Quantity of Sales

A firm's *breakeven point* is the quantity of sales a firm must achieve to just cover its fixed and variable costs. The breakeven quantity is calculated as:

$$Q_{BE} = \frac{\text{total fixed costs}}{\text{price} - \text{variable cost per unit}}$$

The *operating breakeven quantity* considers only fixed operating costs:

$$Q_{OBE} = \frac{\text{fixed operating costs}}{\text{price} - \text{variable cost per unit}}$$

Effects of Operating Leverage and Financial Leverage

A firm with greater operating leverage (greater fixed costs) will have a higher breakeven quantity than an identical firm with less operating leverage. If sales are greater than the breakeven quantity, the firm with greater operating leverage will generate larger profit.

Financial leverage reduces net income by the interest cost, but increases return on equity because the (reduced) net income is generated with less equity (and more debt). A firm with greater financial leverage will have a greater risk of default, but will also offer greater potential returns for its stockholders.

DIVIDENDS AND SHARE REPURCHASES: BASICS
Cross-Reference to CFA Institute Assigned Reading #38

Cash dividends transfer cash from the firm to its shareholders. This reduces the company's assets and the market value of its equity. When the dividend is paid, the stock price should drop by the amount of the per share dividend. Therefore, the dividend does not change the shareholder's wealth.

Types of cash dividends:

- *Regular dividend.* A company pays out a portion of its earnings on a schedule.
- *Special dividend.* One-time cash payment to shareholders.
- *Liquidating dividend.* A company goes out of business and distributes the proceeds to shareholders. These are taxed as a return of capital.

Dividend Payment Chronology

- *Declaration date:* board of directors approves the dividend payment.
- *Ex-dividend date:* first day the stock trades without the dividend (two business days before the record date).
- *Holder-of-record date:* date on which shareholders must own the shares in order to receive the dividend.
- *Payment date:* dividend is paid by check or electronic transfer.

Stock Dividends, Stock Splits, and Reverse Stock Splits

These actions change the number of shares outstanding, but the share price changes proportionately, so a shareholder's wealth and ownership stake are not affected.

- *Stock dividend.* Shareholders receive additional shares of stock (e.g., 10% more shares).
- *Stock split.* Each "old" share is replaced by more than one "new" share (e.g., 3:2 or 2:1).
- *Reverse stock split.* Replace "old" shares with a smaller number of "new" shares.

Share Repurchases

A company can buy back shares of its common stock. Since this uses the company's cash, it can be seen as an alternative to a cash dividend. Taxes aside, neither cash dividends nor share repurchases affect the shareholder's wealth.

Three repurchase methods:

1. Buy in the open market.
2. Make a tender offer for a fixed number of shares at a fixed price.
3. Directly negotiate with a large shareholder.

If a firm borrows funds to repurchase its shares, EPS will rise if the after-tax cost of debt is less than the earnings yield (E/P) of its shares.

For a firm that repurchases its shares with retained earnings, the book value of its shares will increase if the price paid for repurchased shares is less than their book value.

WORKING CAPITAL MANAGEMENT
Cross-Reference to CFA Institute Assigned Reading #39

Primary sources of liquidity are a company's normal sources of short-term cash, such as selling goods and services, collecting receivables, or using trade credit and short-term borrowing. **Secondary sources of liquidity** are the measures a company must take to generate cash when its primary sources are inadequate, such as liquidating assets, renegotiating debt, or filing for bankruptcy.

Drags and pulls on liquidity include uncollectable receivables or debts, obsolete inventory, tight short-term credit, and poor payables management.

Liquidity measures include:

- Current ratio.
- Quick ratio.
- Cash ratio.

Measures of working capital effectiveness include:

- Receivables turnover, number of days receivables.
- Inventory turnover, number of days of inventory.
- Payables turnover, number of days of payables.
- Operating cycle, cash conversion cycle.

operating cycle = days of inventory + days of receivables

cash conversion cycle = days of inventory + days of receivables − days of payables

Managing a Company's Net Daily Cash Position

The purpose of managing a firm's daily cash position is to make sure there is sufficient cash (target balance) but to not keep excess cash balances because of the interest foregone by not investing the cash in short-term securities to earn interest. These short-term securities include:

- U.S. Treasury bills.
- Short-term federal agency securities.
- Bank certificates of deposit.
- Banker's acceptances.
- Time deposits.
- Repurchase agreements.
- Commercial paper.
- Money market mutual funds.
- Adjustable-rate preferred stock.

Adjustable-rate preferred stock has a dividend rate that is reset periodically to current market yields (through an auction in the case of auction-rate preferred) and offers corporate holders a tax advantage because a percentage of the dividends received is exempt from federal tax.

Yield measures used to compare different options for investing excess cash balances include:

$$\% \text{ discount from face value} = \left(\frac{\text{face value} - \text{price}}{\text{face value}} \right)$$

$$\text{discount-basis yield} = \left(\frac{\text{face value} - \text{price}}{\text{face value}} \right) \left(\frac{360}{\text{days}} \right)$$

$$= \% \text{ discount} \left(\frac{360}{\text{days}} \right)$$

$$\text{money market yield} = \left(\frac{\text{face value} - \text{price}}{\text{price}} \right) \left(\frac{360}{\text{days to maturity}} \right)$$

$$\text{bond equivalent yield} = \left(\frac{\text{face value} - \text{price}}{\text{price}} \right) \left(\frac{365}{\text{days to maturity}} \right)$$

$$= \text{HPY} \left(\frac{365}{\text{days}} \right)$$

Note that in Quantitative Methods, the bond equivalent yield was defined differently, as two times the effective semiannual holding period yield.

Cash Management Investment Policy

- An investment policy statement typically begins with a statement of the purpose and objective of the investment portfolio and some general guidelines about the strategy to be employed to achieve those objectives and the types of securities that will be used.
- The investment policy statement will also include specific information about who is allowed to purchase securities, who is responsible for complying with company guidelines, and what steps will be taken if the investment guidelines are not followed.
- Finally, the investment policy statement will include limitations on the specific types of securities permitted for investment of short-term funds, limitations on the credit ratings of portfolio securities, and limitations on the proportions of the total short-term securities portfolio that can be invested in the various types of permitted securities.

An investment policy statement should be evaluated on how well the policy can be expected to satisfy the goals and purpose of short-term investments, generating yield without taking on excessive credit or liquidity risk. The policy should not be overly restrictive in the context of meeting the goals of safety and liquidity.

Evaluating Firm Performance in Managing Receivables, Inventory, and Payables

Receivables

The management of accounts receivable begins with calculation of the average days of receivables and comparison of this ratio to a firm's historical performance or to the average ratios for a group of comparable companies.

More detail about accounts receivable performance can be gained by using an aging schedule that shows amounts of receivables by the length of time they have been outstanding.

Presenting the amounts in an aging schedule as percentages of total outstanding receivables can facilitate analysis of how the aging schedule for receivables is changing over time.

Another useful metric for monitoring accounts receivable performance is the *weighted average collection period*, the average days outstanding per dollar of receivables. The weights are the percentages of total receivables in each category of days outstanding, and these are multiplied by the average days to collect accounts within each aging category.

Analysis of the historical trends and significant changes in a firm's aging schedule and weighted average collection days can give a clearer picture of what is driving changes in the simpler metric of average days of receivables.

The company must always evaluate the tradeoff between more strict credit terms and borrower creditworthiness and the ability to make sales. Terms that are too strict will lead to less-than-optimal sales. Terms that are too lenient will increase sales at the cost of longer average days of receivables, which must be funded at some cost and will increase bad accounts, directly affecting profitability.

Inventory

Inventory management involves a tradeoff as well. Inventory levels that are too low will result in lost sales (stock outs), while inventory that is too large will have costs (carrying costs) because the firm's capital is tied up in inventory.

Reducing inventory will free up cash that can be invested in interest-bearing securities or used to reduce debt or equity funding.

Increasing inventory in terms of average days' inventory or a decreasing inventory turnover ratio can both indicate inventory that is too large. A large inventory can lead to greater losses from obsolete items and can also indicate that items that no longer sell well are included in inventory.

Comparison of average days of inventory and inventory turnover ratios between industries, or even between two firms that have different business strategies, can be misleading.

Payables

Payables must be managed well because they represent a source of working capital to the firm. If the firm pays its payables prior to their due dates, cash is unnecessarily used and interest on it is sacrificed. If a firm pays its payables late, it can damage relationships with suppliers and lead to more restrictive credit terms or even the requirement that purchases be made for cash. Late payment can also result in interest charges that are high compared to those of other sources of short-term financing.

- A company with a short payables period (high payables turnover) may simply be taking advantage of discounts for paying early because it has good low-cost funds available to finance its working capital needs.
- A company with a long payables period may be such an important buyer that it can effectively utilize accounts payable as a source of short-term funding with relatively little cost (suppliers will put up with it).
- Monitoring the changes in days' payables outstanding over time for a single firm will, however, aid the analyst and an extension of days' payables may serve as an early warning of deteriorating short-term liquidity.

A discount is often available for early payment of an invoice (for example, "2/10 net 60" is a 2% discount for paying an invoice within 10 days that is due in full after 60 days). Paying the full invoice later instead of taking the discount is a use of trade credit. The **cost of trade credit** can be calculated as:

$$\text{cost of trade credit} = \left(1 + \frac{PD}{1 - PD}\right)^{\frac{365}{\text{days past discount}}} - 1$$

where:
PD = percent discount (in decimals)
days past discount = the number of days after the end of the discount period

Sources of Short-Term Funding

Bank Sources

- *Uncommitted line of credit:* Non-binding offer of credit.
- *Committed (regular) line of credit:* Binding offer of credit to a certain maximum amount for a specific time period. Requires a fee, called an overdraft line of credit outside the United States.
- *Revolving line of credit:* Most reliable line of credit, typically for longer terms than a committed line of credit, can be listed on a firm's financial statements in the footnotes as a source of liquidity.

Lines of credit are used primarily by large, financially sound companies.

- *Banker's acceptances:* Used by firms that export goods and are a guarantee from the bank of the firm that has ordered the goods, stating that a payment will be made upon receipt of the goods. The exporting company can then sell this acceptance at a discount in order to generate funds.
- *Collateralized borrowing:* Firms with weaker credit can borrow at better rates if they pledge specific collateral (receivables, inventory, equipment). A *blanket lein* gives the lender a claim to all current and future firm assets as collateral additional to specific named collateral.

Non-Bank Sources

- *Factoring:* The actual sale of receivables at a discount from their face value. The factor takes on the responsibility for collecting receivables and the credit risk of the receivables portfolio.
- Smaller firms and firms with poor credit may use *nonbank finance* companies for short-term funding. The cost of such funding is higher than other sources and is used by firms for which normal bank sources of short-term funding are not available.
- Large, creditworthy companies can also issue short-term debt securities called *commercial paper.* Interest costs are typically slightly less than the rate the firm could get from a bank.

Managing Short-Term Funding

In managing its short-term financing, a firm should focus on the objectives of having sufficient sources of funding for current as well as for future foreseeable cash needs, and should seek the most cost-effective rates available given its needs, assets, and creditworthiness. The firm should have the ability to prepay short-term borrowings when cash flow permits and have the flexibility to structure its short-term financing so that the debt matures without peaks and can be matched to expected cash flows.

For large borrowers, it is important that the firm has alternative sources of short-term funding and even alternative lenders for a particular type of financing. It is often worth having slightly higher overall short-term funding costs in order to have flexibility and redundant sources of financing.

CORPORATE GOVERNANCE OF LISTED COMPANIES
Cross-Reference to CFA Institute Assigned Reading #40

Corporate governance refers to the procedures, policies, and controls within a firm that determine how it is managed. In general, good corporate governance will result in protecting and advancing shareholder interests and in a firm management that acts ethically and legally, and also reports accurate financial information in a timely manner.

Board members should be independent of management, not have other employment with the firm, be qualified/experienced, and be annually elected. The board itself should have the authority to hire outside consultants without management approval and have committees devoted to executive compensation, risk management, legal matters, and governance issues.

Shareholder rights should include proxy voting without attending the meeting, confidential voting, cumulative voting, approval over corporate structure changes, and ability to introduce proposals for board consideration. Shareholder rights are enhanced when there are not different classes of stock that separate economic ownership from voting rights.

A board should have a majority of independent members, which means they do not have other relationships with management or the firm itself, and these members should regularly meet outside the presence of management. The audit committee of the board should be completely made up of independent members, be comprised of financial experts, have the authority to approve or reject any non-audit engagements of the auditor with the firm, and control the audit budget. Shareholders should have approval rights on the acceptance of the external auditor.

Members of the compensation committee should be independent and see that executive compensation is appropriate and is tied to the long-term performance/profitability of the firm. Shareholders should insist that the firm provide them with details regarding compensation, see that the terms and conditions of option grants are reasonable, and be alert to instances of option re-pricing.

In general, anti-takeover defenses benefit entrenched management and harm shareholders by decreasing share values.

PORTFOLIO MANAGEMENT

Weight on Exam	7%
SchweserNotes™ Reference	Book 4, Pages 114–199

PORTFOLIO MANAGEMENT: AN OVERVIEW
Cross-Reference to CFA Institute Assigned Reading #41

The Portfolio Perspective

The **portfolio perspective** refers to evaluating individual investments by their contribution to the risk and return of an investor's overall portfolio. The alternative is to examine the risk and return of each security in isolation. An investor who holds all his wealth in a single stock because he believes it to be the best stock available is not taking the portfolio perspective—his portfolio is very risky compared to a diversified portfolio.

Modern portfolio theory concludes that the extra risk from holding only a single security is not rewarded with higher expected investment returns. Conversely, diversification allows an investor to reduce portfolio risk without necessarily reducing the portfolio's expected return.

The **diversification ratio** is calculated as the ratio of the risk of an equal-weighted portfolio of *n* securities (standard deviation of returns) to the risk of a single security selected at random from the portfolio. If the average standard deviation of returns of the *n* stocks is 25%, and the standard deviation of returns of an equal-weighted portfolio of the *n* stocks is 18%, the diversification ratio is 18 / 25 = 0.72.

- Portfolio diversification works best when financial markets are operating normally.
- Diversification provides less reduction of risk during market turmoil.
- During periods of financial crisis, correlations tend to increase, which reduces the benefits of diversification.

Investment Management Clients

Individual investors save and invest for a variety of reasons, including purchasing a house or educating their children. In many countries, special accounts allow citizens to invest for retirement and to defer any taxes on investment income and gains until the funds are withdrawn. Defined contribution pension plans are popular vehicles for these investments.

Many types of **institutions** have large investment portfolios. **Defined benefit pension plans** are funded by company contributions and have an obligation to provide specific benefits to retirees, such as a lifetime income based on employee earnings.

An **endowment** is a fund that is dedicated to providing financial support on an ongoing basis for a specific purpose. A **foundation** is a fund established for charitable purposes to support specific types of activities or to fund research related to a particular disease.

The investment objective of a **bank** is to earn more on the bank's loans and investments than the bank pays for deposits of various types. Banks seek to keep risk low and need adequate liquidity to meet investor withdrawals as they occur.

Insurance companies invest customer premiums with the objective of funding customer claims as they occur.

Investment companies manage the pooled funds of many investors. **Mutual funds** manage these pooled funds in particular styles (e.g., index investing, growth investing, bond investing) and restrict their investments to particular subcategories of investments (e.g., large-firm stocks, energy stocks, speculative bonds) or particular regions (emerging market stocks, international bonds, Asian-firm stocks).

Sovereign wealth funds refer to pools of assets owned by a government.

Figure 1 provides a summary of the risk tolerance, investment horizon, liquidity needs, and income objectives for these different types of investors.

Figure 1: Characteristics of Different Types of Investors

Investor	Risk Tolerance	Investment Horizon	Liquidity Needs	Income Needs
Individuals	Depends on individual	Depends on individual	Depends on individual	Depends on individual
DB pensions	High	Long	Low	Depends on age
Banks	Low	Short	High	Pay interest
Endowments	High	Long	Low	Spending level
Insurance	Low	Long—life Short—P&C	High	Low
Mutual funds	Depends on fund	Depends on fund	High	Depends on fund

Steps in the Portfolio Management Process

Planning begins with an analysis of the investor's risk tolerance, return objectives, time horizon, tax exposure, liquidity needs, income needs, and any unique circumstances or investor preferences.

This analysis results in an **investment policy statement (IPS)** that:

- Details the investor's investment objectives and constraints.
- Specifies an objective benchmark (such as an index return).
- Should be updated at least every few years and anytime the investor's objectives or constraints change significantly.

The **execution** step requires an analysis of the risk and return characteristics of various asset classes to determine the asset allocation. In *top-down* analysis, a portfolio manager examines current macroeconomic conditions to identify the asset classes that are most attractive. In *bottom-up* analysis, portfolio managers seek to identify individual securities that are undervalued.

Feedback is the final step. Over time, investor circumstances will change, risk and return characteristics of asset classes will change, and the actual weights of the assets in the portfolio will change with asset prices. The portfolio manager must monitor changes, **rebalance** the portfolio periodically, and evaluate performance relative to the benchmark portfolio identified in the IPS.

RISK MANAGEMENT: AN INTRODUCTION
Cross-Reference to CFA Institute Assigned Reading #42

Risk (uncertainty) is not something to be avoided by an organization or in an investment portfolio; returns above the risk-free rate are earned only by accepting risk. The risk management process seeks to 1) determine the risk tolerance of the organization, 2) identify and measure the risks the organization faces, and 3) modify and monitor these risks. Through these choices, a firm aligns the risks it takes with its risk tolerance after considering which risks the organization is best able to bear.

An overall risk management framework encompasses several activities, including:

- Establishing processes and policies for risk governance.
- Determining the organization's risk tolerance.
- Identifying and measuring existing risks.
- Managing and mitigating risks to achieve the optimal bundle of risks.
- Monitoring risk exposures over time.
- Communicating across the organization.
- Performing strategic risk analysis.

Risk governance provides organization-wide guidance on which risks should be pursued in an efficient manner, which should be subject to limits, and which should be reduced or avoided. A risk management committee can provide a way for various parts of the organization to bring up issues of risk measurement, integration of risks, and the best ways to mitigate undesirable risks.

Determining an organization's **risk tolerance** involves setting the overall risk exposure the organization will take by identifying the risks the firm can effectively take and the risks that the organization should reduce or avoid. Some of the factors that determine an organization's risk tolerance are its expertise in its lines of business, its skill at responding to negative outside events, its regulatory environment, and its financial strength and ability to withstand losses.

Risk budgeting is the process of allocating firm resources to assets or investments by considering their risk characteristics and how they combine to meet the organization's risk tolerance. The goal is to allocate the overall amount of acceptable risk to the mix of assets or investments that have the greatest expected returns over time. The risk budget may be a single metric, such as portfolio beta, value at risk, portfolio duration, or returns variance.

Financial risks are those that arise from exposure to financial markets. Examples are:

- *Credit risk.* This is the uncertainty about whether the counterparty to a transaction will fulfill its contractual obligations.
- *Liquidity risk.* This is the risk of loss when selling an asset at a time when market conditions make the sales price less than the underlying fair value of the asset.
- *Market risk.* This is the uncertainty about market prices of assets (stocks, commodities, and currencies) and interest rates.

©2015 Kaplan, Inc.

Non-financial risks arise from the operations of the organization and from sources external to the organization. Examples are:

- *Operational risk.* This is the risk that human error or faulty organizational processes will result in losses.
- *Solvency risk.* This is the risk that the organization will be unable to continue to operate because it has run out of cash.
- *Regulatory risk.* This is the risk that the regulatory environment will change, imposing costs on the firm or restricting its activities.
- *Governmental or political risk* (including *tax risk*). This is the risk that political actions outside a specific regulatory framework, such as increases in tax rates, will impose significant costs on an organization.
- *Legal risk.* This is the uncertainty about the organization's exposure to future legal action.
- *Model risk.* This is the risk that asset valuations based on the organization's analytical models are incorrect.
- *Tail risk.* This is the risk that extreme events (those in the tails of the distribution of outcomes) are more likely than the organization's analysis indicates, especially from incorrectly concluding that the distribution of outcomes is normal.
- *Accounting risk.* This is the risk that the organization's accounting policies and estimates are judged to be incorrect.

The various risks an organization faces interact in many ways. Interactions among risks can be especially important during periods of stress in financial markets.

Measures of risk for specific asset types include standard deviation, beta, and duration.

- *Standard deviation* is a measure of the volatility of asset prices and interest rates. Standard deviation may not be the appropriate measure of risk for non-normal probability distributions, especially those with negative skew or positive excess kurtosis (fat tails).
- *Beta* measures the market risk of equity securities and portfolios of equity securities. This measure considers the risk reduction benefits of diversification and is appropriate for securities held in a well-diversified portfolio, whereas standard deviation is a measure of risk on a stand-alone basis.
- *Duration* is a measure of the price sensitivity of debt securities to changes in interest rates.

Derivatives risks (sometimes referred to as "the Greeks") include:

- *Delta.* This is the sensitivity of derivatives values to the price of the underlying asset.
- *Gamma.* This is the sensitivity of delta to changes in the price of the underlying asset.

- *Vega.* This is the sensitivity of derivatives values to the volatility of the price of the underlying asset.
- *Rho.* This is the sensitivity of derivatives values to changes in the risk-free rate.

Tail risk or **downside risk** is the uncertainty about the probability of extreme negative outcomes. Commonly used measures of tail risk include **value at risk (VaR)**, the minimum loss over a period that will occur with a specific probability, and conditional VaR (CVaR), the expected value of a loss, given that the loss exceeds a given amount.

Two methods of risk assessment that are used to supplement measures such as VaR and CVaR are stress testing and scenario analysis. **Stress testing** examines the effects of a specific (usually extreme) change in a key variable. **Scenario analysis** refers to a similar what-if analysis of expected loss but incorporates specific changes in multiple inputs.

Once the risk management team has estimated various risks, management may decide to *avoid* a risk, *prevent* a risk, *accept* a risk, *transfer* a risk, or *shift* a risk.

- One way to *avoid* a risk is to not engage in the activity with the uncertain outcome.
- Some risks can be *prevented* by increasing the level of security and adopting stronger processes.
- For risks that management has decided to *accept*, the organization will seek to bear them efficiently, often through diversification. The term **self-insurance** of a risk refers to a risk an organization has decided to bear.
- With a risk *transfer*, a risk is transferred to another party. Insurance is a type of risk transfer. With a **surety bond**, an insurance company agrees to make a payment if a third party fails to perform under the terms of a contract. A **fidelity bond** pays for losses resulting from employee theft or misconduct.
- Risk *shifting* is a way to change the distribution of possible outcomes and is accomplished primarily with derivative contracts.

PORTFOLIO RISK AND RETURN: PART I
Cross-Reference to CFA Institute Assigned Reading #43

Risk and Return of Major Asset Classes

Based on U.S. data over the period 1926–2008, Figure 2 indicates that small capitalization stocks have had the greatest average returns and greatest risk over the period. T-bills had the lowest average returns and the lowest standard deviation of returns.

©2015 Kaplan, Inc.

Figure 2: Risk and Return of Major Asset Classes in the United States (1926–2008)[1]

Assets Class	Average Annual Return (Geometric Mean)	Standard Deviation (Annualized Monthly)
Small-cap stocks	11.7%	33.0%
Large-cap stocks	9.6%	20.9%
Long-term corporate bonds	5.9%	8.4%
Long-term Treasury bonds	5.7%	9.4%
Treasury bills	3.7%	3.1%
Inflation	3.0%	4.2%

Results for other markets around the world are similar: asset classes with the greatest average returns also have the highest standard deviations of returns.

Variance and Standard Deviation

Variance of the rate of return for a risky asset calculated from expectational data (a probability model) is the probability-weighted sum of the squared differences between the returns in each state and the unconditional expected return.

$$\text{variance} = \sigma^2 = \sum_{i=1}^{n} \left\{ [R_i - E(R)]^2 \times P_i \right\}$$

$$\text{standard deviation} = \sigma = \sqrt{\sigma^2}$$

Covariance and Correlation

Covariance measures the extent to which two variables move together over time. The covariance of returns is an absolute measure of movement and is measured in return units squared.

Using *historical data*, we take the product of the two securities' deviations from their expected returns for each period, sum them, and divide by the number of (paired) observations minus one.

---

1. 2009 Ibbotson SBBI Classic Yearbook

$$\text{cov}_{1,2} = \frac{\sum_{t=1}^{n}\left\{ [R_{t,1} - \overline{R}_1][R_{t,2} - \overline{R}_2] \right\}}{n-1}$$

Covariance can be standardized by dividing by the product of the standard deviations of the two securities. This standardized measure of co-movement is called their *correlation coefficient* or *correlation* and is computed as:

$$\text{correlation of assets 1 and 2} = \rho_{1,2} = \frac{\text{cov}_{1,2}}{\sigma_1\sigma_2} \quad \text{so that, } \text{cov}_{1,2} = \rho_{1,2}\sigma_1\sigma_2$$

Risk Aversion

A **risk-averse** investor is simply one that dislikes risk (i.e., prefers less risk to more risk). Given two investments that have equal expected returns, a risk-averse investor will choose the one with less risk (standard deviation, σ).

A **risk-seeking** (risk-loving) investor actually prefers more risk to less and, given equal expected returns, will choose the more risky investment. A **risk-neutral** investor has no preference regarding risk and would be indifferent between two such investments.

A risk-averse investor may select a very risky portfolio despite being risk averse; a risk-averse investor may hold very risky assets if he feels that the extra return he expects to earn is adequate compensation for the additional risk.

Risk and Return for a Portfolio of Risky Assets

When risky assets are combined into a portfolio, the expected portfolio return is a weighted average of the assets' expected returns, where the weights are the percentages of the total portfolio value invested in each asset.

The standard deviation of returns for a portfolio of risky assets depends on the standard deviations of each asset's return (σ), the proportion of the portfolio in each asset (w), and, crucially, on the covariance (or correlation) of returns between each asset pair in the portfolio.

Portfolio standard deviation for a two-asset portfolio:

$$\sigma_p = \sqrt{w_1^2\sigma_1^2 + w_2^2\sigma_2^2 + 2w_1w_2\sigma_1\sigma_2\rho_{12}}$$

which is equivalent to:

$$\sigma_p = \sqrt{w_1^2\sigma_1^2 + w_2^2\sigma_2^2 + 2w_1w_2\text{Cov}_{12}}$$

If two risky asset returns are perfectly positively correlated, $\rho_{12} = +1$, then the square root of portfolio variance (the portfolio standard deviation of returns) is equal to:

$$\sigma_{portfolio} = \sqrt{Var_{portfolio}} = \sqrt{w_1^2\sigma_1^2 + w_2^2\sigma_2^2 + 2w_1w_2\sigma_1\sigma_2(1)} = w_1\sigma_1 + w_2\sigma_2$$

In this unique case, with $\rho_{12} = +1$, the portfolio standard deviation is simply the weighted average of the standard deviations of the individual asset returns.

Other things equal, the greatest portfolio risk results when the correlation between asset returns is +1. For any value of correlation less than +1, portfolio variance is reduced. Note that for a correlation of zero, the entire third term in the portfolio variance equation is zero. For negative values of correlation ρ_{12}, the third term becomes negative and further reduces portfolio variance and standard deviation.

Efficient Frontier

The Markowitz efficient frontier represents the set of possible portfolios that have the greatest expected return for each level of risk (standard deviation of returns).

Figure 3: Minimum Variance and Efficient Frontiers

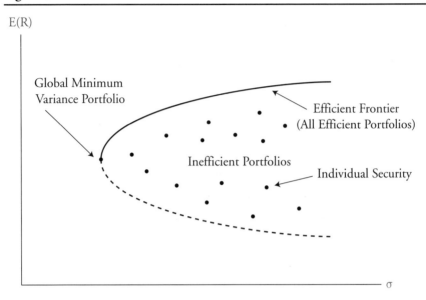

An Investor's Optimal Portfolio

An investor's **expected utility function** depends on his degree of risk aversion. An **indifference curve** plots combinations of risk (standard deviation) and expected return among which an investor is indifferent, as they all have equal expected utility.

Indifference curves slope upward for risk-averse investors because they will only take on more risk if they are compensated with greater expected return. An investor who is relatively more risk averse requires a relatively greater increase in expected return to compensate for taking on greater risk. In other words, a more risk-averse investor will have steeper indifference curves.

In our previous illustration of efficient portfolios available in the market, we included only risky assets. When we add a risk-free asset to the universe of available assets, the efficient frontier is a straight line. Using the formulas:

$$E(R_{portfolio}) = W_A E(R_A) + W_B E(R_B)$$

$$\sigma_{portfolio} = \sqrt{W_A^2 \sigma_A^2 + W_B^2 \sigma_B^2 + 2W_A W_B \rho_{AB} \sigma_A \sigma_B}$$

allow Asset B to be the risk-free asset and Asset A to be a risky portfolio of assets.

Because a risk-free asset has zero standard deviation and zero correlation of returns with those of the risky portfolio, this results in the reduced equation:

$$\sigma_{portfolio} = \sqrt{W_A^2 \sigma_A^2} = W_A \sigma_A$$

If we put X% of our portfolio into the risky asset portfolio, the resulting portfolio will have standard deviation of returns equal to X% of the standard deviation of the risky asset portfolio. The relationship between portfolio risk and return for various portfolio allocations is linear, as illustrated in Figure 4.

Figure 4: Capital Allocation Line and Risky Asset Weights

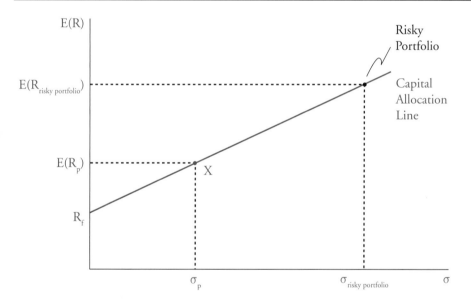

Combining a risky portfolio with a risk-free asset is the process that supports the **two-fund separation theorem**, which states that all investors' optimum portfolios will be made up of some combination of an optimal portfolio of risky assets and the risk-free asset. The line representing these possible combinations of risk-free assets and the optimal risky asset portfolio is referred to as the **capital allocation line**.

Point X on the capital allocation line in Figure 4 represents a portfolio that is 40% invested in the risky asset portfolio and 60% invested in the risk-free asset. Its expected return will be $0.40[E(R_{risky\ asset\ portfolio})] + 0.60(R_f)$ and its standard deviation will be $0.40(\sigma_{risky\ asset\ portfolio})$.

We can combine the capital allocation line with indifference curves to illustrate the logic of selecting an optimal portfolio (i.e., one that maximizes the investor's expected utility). In Figure 5, we can see that an investor with preferences represented by indifference curves I_1, I_2, and I_3 can reach the level of expected utility on I_2 by selecting portfolio X. This is the optimal portfolio for this investor, as any portfolio that lies on I_2 is preferred to all portfolios that lie on I_3 (and in fact to any portfolios that lie between I_2 and I_3). Portfolios on I_1 are preferred to those on I_2, but none of the portfolios that lie on I_1 are available in the market.

Figure 5: Risk-Averse Investor's Indifference Curves

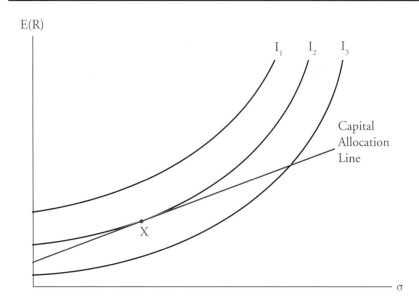

The final result of our analysis here is not surprising; investors who are less risk averse will select portfolios with more risk. As illustrated in Figure 6, the flatter indifference curve for Investor B (I_B) results in an optimal (tangency) portfolio that lies to the right of the one that results from a steeper indifference curve, such as that for Investor A (I_A). An investor who is less risk averse should optimally choose a portfolio with more invested in the risky asset portfolio and less invested in the risk-free asset.

Figure 6: Portfolio Choices Based on Investor's Indifference Curves

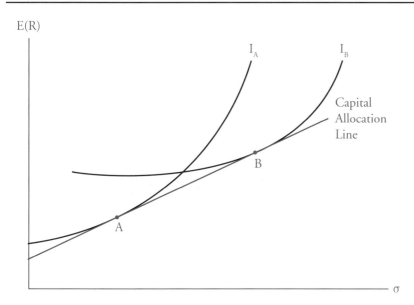

Portfolio Risk And Return: Part II
Cross-Reference to CFA Institute Assigned Reading #44

The following figure illustrates the possible risk-return combinations from combining a risk-free asset with three different (efficient) risky portfolios, X, Y, and M.

Figure 7: Combining a Risk-Free Asset With a Risky Portfolio

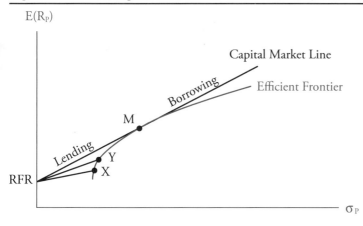

This figure also illustrates the point that combining a risk-free asset with risky Portfolio M (the *tangency* portfolio) results in the best available set of risk and return opportunities. Combining the risk-free asset with either Portfolio X or Portfolio Y results in a less preferred set of possible portfolios.

Since all investors who hold any risky assets will choose to hold Portfolio M, it must contain *all* available risky assets, and we can describe it as the "market portfolio."

Investors at Point M have 100% of their funds invested in Portfolio M. Between R_f and M, investors hold both the risk-free asset and Portfolio M. This means investors are *lending* some of their funds at the risk-free rate and investing the rest in the risky market Portfolio M. To the right of M, investors hold more than 100% of Portfolio M. This means they are *borrowing* funds to buy more of Portfolio M. The *levered positions* represent a 100% investment in Portfolio M and borrowing to invest even more in Portfolio M.

In short, adding a risk-free asset to the set of risky assets considered in the Markowitz portfolio theory results in a new efficient frontier that is now a straight line, the capital market line (CML).

Security Market Line: Systematic and Unsystematic Risk

Under the assumptions of capital market theory, diversification is costless, and investors will only hold efficient portfolios. The risk that is eliminated by diversification is called *unsystematic risk* (also referred to as unique, diversifiable, or firm-specific risk). Since unsystematic risk is assumed to be eliminated at no cost, investors need not be compensated in equilibrium for bearing unsystematic risk.

The risk that remains in efficient portfolios is termed *systematic risk* (also referred to as non-diversifiable or market risk), which is measured by an asset's or portfolio's beta. This crucial result is the basis for the capital asset pricing model (CAPM). The equilibrium relationship between systematic risk and expected return is illustrated by the security market line (SML) as shown in Figure 8.

The *total risk* (standard deviation of returns) for any asset or portfolio of assets can be separated into systematic and unsystematic risk.

$$\text{total risk} = \text{systematic risk} + \text{unsystematic risk}$$

Well-diversified (efficient) portfolios have no unsystematic risk, and a risk-free asset has no systematic (market) risk either. Systematic risk is measured in units of market risk, referred to as the beta of an asset or portfolio, so that the beta of the market portfolio is equal to one. The market portfolio simply has one "unit" of market risk.

Figure 8: Security Market Line

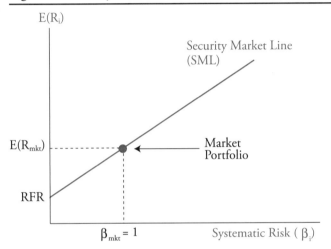

$$\text{CAPM: } E(R_i) = RFR + [E(R_{MKT}) - RFR] \times \text{beta}_i$$

Note that required return and expected return are the same in equilibrium.

Return Generating Models

Return generating models are used to estimate the expected returns on risky securities based on specific factors. For each security, we must estimate the sensitivity of its returns to each factor included in the model. Factors that explain security returns can be classified as macroeconomic, fundamental, and statistical factors.

Multifactor models most commonly use macroeconomic factors such as GDP growth, inflation, or consumer confidence, along with fundamental factors such as earnings, earnings growth, firm size, and research expenditures.

The general form of a multifactor model with k risk factors is as follows:

$$E(R_i) - R_f = \beta_{i1} \times E(\text{Factor 1}) + \beta_{i2} \times E(\text{Factor 2}) + \dots + \beta_{ik} \times E(\text{Factor k})$$

This model states that the expected excess return (above the risk-free rate) for Asset i is the sum of each **factor sensitivity** or **factor loading** (the βs) for Asset i multiplied by the expected value of that factor for the period. The first factor is often the expected excess return on the market, $E(R_m) - R_f$.

One multifactor model that is often used is that of Fama and French. They estimated the sensitivity of security returns to three factors: firm size, firm book value to market value ratio, and the return on the market portfolio minus the risk-free rate (excess return on the market portfolio). Carhart suggests a fourth factor that measures price momentum using prior period returns. Together, these four factors do a relatively good job of explaining returns differences for U.S. equity securities over the period for which the model has been estimated.

The **market model** is a single factor (sometimes termed single index) model. The only factor is the expected return on the market portfolio (market index).

The form of the market model is:

$$R_i = \alpha_i + \beta_i R_m + e_i$$

where:
R_i = Return on Asset i
R_m = Market return
β_i = Slope coefficient
α_i = Intercept
e_i = Abnormal return on Asset i

In the market model, the beta (factor sensitivity) of Asset i is a measure of the sensitivity of the return on Asset i to the return on the market portfolio.

Beta

The sensitivity of an asset's return to the return on the market index in the context of the market model is referred to as its **beta**. Beta is a standardized measure of the covariance of the asset's return with the market return. Beta can be calculated as follows:

$$\beta_i = \frac{\text{covariance of Asset } i\text{'s return with the market return}}{\text{variance of the market return}} = \frac{\text{Cov}_{im}}{\sigma_m^2}$$

©2015 Kaplan, Inc.

We can use the definition of the correlation between the returns on Asset i with the returns on the market index:

$$\rho_{im} = \frac{Cov_{im}}{\sigma_i \sigma_m}$$

to get $Cov_{im} = \rho_{im}\sigma_i\sigma_m$.

Substituting for Cov_{im} in the equation for B_i, we can also calculate beta as:

$$\beta_i = \frac{\rho_{im}\sigma_i\sigma_m}{\sigma_m^2} = \rho_{im}\frac{\sigma_i}{\sigma_m}$$

SML and Equilibrium

You should be able to compute an asset's expected return using the SML and determine whether the aseet is underpriced or overpriced relative to its equilibrium value. In solving problems, be careful to note whether you are given the expected return on the market, $E(R_M)$, or the market risk premium, $E(R_M) - R_f$.

An analyst may identify assets for which his forecasted returns differ from the expected return based on the asset's beta. Assets for which the forecasted return differs from its equilibrium expected returns will plot either above or below the SML. Consider three stocks, A, B, and C, that are plotted on the SML diagram in Figure 9 based on their forecasted returns.

Figure 9: Identifying Mispriced Securities

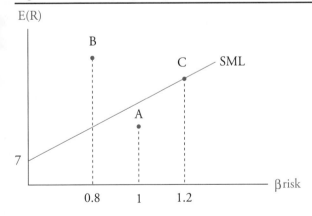

According to the forecasts, Asset B is underpriced, Asset A is overpriced, and Asset C is priced at its equilibrium value.

There are several measures of risk-adjusted returns that are used to evaluate relative portfolio performance.

One such measure is the **Sharpe ratio** $\left(\dfrac{R_P - R_f}{\sigma_P} \right)$.

The Sharpe ratio of a portfolio is its *excess returns per unit of total portfolio risk*, and higher Sharpe ratios indicate better risk-adjusted portfolio performance. Note that this is a slope measure and, as illustrated in Figure 10, the Sharpe ratios of all portfolios along the CML are equal. Because the Sharpe ratio uses total risk, rather than systematic risk, it accounts for any unsystematic risk that the portfolio manager has taken.

In Figure 10, we illustrate that the Sharpe ratio is the slope of the CAL for a portfolio and can be compared to the slope of the CML to evaluate risk-adjusted performance.

Figure 10: Sharpe Ratios as Slopes

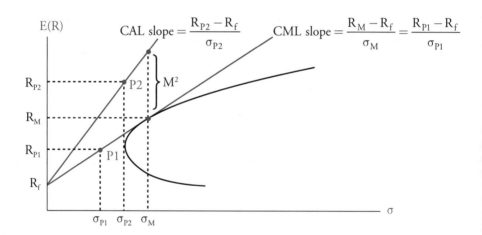

The **M-squared** (M^2) measure produces the same portfolio rankings as the Sharpe ratio but is stated in percentage terms (as illustrated in Figure 10). It is calculated for Portfolio 2 as:

$$(R_{P2} - R_f)\frac{\sigma_M}{\sigma_{P2}} - (R_M - R_f)$$

Two measures of risk-adjusted returns based on systematic risk (beta) rather than total risk are the **Treynor measure** and **Jensen's alpha**. They are similar to the Sharpe ratio and M^2 measures in that the Treynor measure is a slope and Jensen's alpha is in percentage returns.

The Treynor measure is calculated as $\dfrac{R_P - R_f}{\beta_P}$, interpreted as excess returns per unit of systematic risk, and represented by the slope of a line as illustrated in Figure 11.

Jensen's alpha for Portfolio P is calculated as $\alpha_P = (R_P - R_f) - \beta_P(R_M - R_f)$ and is the percentage portfolio return above that of a portfolio (or security) with the same beta as the portfolio that lies on the SML, as illustrated in Figure 11.

Figure 11: Treynor Measure and Jensen's Alpha

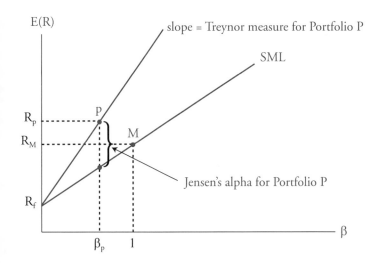

Basics Of Portfolio Planning And Construction
Cross-Reference to CFA Institute Assigned Reading #45

Importance of Investment Policy Statement

Understand the basic inputs to an investment policy statement and how these inputs relate to individuals, pensions, and endowments.

- The policy statement requires that risks and costs of investing, as well as the return requirements, all be objectively and realistically articulated.
- The policy statement imposes investment discipline on, and provides guidance for, both the client and the portfolio manager.

The major components of an IPS typically address the following:

- *Description of Client* circumstances, situation, and investment objectives.
- *Statement of the Purpose* of the IPS.
- *Statement of Duties and Responsibilities* of investment manager, custodian of assets, and the client.
- *Procedures* to update IPS and to respond to various possible situations.
- *Investment Objectives* derived from communications with the client.
- *Investment Constraints* that must be considered in the plan.
- *Investment Guidelines* such as how the policy will be executed, asset types permitted, and leverage to be used.
- *Evaluation of Performance,* the benchmark portfolio for evaluating investment performance, and other information on evaluation of investment results.
- *Appendices* containing information on strategic (baseline) asset allocation and permitted deviations from policy portfolio allocations, as well as how and when the portfolio allocations should be rebalanced.

Risk and Return Objectives

Absolute risk objectives can be stated in terms of the probability of specific portfolio results, either percentage losses or dollar losses, or in terms of strict limits on portfolio results. An absolute return objective may be stated in nominal terms, such as "an overall return of at least 6% per annum," or in real returns, such as "a return of 3% more than the annual inflation rate each year."

Relative risk objectives relate to a specific benchmark and can also be strict, such as, "Returns will not be less than 12-month euro LIBOR over any 12-month period," or stated in terms of probability, such as, "No greater than a 5% probability of returns more than 4% below the return on the MSCI World Index over any 12-month period."

The account manager must make sure that the stated risk and **return objectives** are compatible, given the reality of expected investment results and uncertainty over time.

Risk Tolerance

An investor's **ability to bear risk** depends on financial circumstances. Longer investment horizons (20 years rather than 2 years), greater assets versus liabilities (more wealth), more insurance against unexpected occurrences, and a secure job all suggest a greater ability to bear investment risk.

An investor's **willingness to bear risk** is based primarily on the investor's attitudes and beliefs about investments (various asset types).

©2015 Kaplan, Inc.

If the investor's willingness to take on investment risk is high but the investor's ability to take on risk is low, the low ability to take on investment risk will prevail in the advisor's assessment.

In situations where ability is high but willingness is low, the advisor may attempt to educate the investor about investment risk and correct any misconceptions.

Investment Objectives and Constraints

The investment policy statement should include the following:

Investment objectives:

- Return objectives.
- Risk tolerance.

Constraints:

- Liquidity needs.
- Time horizon.
- Tax concerns.
- Legal and regulatory factors.
- Unique needs and preferences.

Asset Allocation

After having determined the investor objectives and constraints, a **strategic asset allocation** is developed which specifies the percentage allocations to the included asset classes. In choosing asset classes for an account, the correlations of returns *within* an asset class should be relatively high, and the correlations of returns *between* asset classes should be relatively low in comparison.

Once the portfolio manager has identified the investable asset classes for the portfolio, an *efficient frontier* can be constructed and the manager can identify that portfolio (the strategic asset allocation) which best meets the risk and return requirements of the investor.

A manager who varies from strategic asset allocation weights in order to take advantage of perceived short-term opportunities is adding **tactical asset allocation** to the portfolio strategy. **Security selection** refers to deviations from index weights on individual securities within an asset class.

SECURITIES MARKETS AND EQUITY INVESTMENTS

Weight on Exam	10%
SchweserNotes™ Reference	Book 4, Pages 200–326

STUDY SESSION 13: MARKET ORGANIZATION, MARKET INDICES, AND MARKET EFFICIENCY

MARKET ORGANIZATION AND STRUCTURE
Cross-Reference to CFA Institute Assigned Reading #46

The three main functions of the financial system are to:

1. Allow entities to save and borrow money, raise equity capital, manage risks, trade assets currently or in the future, and trade based on their estimates of asset values.

2. Determine the returns (i.e., interest rates) that equate the total supply of savings with the total demand for borrowing.

3. Allocate capital to its most efficient uses.

Assets and Markets

Financial assets include securities (stocks and bonds), derivative contracts, and currencies. **Real assets** include real estate, equipment, commodities, and other physical assets.

Debt securities are promises to repay borrowed funds. **Equity securities** represent ownership positions.

Public securities are traded on exchanges or through securities dealers and are subject to regulatory oversight. Securities that are not traded in public markets are referred to as **private securities**. Private securities are often illiquid and not subject to regulation.

Derivative contracts have values that are derived from the values of other assets. **Financial derivative contracts** are based on equities, equity indexes, debt, debt indexes, or other financial contracts. **Physical derivative contracts** derive their values from the values of physical assets such as gold, oil, and wheat.

Markets for immediate delivery are referred to as **spot markets**. Contracts for the future delivery of physical and financial assets include forwards, futures, and options.

The **primary market** is the market for newly issued securities. Subsequent sales of securities are said to occur in the **secondary market**.

Money markets refer to markets for debt securities with maturities of one year or less. **Capital markets** refer to markets for longer-term debt securities and equity securities that have no specific maturity date.

Traditional investment markets refer to those for debt and equity. **Alternative markets** refer to those for hedge funds, commodities, real estate, collectibles, gemstones, leases, and equipment. Alternative assets often are more difficult to value, illiquid, and require investor due diligence.

Types of Securities

Fixed income securities typically refer to debt securities that are promises to repay borrowed money in the future.

Convertible debt is debt that an investor can exchange for a specified number of equity shares of the issuing firm.

Equity securities represent ownership in a firm and include common stock, preferred stock, and warrants.

- **Common stock** is a residual claim on a firm's assets.
- **Preferred stock** is an equity security with scheduled dividends that typically do not change over the security's life and must be paid before any dividends on common stock may be paid.
- **Warrants** are similar to options in that they give the holder the right to buy a firm's equity shares at a fixed exercise price prior to the warrant's expiration.

Pooled investment vehicles include mutual funds, depositories, and hedge funds. The investor's ownership interests are referred to as *shares, units, depository receipts,* or *limited partnership interests.*

- **Mutual funds** are pooled investment vehicles in which investors can purchase shares, either from the fund itself (open-end funds) or in the secondary market (closed-end funds).
- **Exchange-traded funds** (ETFs) and **exchange-traded notes** (ETNs) trade like closed-end funds, but have special provisions for in-kind creation and redemption.
- **Asset-backed securities** represent a claim to a portion of the cash flows from a pool of financial assets such as mortgages, car loans, or credit card debt.
- **Hedge funds** are organized as limited partnerships, and purchase is usually restricted to investors of substantial wealth and investment knowledge.

Contracts

Financial contracts are often based on securities, currencies, commodities, or security indexes (portfolios). They include futures, forwards, options, swaps, and insurance contracts.

Forward contracts are agreements to buy or sell an asset in the future at a price specified in the contract at its inception and are not typically traded on exchanges or in dealer markets.

Futures contracts are similar to forward contracts except that they are standardized as to amount, asset characteristics, and delivery time, and are traded on an exchange.

In a **swap contract**, two parties make payments that are equivalent to one asset or portfolio being traded for another. In a simple *interest rate swap*, floating rate interest payments are exchanged for fixed rate payments over multiple settlement dates. A *currency swap* involves a loan in one currency for the loan of another currency for a period of time. An *equity swap* involves the exchange of the return on an equity index or portfolio for the interest payment on a debt instrument.

A **call option** gives the option buyer the right (but not the obligation) to buy an asset. A **put option** gives the option buyer the right (but not the obligation) to sell an asset.

An **insurance contract** pays a cash amount if a future event occurs.

Credit default swaps are a form of insurance that makes a payment if an issuer defaults on its bonds.

Currencies, Commodities, and Real Assets

Currencies are issued by a government's central bank. Some are referred to as **reserve currencies**, which are those held by governments and central banks worldwide and include the dollar and euro, and secondarily the British pound, Japanese yen, and Swiss franc.

Commodities trade in spot, forward, and futures markets. They include precious metals, industrial metals, agricultural products, energy products, and credits for carbon reduction.

Examples of **real assets** are real estate, equipment, and machinery. Although they have been traditionally held by firms for their use in production, real assets are increasingly held by institutional investors both directly and indirectly.

Brokers, Dealers, and Exchanges

Brokers help their clients buy and sell securities by finding counterparties to trades in a cost efficient manner.

Block brokers help with the placement of large trades.

Investment banks help corporations sell common stock, preferred stock, and debt securities to investors. They also provide advice to firms, notably about mergers, acquisitions, and raising capital.

Exchanges provide a venue where traders can meet. Exchanges sometimes act as brokers by providing electronic order matching.

Alternative trading systems (ATS), which serve the same trading function as exchanges but have no regulatory function, are also known as **electronic communication networks** or **multilateral trading facilities**. ATS that do not reveal current client orders are known as *dark pools*.

Dealers facilitate trading by buying for or selling from their own inventory.

Some dealers also act as brokers. **Broker-dealers** have an inherent conflict of interest. As brokers, they should seek the best prices for their clients, but as dealers, their goal is to profit through prices or spreads. As a result, traders typically place limits on how their orders are filled when they transact with broker-dealers.

Dealers that trade with central banks when the banks buy or sell government securities in order to affect the money supply are referred to as **primary dealers**.

Investment Positions

An investor who owns an asset, or has the right or obligation under a contract to purchase an asset, is said to have a **long position**. A **short position** can result from borrowing an asset and selling it, with the obligation to replace the asset in the future (a short sale). The party to a contract who must sell or deliver an asset in the future is also said to have a short position. In general, investors who are long benefit from an increase in the price of an asset and those who are short benefit when the asset price declines.

In a **short sale**, the short seller (1) simultaneously borrows and sells securities through a broker, (2) must return the securities at the request of the lender or when the short sale is closed out, and (3) must keep a portion of the proceeds of the short sale on deposit with the broker. Short sellers hope to profit from a fall in the price of the security or asset sold short. The repayment of the borrowed security or other asset is referred to as "covering the short position."

Margin Transactions

Margin purchase transactions involve paying for part of the cost of a security, a loan for the rest from a broker, and leaving the securities on deposit with the broker as collateral. Currently a maximum of 50% of the purchase price can be borrowed. A minimum of 50% of the purchase price must be deposited in cash which is referred to as the *initial margin*.

The *equity* in a margin account for a long position is the market value of the securities minus the loan amount. At any point in time, the *margin percentage* in an account is the equity in the account as a percentage of the market value of the securities held. *Maintenance margin*, or minimum margin, is the minimum percentage of equity permitted; if the margin percentage falls below this minimum, more cash or securities must be deposited in order to maintain the position.

To calculate the rate of return on a margin transaction, divide the gain or loss on the security position by the margin deposit.

The following formula indicates how to calculate the stock price that will trigger a margin call based on the initial price, P_0 (for a long position).

$$\text{trigger price (margin purchases)} = P_0 \left(\frac{1 - \text{initial margin\%}}{1 - \text{maintenance margin\%}} \right)$$

Bid and Ask Prices

Securities dealers provide prices at which they will buy and sell shares. The **bid price** is the price at which a dealer will buy a security. The **ask** or **offer price** is the price at which a dealer will sell a security. The difference between the bid and ask prices is referred to as the **bid-ask spread** and is the source of a dealer's compensation. The bid and ask are quoted for specific trade sizes (**bid size** and **ask size**).

The quotation in the market is the highest dealer bid and lowest dealer ask from among all dealers in a particular security. More liquid securities have market quotations with bid-ask spreads that are lower (as a percentage of share price) and therefore have lower transactions costs for investors. Traders who post bids and offers are said to *make a market*, while those who trade with them at posted prices are said to *take the market*.

Execution Instructions

The most common orders, in terms of execution instructions, are market or limit orders. A **market order** instructs the broker to execute the trade immediately at the best available price. A **limit order** places a *minimum* execution price on sell orders and a *maximum* execution price on buy orders. The disadvantage of a limit order is that it might not be filled.

Validity Instructions

Validity instructions specify *when* an order should be executed. Most orders are **day orders**, meaning they expire if unfilled by the end of the trading day. Good-till-cancelled orders remain open until they are filled. **Immediate or cancel** orders (also known as **fill or kill** orders) are cancelled unless they can be filled immediately. **Good-on-close** orders are only filled at the end of the trading day. If they are market orders, they are referred to as **market-on-close** orders. These are often used by mutual funds because their portfolios are valued using closing prices. There are also **good-on-open** orders.

Stop (stop loss) orders are not executed unless the stop price has been reached. A **stop sell order** is placed at a "stop" price below the current market price, executes if the stock trades at or below the stop price, and can limit the losses on a long position. A **stop buy order** is placed at a "stop" price above the current market price, executes if the stock trades at or above the stop price, and can limit losses on a short position.

Primary and Secondary Markets

Primary capital markets refers to the markets for newly issued securities, either:

- **Initial public offerings** (IPOs).
- **Seasoned offerings** (secondary issues).

Secondary financial markets refers to markets where previously issued securities trade.

Market Structures

In **call markets**, orders are accumulated and securities trade only at specific times. Call markets are potentially very liquid when in session because all traders are present, but they are obviously illiquid between sessions. In a call market, all trades, bids, and asks are at prices that are set to equate supply and demand.

In **continuous markets**, trades occur at any time the market is open with prices set either by the auction process or by dealer bid-ask quotes.

There are three main categories of securities markets: *quote-driven markets* where investors trade with dealers, *order-driven markets* where rules are used to match buyers and sellers, and *brokered markets* where investors use brokers to locate a counterparty to a trade.

In **quote-driven markets**, traders transact with dealers (market makers) who post bid and ask prices. Dealers maintain an inventory of securities. Quote-driven markets are thus sometimes called **dealer markets**, **price-driven markets**, or **over-the-counter markets**. Most securities other than stocks trade in quote-driven markets. Trading often takes place electronically.

In **order-driven markets**, orders are executed using trading rules, which are necessary because traders are usually anonymous. Exchanges and automated trading systems are examples of order-driven markets.

In **brokered markets**, brokers find the counterparty in order to execute a trade. This service is especially valuable when the trader has a security that is unique or illiquid. Examples are large blocks of stock, real estate, and artwork. Dealers typically do not carry an inventory of these assets and there are too few trades for these assets to trade in order-driven markets.

Characteristics of a Well-Functioning Financial System

A market is said to be **complete** if:

- Investors can save for the future at fair rates of return.
- Creditworthy borrowers can obtain funds.
- Hedgers can manage their risks.
- Traders can obtain the currencies, commodities, and other assets they need.

If a market can perform these functions at low trading costs (including commissions, bid-ask spreads, and price impacts) it is said to be **operationally efficient**. If security prices reflect all public information associated with fundamental value in a timely fashion, then the financial system is **informationally efficient**. A well-functioning financial system has complete markets that are operationally and informationally efficient, with prices that reflect fundamental values. Furthermore, in informationally efficiently markets, capital is allocated to its most productive uses. That is, markets are also **allocationally efficient**.

SECURITY MARKET INDICES
Cross-Reference to CFA Institute Assigned Reading #47

A **security market index** is used to represent the performance of an asset class, security market, or segment of a market. Individual securities are referred to as the **constituent securities** of an index.

A price index is based on security prices, and the percentage change in a price index is referred to as its **price return**. The price return on an index plus the return from dividends paid on index stocks is referred to as the **total return** of an index.

Index Weighting Methods

A **price-weighted index** is the arithmetic average of the prices of its constituent securities. The divisor of a price-weighted index must be adjusted for stock splits and for changes in the composition of the index so that the index value is unaffected by such changes.

$$\text{price-weighted index} = \frac{\text{sum of stock prices}}{\text{number of stocks in index}}$$

A given percentage price change on a high-priced stock will have a greater impact on index returns than it will on a low-priced stock. Weights based on prices are considered somewhat arbitrary, and the weights of all index stocks must be adjusted when an index stock splits. A portfolio with equal numbers of shares of each index stock will match the performance of a price-weighted index.

An **equal-weighted index** is calculated as the arithmetic average of the returns of index stocks and would be matched by the returns on a portfolio that had equal dollar amounts invested in each index stock. When stock prices change, however, portfolio weights change and the portfolio must be rebalanced periodically to restore equal weights to each index security. Compared to a price-weighted index, an equal-weighted index places more (less) weight on the returns of low-priced (high-priced) stocks. Compared to a market capitalization-weighted index, an equal-weighted index places more (less) weight on returns of stocks with small (large) market capitalizations.

In a **market capitalization-weighted index** (or **value-weighted index**), returns are weights based on the market capitalization of each index stock (current stock price times the number of shares outstanding) as a proportion of the total market capitalization of all the stocks in the index. A market capitalization-weighted index does not need to be adjusted when a stock splits or pays a stock dividend.

$$\text{current index value} = \frac{\text{current total market value of index stocks}}{\text{base year total market value of index stocks}} \times \text{base year index value}$$

A **float-adjusted market capitalization-weighted index** is constructed like a market capitalization-weighted index. The weights, however, are based on the proportionate value of each firm's shares that are available to investors to the total market value of the shares of index stocks that are available to investors. Firms with relatively large percentages of their shares held by controlling stockholders will have less weight than they have in an unadjusted market-capitalization index.

The advantage of market capitalization-weighted indexes of either type is that index security weights represent proportions of total market value.

An index that uses **fundamental weighting** uses weights based on firm fundamentals, such as earnings, dividends, or cash flow. An advantage of a fundamental-weighted index is that it avoids the bias of market capitalization-weighted indexes toward the performance of the shares of overvalued firms and away from the performance of the shares of undervalued firms.

Rebalancing and Reconstitution

Rebalancing refers to periodically adjusting the weights of securities in an index or portfolio to their target weights, and it is important for equal-weighted indexes as portfolio weights change as prices change.

Index **reconstitution** occurs when the securities that make up an index are changed. Securities are deleted if they no longer meet the index criteria and are replaced by securities that do.

Index Types

Equity indexes can be classified as follows:

- *Broad market index.* Provides a measure of a market's overall performance and usually contains more than 90% of the market's total value.
- *Multi-market index.* Typically constructed from the indexes of markets in several countries and is used to measure the equity returns of a geographic region, markets based on their stage of economic development, or the entire world.
- *Multi-market index with fundamental weighting.* Uses market capitalization-weighting for the country indexes, but then weights the country index returns in the global index by a fundamental factor (e.g., GDP).
- *Sector index.* Measures the returns for an industry sector such as health care, financial, or consumer goods firms.
- *Style index.* Measures the returns to market capitalization and value or growth strategies. Some indexes reflect a combination of the two (e.g., small-cap value fund).

Many different **fixed income indexes** are available to investors. The fixed income security universe is much broader than the universe of stocks. Also, unlike stocks, bonds mature and must be replaced in fixed income indexes. As a result, turnover is high in fixed income indexes.

Because fixed income securities often trade infrequently, index providers must often estimate the value of index securities from recent prices of securities with similar characteristics.

Illiquidity, transactions costs, and high turnover of constituent securities make it both difficult and expensive for fixed income portfolio managers to replicate a fixed income index.

Commodity indexes are based on futures contract prices for commodities such as grains, livestock, metals, and energy. Different indexes have significantly different commodity exposures and risk and return characteristics.

Real estate indexes can be constructed using returns based on appraised values, repeat property sales, or the performance of Real Estate Investment Trusts (REITs).

Most **hedge fund indexes** equally weight the returns of the hedge funds included in the index.

Hedge funds are largely unregulated and are not required to report their performance to index providers. It is often the case that those funds that report are the funds that have been successful, as the poorly performing funds do not choose to report their performance. This results in an upward bias in index returns, with hedge funds appearing to be better investments than they actually are.

Market Efficiency
Cross-Reference to CFA Institute Assigned Reading #48

An **informationally efficient capital market** is one in which the current price of a security fully and quickly reflects all available information about that security without bias.

In a perfectly efficient market, investors should use a passive investment strategy (i.e., buying a broad market index of stocks and holding it) because active investment strategies will underperform on average by the amount of transactions costs and management fees. However, to the extent that market prices are inefficient, active investment strategies can generate positive risk-adjusted returns.

Market efficiency increases with:

- Larger numbers of market participants.
- More information available to investors.
- Fewer impediments to trading such as restrictions on short sales.
- Lower transactions costs.

Forms of the Efficient Markets Hypothesis

1. The *weak form* of the hypothesis states that current stock prices fully reflect all price and trading volume (market) information. If weak-form efficiency holds, purely technical analysis has no value.

2. The *semistrong form* of the hypothesis holds that public information cannot be used to beat the market. If stock prices are semistrong-form efficient, neither technical nor fundamental analysis has any value in stock selection.

3. *Strong-form* efficiency states that stock prices fully reflect all information, both public and private. If markets were strong-form efficient, even private (inside) information would be of no value in selecting securities.

Identified Market Pricing Anomalies

A **market anomaly** is something that would lead us to reject the hypothesis of market efficiency.

- The **January effect** or **turn-of-the-year effect** is the finding that during the first five days of January, stock returns, especially for small firms, are significantly higher than they are the rest of the year.
- The **overreaction effect** refers to the finding that firms with poor stock returns over the previous three or five years (losers) have better subsequent returns than firms that had high stock returns over the prior period.
- **Momentum effects** have also been found where high short-term returns are followed by continued high returns.
- The **size effect** refers to evidence that small-cap stocks outperform large-cap stocks. This effect could not be confirmed in later studies, suggesting that either investors had traded on, and thereby eliminated, this anomaly or that the initial finding was simply a random result for the time period examined.
- The **value effect** refers to the finding that value stocks have outperformed growth stocks. Some researchers attribute the value effect to greater risk of value stocks that is not captured in the risk adjustment procedure used in the studies.

The majority of the evidence suggests that reported anomalies are not violations of market efficiency but are due to the methodologies used in the tests of market efficiency. Furthermore, both underreaction and overreaction have been found in the markets, meaning that prices are efficient on average. Other explanations for the evidence of anomalies are that they are transient relations, too small to profit from, or simply reflect returns to risk that the researchers have failed to account for.

Portfolio management based on previously identified anomalies will likely be unprofitable. Investment management based solely on anomalies has no sound economic basis.

Behavioral Finance

Behavioral finance examines investor behavior, its effect on financial markets, how cognitive biases may result in anomalies, and whether investors are rational.

- **Loss aversion** refers to the tendency for investors to dislike losses more than they like gains of equal amounts.
- **Investor overconfidence.** Securities will be mispriced if investors overestimate their ability to value securities. However, it appears that this mispricing may be hard to predict, may only be temporary, may not be exploitable for abnormal profits, and may only exist for high-growth firms.

- **Representativeness.** Investors assume good companies or good markets are good investments.
- **Mental accounting.** Investors classify different investments into separate mental accounts instead of viewing them as a total portfolio.
- **Conservatism.** Investors react slowly to changes.
- **Narrow framing.** Investors view events in isolation.

Although investor biases may help explain the existence of security mispricing and anomalies, it is not clear that they are predictable enough so that abnormal profits could be earned by exploiting them.

STUDY SESSION 14: EQUITY ANALYSIS AND VALUATION

OVERVIEW OF EQUITY SECURITIES
Cross-Reference to CFA Institute Assigned Reading #49

Types of Equity Securities

- **Common shares** represent a residual claim (after the claims of debt holders and preferred stockholders) on firm assets.
- **Callable common shares** give the firm the right to repurchase the stock at a pre-specified call price.
- **Putable common shares** give the shareholder the right to sell the shares back to the firm at a specific price.
- **Preference shares** (or **preferred stock**) have features of both common stock and debt. As with common stock, preferred stock dividends are not a contractual obligation, the shares usually do not mature, and the shares can have put or call features. Like debt, preferred shares typically make fixed periodic payments to investors and do not usually have voting rights.
- **Cumulative preference shares** require that current period dividends and any dividends that were not paid must be made up before common shareholders can receive dividends. The dividends of **non-cumulative preference shares** do not accumulate over time when they are not paid, but dividends for the current period must be paid before common shareholders can receive dividends.
- Investors in **participating preference shares** receive extra dividends if firm profits exceed a predetermined level and may receive a value greater than the par value of the preferred stock if the firm is liquidated. **Non-participating preference shares** have a claim equal to par value in the event of liquidation and do not share in firm profits.
- **Convertible preference shares** can be exchanged for common stock at a conversion ratio determined when the shares are originally issued.

Private Equity

Private equity is usually issued to institutional investors via private placements. Private equity markets are smaller than public markets but are growing rapidly.

Compared to public equity, private equity has the following characteristics:

- Less liquidity because no public market for the shares exists.
- Share price is negotiated between the firm and its investors, not determined in a market.
- More limited firm financial disclosure because there is no government or exchange requirement to do so.
- Lower reporting costs because of less onerous reporting requirements.
- Potentially weaker corporate governance because of reduced reporting requirements and less public scrutiny.
- Greater ability to focus on long-term prospects because there is no public pressure for short-term results.
- Potentially greater return for investors once the firm goes public.

The three main types of private equity investments are venture capital, leveraged buyouts, and private investments in public equity.

Voting Rights

In a **statutory voting** system, each share held is assigned one vote in the election of each member of the board of directors. Under **cumulative voting**, shareholders can allocate their votes to one or more candidates as they choose.

A firm may have different classes of common stock (e.g., "Class A" and "Class B" shares). One class may have greater voting power and seniority if the firm's assets are liquidated. The classes may also be treated differently with respect to dividends, stock splits, and other transactions with shareholders.

Foreign Equity

Direct investing in the securities of foreign companies simply refers to buying a foreign firm's securities in foreign markets. Some obstacles to direct foreign investment are that:

- The investment and return are denominated in a foreign currency.
- The foreign stock exchange may be illiquid.
- The reporting requirements of foreign stock exchanges may be less strict, impeding analysis.
- Investors must be familiar with the regulations and procedures of each market in which they invest.

Methods for Investing in Foreign Companies

Depository receipts (DRs) trade like domestic shares but represent an interest in shares of a foreign firm that are held by a bank in the country in which they trade. When the foreign firm is involved with the issue, they are termed **sponsored DRs**, and investors receive the voting rights for the shares their DRs represent. When the foreign firm is not involved, they are termed **unsponsored DRs**, face less strict reporting requirements, and the depository bank retains the voting rights on the shares.

Global depository receipts (GDRs) are issued outside the U.S. and the issuer's home country, are traded primarily on the London and Luxembourg exchanges, are usually denominated in U.S. dollars, and can be sold to U.S. institutional investors.

American depository receipts (ADRs) are denominated in U.S. dollars and trade in the United States.

Global registered shares (GRS) are traded in different currencies on stock exchanges around the world.

A **basket of listed depository receipts** (BLDR) is an exchange-traded fund (ETF) that is a collection of DRs. ETF shares trade in markets just like common stocks.

Equity Risk and Return Characteristics

The risk of equity securities is most commonly measured as the standard deviation of returns. Preferred shares are less risky than common stock because preferred shares pay a known, fixed dividend. Because they are less risky, preferred shares have lower average returns than common shares.

Cumulative preferred shares have less risk than non-cumulative preferred shares.

For both common and preferred shares, putable shares are less risky and callable shares are more risky compared to shares with neither option.

Callable shares are the most risky because if the market price rises, the firm can call the shares, limiting the upside potential of the shares.

Market and Book Value of Equity

A firm's **book value of equity** is the value of the firm's assets on the balance sheet minus its liabilities.

The **market value of equity** is the total value of a firm's outstanding equity shares based on market prices and reflects the expectations of investors about the firm's future performance.

A key ratio used to determine management efficiency is the **accounting return on equity**, usually referred to simply as the **return on equity** (ROE):

$$\text{ROE}_t = \frac{\text{NI}_t}{\text{average BV}_t} = \frac{\text{NI}_t}{(\text{BV}_t + \text{BV}_{t-1})/2}$$

A firm's **cost of equity** is the expected equilibrium total return (including dividends) on its shares in the market.

Introduction to Industry and Company Analysis

Cross-Reference to CFA Institute Assigned Reading #50

Industry analysis is important for company analysis because it provides a framework for understanding the firm. Understanding a firm's business environment can provide insight about the firm's potential growth, competition, and risks. For a credit analyst, industry conditions can provide important information about whether a firm will be able to meet its obligations during the next recession.

Industry Classification Systems

One way to group companies into an industry group is by the *products and services* they offer. For example, the firms that produce automobiles constitute the auto industry. A **sector** is a group of similar industries. Systems that group firms by products and services usually use a firm's **principal business activity** (the largest source of sales or earnings) to classify firms.

Sectors representative of those used by commercial providers include the following:

- Basic materials and processing.
- Consumer discretionary.
- Consumer staples.
- Energy.
- Financial services.
- Health care.
- Industrial and producer durables.
- Technology.
- Telecommunications and utilities.

Several government bodies provide industry classification of firms.

- *International Standard Industrial Classification of All Economic Activities* (ISIC) was produced by the United Nations in 1948 to increase global comparability of data.
- *Statistical Classification of Economic Activities in the European Community* is similar to the ISIC, but is designed for Europe.
- *Australian and New Zealand Standard Industrial Classification* was jointly developed by those countries.
- *North American Industry Classification System* (NAICS) was jointly developed by the U.S., Canada, and Mexico.

Other Classification Methods

Firms can be classified by their *sensitivity to business cycles*. This system has two main classifications: cyclical and non-cyclical firms.

A **cyclical firm** is one whose earnings are highly dependent on the stage of the business cycle.

A **non-cyclical firm** produces goods and services for which demand is relatively stable over the business cycle. Examples of non-cyclical industries include health care, utilities, and food and beverage.

Cyclical sector examples include energy, financials, technology, materials, and consumer discretionary. Non-cyclical sector examples include health care, utilities, and consumer staples.

Non-cyclical industries can be further separated into defensive (stable) or growth industries. **Defensive industries** are those that are least affected by the stage of the business cycle and include utilities, consumer staples (such as food producers), and basic services (such as drug stores). **Growth industries** have demand so strong they are largely unaffected by the stage of the business cycle.

Statistical methods, such as cluster analysis, can also be used. This method groups firms that historically have had highly correlated returns.

This method has several limitations:

- Historical correlations may not be the same as future correlations.
- The groupings of firms may differ over time and across countries.
- The grouping of firms is sometimes non-intuitive.
- The method is susceptible to a central issue in statistics, i.e., firms can be grouped by a relationship that occurs by chance or not grouped together when they should be.

©2015 Kaplan, Inc.

Peer Groups

A **peer group** is a set of companies with similar business activities, demand drivers, cost structure drivers, and availability of capital.

To form a peer group, an analyst will often start by identifying companies in the same industry classification, using the commercial classification providers previously described. Usually, the analyst will use other information to verify that the firms in an industry are indeed peers. An analyst might include a company in more than one peer group.

Elements of an Industry Analysis

A thorough industry analysis should include the following elements:

- Evaluate the relationships between macroeconomic variables and industry trends using information from industry groups, firms in the industry, competitors, suppliers, and customers.
- Estimate industry variables using different approaches and scenarios.
- Compare with other analysts' forecasts of industry variables to confirm the validity of the analysis, and potentially find industries that are misvalued as a result of consensus forecasts.
- Determine the relative valuation of different industries.
- Compare the valuations of industries across time to determine the volatility of their performance over the long run and during different phases of the business cycle. This is useful for long-term investing as well as short-term industry rotation based on the current economic environment.
- Analyze industry prospects based on **strategic groups**, which are groups of firms that are distinct from the rest of the industry due to the delivery or complexity of their products or barriers to entry. For example, full-service hotels are a distinct market segment within the hotel industry.
- Classify industries by **life-cycle stage**, whether it is embryonic, growth, shakeout, mature, or declining.
- Position the industry on the **experience curve**, which shows the cost per unit relative to output. The curve declines because of increases in productivity and economies of scale, especially in industries with high fixed costs.
- Consider the forces that affect industries, which include demographic, macroeconomic, governmental, social, and technological influences.
- Examine the forces that determine competition within an industry.

External Influences on Industries

The external influences on industry growth, profitability, and risk should be a component of an analyst's strategic analysis. These external factors include macroeconomic, technological, demographic, governmental, and social influences.

Macroeconomic factors can be cyclical or structural (longer-term) trends, most notably economic output as measured by GDP or some other measure. Interest rates affect financing costs for firms and individuals, as well as financial institution profitability. Credit availability affects consumer and business expenditures and funding. Inflation affects costs, prices, interest rates, and business and consumer confidence.

Technology can change an industry dramatically through the introduction of new or improved products. Computer hardware is an example of an industry that has undergone dramatic transformation. Radical improvements in circuitry were assisted by transformations in other industries, including the computer software and telecommunications industries. Another example of an industry that has been changed by technology is photography, which has largely moved from film to digital media.

Demographic factors include age distribution and population size, as well as other changes in the composition of the population. As a large segment of the population reaches their twenties, residential construction, furniture, and related industries see increased demand. An aging of the overall population can mean significant growth for the health care industry and developers of retirement communities.

Governments have an important effect on businesses through taxes and regulation. Entry into the health care industry, for example, is controlled by governments that license providers. Some industries, such as the U.S. defense industry, depend heavily on government purchases of goods and services.

Social influences relate to how people work, play, spend their money, and conduct their lives; these factors can have a large impact on industries. For example, when women entered the U.S. work force, the restaurant industry benefitted because there was less cooking at home. Child care, women's clothing, and other industries were also dramatically affected.

Industry Life Cycle

Industry life cycle analysis should be a component of an analyst's strategic analysis. The five phases of the industry life-cycle model are illustrated in Figure 1.

Figure 1: Stages of the Industry Life Cycle

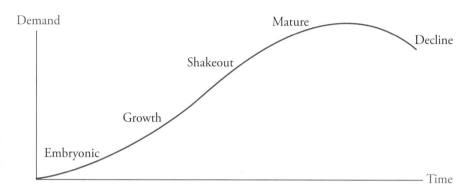

In the **embryonic stage**, the industry has just started. The characteristics of this stage are as follows:

- *Slow growth:* customers are unfamiliar with the product.
- *High prices:* the volume necessary for economies of scale has not been reached.
- *Large investment required:* to develop the product.
- *High risk of failure:* most embryonic firms fail.

In the **growth stage**, industry growth is rapid. The characteristics of this stage are as follows:

- *Rapid growth:* new consumers discover the product.
- *Limited competitive pressures:* The threat of new firms coming into the market peaks during the growth phase, but rapid growth allows firms to grow without competing on price.
- *Falling prices:* economies of scale are reached and distribution channels increase.
- *Increasing profitability:* due to economies of scale.

In the **shakeout stage**, industry growth and profitability are slowing due to strong competition. The characteristics of this stage are as follows:

- *Growth has slowed:* demand reaches saturation level with few new customers to be found.
- *Intense competition:* industry growth has slowed, so firm growth must come at the expense of competitors.
- *Increasing industry overcapacity:* firm investment exceeds increases in demand.
- *Declining profitability:* due to overcapacity.
- *Increased cost cutting:* firms restructure to survive and attempt to build brand loyalty.
- *Increased failures:* weaker firms liquidate or are acquired.

In the **mature stage**, there is little industry growth and firms begin to consolidate. The characteristics of this stage are as follows:

- *Slow growth:* market is saturated and demand is only for replacement.
- *Consolidation:* market evolves to an oligopoly.
- *High barriers to entry:* surviving firms have brand loyalty and low cost structures.
- *Stable pricing:* firms try to avoid price wars, although periodic price wars may occur during recessions.
- *Superior firms gain market share:* the firms with better products may grow faster than the industry average.

In the **decline stage**, industry growth is negative. The characteristics of this stage are as follows:

- *Negative growth:* due to development of substitute products, societal changes, or global competition.
- *Declining prices:* competition is intense and there are price wars due to overcapacity.
- *Consolidation:* failing firms exit or merge.

Industry Concentration

High industry concentration does not guarantee pricing power.

- Absolute market share may not matter as much as a firm's market share relative to its competitors.
- If industry products are undifferentiated and commodity-like, then consumers will switch to the lowest-priced producer. Firms in industries with greater product differentiation in regard to features, reliability, and service after the sale will have greater pricing power.
- If an industry is capital intensive, and therefore costly to enter or exit, overcapacity can result in intense price competition.

Tobacco, alcohol, and confections are examples of highly concentrated industries in which firms' pricing power is relatively strong. Automobiles, aircraft, and oil refining are examples of highly concentrated industries with relatively weak pricing power.

Although industry concentration does not guarantee pricing power, a fragmented market usually does result in strong price competition.

Ease of Entry

High barriers to entry benefit existing industry firms because they prevent new competitors from competing for market share. In industries with low barriers to entry, firms have little pricing power. To assess the ease of entry, the analyst should

©2015 Kaplan, Inc.

determine how easily a new entrant to the industry could obtain the capital, intellectual property, and customer base needed to be successful. One method of determining the ease of entry is to examine the composition of the industry over time. If the same firms dominate the industry today as ten years ago, entry is probably difficult.

High barriers to entry do not necessarily mean firm pricing power is high. Industries with high barriers to entry may have strong price competition when the products sold are undifferentiated or when high barriers to exit result in overcapacity.

Capacity

Industry capacity has a clear impact on pricing power. Undercapacity, a situation in which demand exceeds supply at current prices, results in pricing power. Overcapacity, with supply greater than demand at current prices, will result in downward pressure on price.

Market Share Stability

An analyst should examine whether firms' market shares in an industry have been stable over time. Market shares that are highly variable likely indicate a highly competitive industry in which firms have little pricing power. More stable market shares likely indicate less intense competition in the industry.

Factors that affect market share stability include barriers to entry, introductions of new products and innovations, and the **switching costs** that customers face when changing from one firm's products to another. High switching costs contribute to market share stability and pricing power.

Five Forces that Determine Industry Competition

The analysis framework developed by Michael Porter[1] delineates five forces that determine industry competition.

1. Rivalry among existing competitors.

2. Threat of entry.

3. Threat of substitutes.

4. Power of buyers.

5. Power of suppliers.

---

1. Michael Porter, "The Five Competitive Forces That Shape Strategy," *Harvard Business Review,* Volume 86, No. 1: pp. 78–93.

Industry competition is less intensive and firm profitability is greater when there is (1) less rivalry among existing industry firms, (2) less threat of new entrants, (3) less threat of substitute products, (4) less bargaining power of buyers (customers), and (5) less bargaining power of suppliers.

Company Analysis

Having gained understanding of an industry's external environment, an analyst can then focus on **company analysis**. This involves analyzing the firm's financial condition, products and services, and **competitive strategy**. Competitive strategy is how a firm responds to the opportunities and threats of the external environment.

Porter has identified two important competitive strategies that can be employed by firms within an industry: a **cost leadership (low-cost) strategy** or a **product or service differentiation strategy**. According to Porter, a firm must decide to focus on one of these two areas to compete effectively.

In a *low-cost strategy*, the firm seeks to have the lowest costs of production in its industry, offer the lowest prices, and generate enough volume to make a superior return. In **predatory pricing**, the firm hopes to drive out competitors and later increase prices. A low-cost strategy firm should have managerial incentives that are geared toward improving operating efficiency.

In a *differentiation strategy*, the firm's products and services should be distinctive in terms of type, quality, or delivery. For success, the firm's cost of differentiation must be less than the price premium buyers place on product differentiation. The price premium should also be sustainable over time. Successful differentiators will have outstanding marketing research teams and creative personnel.

A company analysis should include the following elements:

- Firm overview, including information on operations, governance, and strengths and weaknesses.
- Industry characteristics.
- Product demand.
- Product costs.
- Pricing environment.
- Financial ratios, with comparisons to other firms and over time.
- Projected financial statements and firm valuation.

A firm's return on equity (ROE) should be part of the financial analysis. The ROE is a function of profitability, total asset turnover, and financial leverage (debt).

Equity Valuation: Concepts and Basic Tools
Cross-Reference to CFA Institute Assigned Reading #51

Categories of Equity Valuation Models

In **discounted cash flow models** (or **present value models**), a stock's value is estimated as the present value of cash distributed to shareholders (*dividend discount models*) or the present value of cash available to shareholders after the firm meets its necessary capital expenditures and working capital expenses (*free cash flow to equity models*).

There are two basic types of **multiplier models** (or **market multiple models**) that can be used estimate intrinsic values. In the first type, the ratio of stock price to such fundamentals as earnings, sales, book value, or cash flow per share is used to determine if a stock is fairly valued. For example, the price to earnings (P/E) ratio is frequently used by analysts.

The second type of multiplier model is based on the ratio of **enterprise value** to either earnings before interest, taxes, depreciation, and amortization (EBITDA) or revenue. Enterprise value is the market value of all a firm's outstanding securities minus cash and short-term investments. Common stock value can be estimated by subtracting the value of liabilities and preferred stock from an estimate of enterprise value.

In **asset-based models**, the intrinsic value of common stock is estimated as total asset value minus liabilities and preferred stock. Analysts typically adjust the book values of the firm's assets and liabilities to their fair values when estimating the market value of its equity with an asset-based model.

Preferred Stock Valuation

The dividend is fixed and the income stream (dividends) theoretically continues forever so we use the formula for the present value of a perpetuity.

$$\text{preferred stock value} = \frac{D_p}{k_p}$$

Dividend Discount Models (DDM)

All of the valuation models here are based on taking the present value of expected future cash flows.

One-year holding period:

For the purposes of this valuation model, we assume that dividends are received annually at the end of the year; so, if you hold the stock one year, you will receive the dividend and the estimated sale price P_1. To calculate the present value of these cash flows one year from now:

$$\text{one-period model: } P_0 = \frac{\begin{pmatrix} \text{dividend to} \\ \text{be received} \end{pmatrix}}{(1+k_e)} + \frac{\begin{pmatrix} \text{year -} \\ \text{end price} \end{pmatrix}}{(1+k_e)} \text{ or } P_0 = \frac{D_1 + P_1}{(1+k_e)}$$

Be sure to use the *expected* dividend, D_1, in the calculation.

Multiple-year holding periods:

With a multiple-year holding period, estimate all the dividends to be received as well as the expected selling price at the end of the holding period.

$$\text{n-period model: } P_0 = \frac{D_1}{(1+k_e)^1} + \frac{D_2}{(1+k_e)^2} + \ldots + \frac{D_n}{(1+k_e)^n} + \frac{P_n}{(1+k_e)^n}$$

Infinite period model (constant growth model):

We can take the present value of an infinite stream of dividends that grows at a *constant rate* as long as the assumed growth rate, g_c, is less than the appropriate discount rate, k_e.

$$\text{constant growth model: } P_0 = \frac{D_1}{k_e - g_c}, \text{note that } D_1 = D_0(1+g_c)$$

Other things held constant, the higher the growth rate and the higher the dividend, the greater the present value.

In practice, however, increasing the dividend will decrease retained earnings and the firm's sustainable growth rate, so we cannot assume that a firm that increases its dividend will increase firm value.

Temporary supernormal growth or multi-stage DDM:

This model assumes that a company's dividends will grow at a high rate for a period of time before declining to a constant growth rate. To calculate the stock price, discount each of the dividends during the high growth period individually and then use the formula for the infinite growth model to find the terminal stock value at the end of the supernormal growth period. Finally, add together the present values of all dividends and of the terminal stock value.

$$\text{value}_{\text{supernormal growth}} = \frac{D_1}{(1+k_e)} + \frac{D_2}{(1+k_e)^2} + \ldots + \frac{D_n}{(1+k_e)^n} + \frac{P_n}{(1+k_e)^n}$$

D_n is the last dividend of the supernormal growth period.

$$P_n = \frac{D_{n+1}}{k_e - \overline{g}c}, \text{ where } D_{n+1} \text{ is expected to grow at the constant/normal rate}$$

Earnings multiplier model (P/E ratio):

Understand how the DDM relates to the fundamental P/E ratio.

Start with the DDM and then divide both sides of the equation by next year's projected earnings, E_1:

$$\text{If constant growth DDM holds: } P_0 = \frac{D_1}{k-g} \text{ then } \frac{P_0}{E_1} = \frac{D_1 / E_1}{k-g}$$

Other things held constant, the P/E ratio:

- Increases with D_1/E_1, the dividend payout ratio.
- Increases with *g*, the growth rate of dividends.
- Decreases with increases in *k*, the required rate of return.
- Increases with ROE, since *g* = ROE × retention ratio.

ROE = (net income / sales)(sales / total assets)(total assets / equity)

Problems with using P/E analysis:

- Earnings are historical accounting numbers and may be of differing quality.
- Business cycles may affect P/E ratios. Currently reported earnings may be quite different from expected future earnings (E_1).
- As with the infinite growth model, when k < g, the P/E implied by the DDM is meaningless.

Estimating the Growth Rate in Dividends

To estimate the growth rate in dividends, the analyst can use three methods:

1. Use the historical growth in dividends for the firm.

2. Use the median industry dividend growth rate.

3. Estimate the sustainable growth rate.

The **sustainable growth rate** is the rate at which equity, earnings, and dividends can continue to grow indefinitely assuming that ROE is constant, the dividend payout ratio is constant, and no new equity is issued.

$$\text{sustainable growth} = (1 - \text{dividend payout ratio}) \times \text{ROE}$$

The quantity (1 – dividend payout ratio) is referred to as the **retention rate**, the proportion of net income that is not paid out as dividends and goes to retained earnings, thus increasing equity.

Some firms do not currently pay dividends but are expected to begin paying dividends at some point in the future. A firm may not currently pay a dividend because it is in financial distress and cannot afford to pay out cash, or because the return the firm can earn by reinvesting cash is greater than what stockholders could expect to earn by investing dividends elsewhere.

For firms that do not currently pay dividends, an analyst must estimate the amount and timing of the first dividend in order to use the Gordon growth model. Because these parameters are highly uncertain, the analyst should compare the estimated value from the Gordon growth model with value estimates from other models.

Using Price Multiples to Value Equity

Because the dividend discount model is very sensitive to its inputs, many investors rely on other methods. In a **price multiple** approach, an analyst compares a stock's price multiple to a benchmark value based on an index, industry group of firms, or a peer group of firms within an industry.

©2015 Kaplan, Inc.

Common price multiples used for valuation include price-to earnings, price-to-cash flow, price-to-sales, and price-to-book value ratios. Many of these ratios have been shown to be useful for predicting stock returns, with low multiples associated with higher future returns.

When we compare a price multiple, such as P/E, for a firm to those of other firms based on market prices, we are using price multiples based on comparables. By contrast, price multiples based on fundamentals tell us what a multiple should be based on some valuation models.

One criticism of price multiples is that they reflect only the past because historical (trailing) data are often used in the denominator. For this reason, many practitioners use forward (leading or prospective) values in the denominator (sales, book value, earnings, etc.) The use of projected values can result in much different ratios. An analyst should be sure to use price multiple calculations consistently across firms.

Trailing P/E uses earnings over the *most recent* 12 months in the denominator. The *leading P/E ratio* (also known as forward or prospective P/E) uses expected earnings for the next four quarters or fiscal year.

$$\text{trailing P/E} = \frac{\text{market price per share}}{\text{EPS over previous 12 months}}$$

$$\text{leading P/E} = \frac{\text{market price per share}}{\text{forecasted EPS over next 12 months}}$$

The *price-to-book (P/B) ratio* is calculated as:

$$\text{P/B ratio} = \frac{\text{market value of equity}}{\text{book value of equity}} = \frac{\text{market price per share}}{\text{book value per share}}$$

A common adjustment is to use *tangible book value*, which is equal to book value of equity less intangible assets (e.g., goodwill, patents).

Furthermore, balance sheets should be adjusted for significant off-balance-sheet assets and liabilities and for differences between the fair and recorded values of assets and liabilities. Finally, book values often need to be adjusted for differences in accounting methods to ensure comparability.

Price-to-sales (P/S) ratios are computed by dividing a stock's price per share by sales or revenue per share or by dividing the market value of the firm's equity by its total sales:

$$\text{P/S ratio} = \frac{\text{market value of equity}}{\text{total sales}} = \frac{\text{market price per share}}{\text{sales per share}}$$

Given one of the definitions of cash flow, the *price-to-cash-flow (P/CF) ratio* is calculated as:

$$\text{P/CF ratio} = \frac{\text{market value of equity}}{\text{cash flow}} = \frac{\text{market price per share}}{\text{cash flow per share}}$$

where:
cash flow = CF, adjusted CFO, FCFE, or EBITDA

Enterprise Value Multiples

Enterprise value (EV) is a measure of total company value and can be viewed as what it would cost to acquire the firm.

EV = market value of common stock + market value of debt – cash and short-term investments

Cash and short-term investments are subtracted because an acquirer's cost for a firm would be decreased by the amount of the target's liquid assets. Although an acquirer assumes the firm's debt, it receives the firm's cash and short-term investments. Enterprise value is appropriate when an analyst wants to compare the values of firms that have significant *differences in capital structure*.

EBITDA (earnings before interest, taxes, depreciation, and amortization are subtracted) is probably the most frequently used denominator for EV multiples; operating income can also be used. An advantage of using EBITDA instead of net income is that EBITDA is usually positive even when earnings are not. A disadvantage of using EBITDA is that it often includes non-cash revenues and expenses.

Asset-Based Valuation Models

Asset-based models are appropriate when equity value is the market or fair value of assets minus the market or fair value of liabilities. Because market values of firm assets are usually difficult to obtain, the analyst typically starts with the balance sheet to determine the values of assets and liabilities. In most cases, market values are not equal to book values. Possible approaches to valuing assets are to value them at their depreciated values, inflation-adjusted depreciated values, or estimated replacement values.

Applying asset-based models is especially problematic for firms that have a large amount of intangible assets, on or off the balance sheet. The effect of the loss of the current owners' talents and customer relationships on forward earnings may be quite difficult to measure. Analysts often consider asset-based model values as floor or minimum values when significant intangibles, such as business reputation, are involved.

Asset-based model valuations are most reliable when the firm has primarily tangible short-term assets, assets with ready market values (e.g., financial or natural resource firms), or when the firm will cease to operate and is being liquidated.

Advantages and Disadvantages of Valuation Models

Advantages of discounted cash flow models:

- They are based on the fundamental concept of discounted present value and are well grounded in finance theory.
- They are widely accepted in the analyst community.

Disadvantages of discounted cash flow models:

- Their inputs must be estimated.
- Value estimates are very sensitive to input values.

Advantages of comparable valuation using price multiples:

- Evidence that some price multiples are useful for predicting stock returns.
- Price multiples are widely used by analysts.
- Price multiples are readily available.
- They can be used in time series and cross-sectional comparisons.
- EV/EBITDA multiples are useful when comparing firm values independent of capital structure or when earnings are negative and the P/E ratio cannot be used.

Disadvantages of comparable valuation using price multiples:

- Lagging price multiples reflect the past.
- Price multiples may not be comparable across firms if the firms have different size, products, and growth.
- Price multiples for cyclical firms may be greatly affected by economic conditions at a given point in time.
- A stock may appear overvalued by the comparable method but undervalued by a fundamental method, or vice versa.
- Different accounting methods can result in price multiples that are not comparable across firms, especially internationally.
- A negative denominator in a price multiple results in a meaningless ratio. The P/E ratio is especially susceptible to this problem.

Advantages of price multiple valuations based on fundamentals:

- They are based on theoretically sound valuation models.
- They correspond to widely accepted value metrics.

Disadvantages of price multiple valuations based on fundamentals:

- Price multiples based on fundamentals will be very sensitive to the inputs (especially the k – g denominator).

Advantages of asset-based models:

- They can provide floor values.
- They are most reliable when the firm has primarily tangible short-term assets, assets with ready market values, or when the firm is being liquidated.
- They are increasingly useful for valuing public firms that report fair values.

Disadvantages of asset-based models:

- Market values are often difficult to obtain.
- Market values are usually different than book values.
- They are inaccurate when a firm has a high proportion of intangible assets or future cash flows not reflected in asset values.
- Assets can be difficult to value during periods of hyperinflation.

FIXED INCOME

Weight on Exam	10%
SchweserNotes™ Reference	Book 5, Pages 1–153

STUDY SESSION 15: FIXED INCOME—BASIC CONCEPTS

FIXED-INCOME SECURITIES: DEFINING ELEMENTS
Cross-Reference to CFA Institute Assigned Reading #52

Basic features of fixed income securities include:

- *Issuer.*
- *Maturity date*, also known as a bond's tenor.
- *Par value*, also known as *face value, maturity value*, or *redemption value*.
- *Coupon rate.*
- *Coupon frequency*, also known as a bond's *periodicity*.
- *Currency denomination* in which interest and principal will be paid. A *dual-currency bond* pays interest in one currency and principal in another.

The *trust deed* or *indenture* details the issuer's obligations and the bondholder's rights. Legal and regulatory issues addressed include:

- Legal information about the entity issuing the bond.
- Any *collateral* pledged to support repayment of the bond.
  - *Secured bonds* are backed by a claim to specific assets.
  - *Unsecured bonds* represent a claim to the overall assets and cash flows of the issuer.
- *Credit enhancements* increase the probability of repayment and can be internal (built into the structure of a bond issue) or external (provided by a third party).
- *Covenants* describing any actions the firm must take (affirmative covenants) and any actions the firm is prohibited from taking (negative covenants).

A country's *national bond market* includes bonds that trade in that country and are denominated in its currency. These include *domestic bonds* from domestic issuers and *foreign bonds* from foreign issuers.

Eurobonds are issued outside the jurisdiction of any one country and are denominated in a currency different from the currency of the countries in which they are sold. They are subject to less regulation and are often issued as *bearer bonds* (rather than *registered bonds*), which may offer a tax advantage.

Global bonds trade in both the eurobond market and a national bond market.

Interest income paid to bondholders is typically taxed as ordinary income at the same rate as wage and salary income. The interest income from most bonds issued by municipal governments in the United States is exempt from federal income tax and income tax in the state of issue.

When a bondholder sells a bond prior to maturity, the transaction may generate a *capital gain* or *loss*, depending on the sale price. Capital gains are often taxed at a lower rate than ordinary income. If the assets have been owned for more than a specified length of time, they are often taxed at an even lower rate.

Pure-discount bonds and other bonds sold at significant discounts to par when issued are termed *original issue discount* (OID) bonds. The increase in value of OID bonds due to the passage of time may be treated as taxable interest income and, as a result, these bonds can generate a tax liability even though no cash interest payment has been received.

How Fixed Income Cash Flows are Structured

A typical "plain vanilla" bond has a *bullet structure*. Periodic coupon interest payments are made over the life of the bond, and the principal value is paid with the final interest payment at maturity.

For a bond with an *amortizing structure*, the periodic payments include both interest and some repayment of principal. If a bond is *fully amortizing*, the principal is fully paid off when the last periodic payment is made. A bond can also be structured to be *partially amortizing* so there is a *balloon payment* at bond maturity that includes the unamortized principal.

A *floating-rate note* (FRN) has a coupon rate that is based on a *reference rate*, such as 90-day LIBOR, plus (or possibly minus) a margin that reflects the issuer's creditworthiness relative to the reference rate. A *variable-rate note* is an FRN with a variable margin. An *inverse floater* has a coupon rate that increases when the reference rate decreases and decreases when the reference rate increases.

An FRN may have a *cap*, which benefits the issuer by placing a limit on how high the coupon rate can rise. Often, FRNs with caps also have a *floor*, which benefits the bondholder by placing a minimum on the coupon rate, regardless of how low the reference rate falls.

An *index-linked bond* has coupon payments and/or a principal value that is based on a commodity index, an equity index, or some other published index number.

Some index-linked bonds are *principal-protected*, which means they will not pay less than their original par value at maturity, even if the index has decreased.

The most common type of index-linked bonds is *inflation-linked bonds* (or *linkers*) for which payments are based on the change in an inflation index, such as the Consumer Price Index (CPI) in the United States.

The different structures of inflation-indexed bonds include:

- *Indexed-annuity bonds.* Fully amortizing bonds with the periodic payments directly adjusted for inflation or deflation.
- *Indexed zero-coupon bonds.* The payment at maturity is adjusted for inflation.
- *Interest-indexed bonds.* The coupon rate is adjusted for inflation while the principal value remains unchanged.
- *Capital-indexed bonds.* This is the most common structure. An example is U.S. Treasury Inflation Protected Securities (TIPS). The coupon rate remains constant, and the principal value of the bonds is increased by the rate of inflation (or decreased by deflation). TIPS are principal-protected.

Other coupon structures include:

- *Step-up coupon bonds.* The coupon rate increases over time according to a predetermined schedule. These bonds are typically callable.
- *Credit-linked coupon bonds.* The coupon rate increases by a certain amount if the credit rating of the issuer falls, and decreases if the credit rating of the issuer improves.
- *Payment-in-kind bonds.* The issuer may make coupon payments by increasing the principal amount, essentially paying bond interest with more bonds.
- *Deferred coupon (split coupon) bonds.* Regular coupon payments do not begin until a period of time after issuance.

A *sinking fund* provision provides for the periodic retirement of a portion of the bonds issued over the life of the issue. In general, bonds with a sinking fund provision have less credit risk but greater reinvestment risk.

Contingency Provisions in Bonds

A contingency provision describes an action that may be taken if a specific event occurs. Contingency provisions in bond indentures are referred to as *embedded options*. Embedded options may benefit the bond issuer, increasing the required market yield, or benefit the bondholder, decreasing the required market yield. Bonds that do not have contingency provisions are referred to as *straight bonds* or *option-free bonds*.

A *call option* gives the issuer the right to redeem all or part of a bond issue at a specific call price. A *call schedule* specifies a callable bond's *call dates* and call prices. A call price may be par value or include a *call premium* above par. The time from issuance until a callable bond's first call date is referred to as the bond's period of *call protection* (or *lockout period, cushion*, or *deferment period*).

The issuer may exercise a call option because market yields have fallen in order to reduce interest expense. Bondholders have more reinvestment risk as a result, as they must reinvest the proceeds of called bonds at lower yields. For this reason, a callable bond must offer a higher yield (sell at a lower price) than an otherwise identical noncallable bond.

To avoid the higher interest rates required on callable bonds but still preserve the option to redeem bonds early for corporate (rather than financial) reasons, issuers have introduced bonds with *make-whole call provisions*. With a make-whole bond, the call price is not fixed but includes a lump-sum payment based on the present value of the future coupons the bondholder will not receive if the bond is called early. Thus, the issuer is unlikely to call the bond except when corporate circumstances, such as an acquisition or restructuring, require it.

There are three styles of exercise for callable bonds. Note that these are only style names and are not indicative of where the bonds are issued:

1. American style—the bonds can be called anytime after the first call date.

2. European style—the bonds can only be called on the call date specified.

3. Bermuda style—the bonds can be called on specified dates after the first call date, often on coupon payment dates.

A *put option* gives the bondholder the right to sell the bond back to the issuing company at a given price, typically par. Bondholders are likely to exercise a put option when the fair value of the bond is less than the put price because interest rates have risen or the credit quality of the issuer has fallen. Unlike a call option, a put option is exercised by the bondholder so a putable bond will trade at a lower yield (sell at a higher price) relative to an otherwise identical option-free bond.

Convertible bonds give bondholders the option to exchange the bond for a specific number of shares of the issuing corporation's common stock and can have the characteristics of both a debt and equity security as a result. The possibility of profit from increases in the value of the common shares reduces the required yield on the bonds, compared to the yield of an option-free bond. The value of a convertible bond is the value of the bond plus the value of the conversion option.

Contingent convertible bonds (referred to as "CoCos") are bonds that convert from debt to common equity automatically if a specific event occurs and can increase the equity of financial institutions when it falls below the percentage required by regulators.

Sometimes bonds, especially those of riskier, less mature companies, are sold with *warrants* attached. Warrants give their holders the right to buy the firm's common shares at a given price until an expiration date. Warrants provide potential gains to bondholders and do not require the bonds to be retired at exercise, as convertible bonds do.

FIXED-INCOME MARKETS: ISSUANCE, TRADING, AND FUNDING
Cross-Reference to CFA Institute Assigned Reading #53

Interbank Rates

The most widely used reference rate for floating-rate bonds is the London Interbank Offered Rate (LIBOR), although other reference rates, such as Euribor, are also used. Libor rates are published daily for several currencies and for maturities of one day (overnight rates) to one year. Thus, there is no single "LIBOR rate" but rather a set of rates, such as "30-day U.S. dollar LIBOR" or "90-day Swiss franc LIBOR."

The rates are based on expected rates for unsecured loans from one bank to another in the interbank money market, based on a survey of banks.

For floating-rate bonds, the reference rate must match the frequency with which the coupon rate on the bond is reset. For example, a bond denominated in euros with a coupon rate that is reset twice each year might use six-month euro LIBOR or six-month Euribor as a reference rate.

Primary Market for Bonds

Primary market transactions are sales of newly issued bonds. Bonds can be registered with securities regulators for sale in a *public offering* or sold only to *qualified* investors in a *private placement*. A public offering is typically done with the help of an investment bank, which has expertise in executing a public offering.

In an *underwritten offering*, the investment bank (underwriter), or a *syndicate* of investment banks, purchases the entire bond issue from the issuing firm and then sells them to dealers and investors. Bonds are priced based on indications of interest from buyers. Some bonds are traded on a prior to issue (on a when-issued basis) in what is called the *grey market*, which helps underwriters determine the offering price.

In a *best efforts offering*, the investment banks sell the bonds on a commission basis. Unlike an underwritten offering, the investment banks do not commit to purchase the whole issue.

Some bonds, especially government bonds, are sold through an auction. For example, U.S. Treasury securities are sold through single-price auctions with the majority of purchases made by *primary dealers*.

In a *shelf registration*, a bond issue is registered with securities regulators in its aggregate value with a master prospectus. Portions of the registered issue can then be issued over time when the issuer needs to raise funds. Individual offerings under a shelf registration require less disclosure than a separate registration of a bond issue.

Secondary Market for Bonds

Secondary markets refer to the trading of previously issued bonds. While some government bonds and corporate bonds are traded on exchanges, the great majority of bond trading in the secondary market is made in the dealer, or over-the-counter, market. Dealers post bid (purchase) prices and ask or offer (selling) prices for various bond issues. The difference between the bid and ask prices is the dealer's spread.

Bond trades are cleared through a clearing system, just as equities trades are. Settlement typically occurs on T + 2 or T + 3 for corporate bonds, on T + 1 or cash settlement for government and quasi-government bonds, and cash settlement for some money market securities.

Government and Agency Bonds

National governments or their treasuries issue *sovereign bonds* that are backed by the taxing power of the government. Both a sovereign's ability to collect taxes and its ability to print the local currency lead to higher ratings on bonds issued in the local currency compared to sovereign debt issued in the currency of a developed economy (e.g., USD or euros). Sovereign bonds include fixed-rate, floating-rate, and inflation-indexed bond issues.

Trading is most active and prices most informative for the most recently issued government securities of a particular maturity. These issues are referred to as *on-the-run bonds* or *benchmark bonds*. Yields of other bonds are determined relative to the benchmark yields of sovereign bonds with similar maturities.

Nonsovereign government bonds are issued by states, provinces, counties, and sometimes by entities created to fund and provide services such as for the construction of hospitals, airports, and other municipal services. Payments on the bonds may be supported by the revenues of a specific project, from general tax revenues, or from special taxes or fees dedicated to the repayment of project debt. Nonsovereign bonds are typically of high credit quality, but sovereign bonds typically trade with lower yields because their credit risk is perceived to be less than that of nonsovereign bonds.

Agency bonds or *quasi-government bonds* are issued by entities created by national governments for specific purposes such as financing small businesses or providing mortgage financing. *Supranational bonds* are issued by supranational agencies (also known as multilateral agencies) such as the World Bank, the IMF, and the Asian Development Bank.

Corporate Debt

Bank loans to corporations are typically LIBOR-based variable-rate loans. When the loan involves only one bank, it is referred to as a *bilateral loan*. In contrast, when a loan is funded by several banks, it is referred to as a *syndicated loan*.

For larger creditworthy corporations, funding costs can be reduced by issuing short-term debt securities referred to as *commercial paper*. Firms use commercial paper to fund working capital and as a temporary source of funds prior to issuing longer term debt. Debt that is temporary until permanent financing can be secured is referred to as *bridge financing*. To get an acceptable credit rating from the ratings services on their commercial paper, corporations maintain *backup lines of credit* with banks.

Commercial paper is short-term unsecured debt, issued with maturities as short as one day (overnight paper), with most issues maturing in about 90 days. In the United States, commercial paper is issued with maturities of 270 days or less so it is exempt from SEC registration, and is typically issued as a pure discount security.

Eurocommercial paper (ECP) is issued in several countries with maturities as long as 364 days. ECP rates are quoted as add-on (rather than discount) yields.

A bond issue is said to have a *term maturity structure* if all the bonds mature on the same date. An alternative is a *serial bond issue* in which bonds are issued with several maturity dates so a portion of the issue is redeemed periodically. The difference between a serial bond issue and an issue with a sinking fund is that with a serial bond issue, investors know the dates when specific bonds will be redeemed.

In general, corporate bonds are referred to as short-term if they are issued with maturities of up to 5 years, medium-term when issued with maturities from 5 to 12 years, and long-term when maturities exceed 12 years.

Corporations issue debt securities called medium-term notes (MTNs), which are not necessarily medium-term in maturity. MTNs are issued in various maturities, ranging from nine months to periods as long as 100 years. MTNs are offered continuously through agents and can be customized to some extent to match a bond buyer's preferences. Most MTNs, other than long-term MTNs, are issued by financial corporations and most buyers are financial institutions.

Funding Alternatives for Banks

Retail customer deposits, including checking accounts, savings accounts, and money market mutual funds, are a short-term funding source for banks. In addition to funds from retail accounts, banks offer interest-bearing certificates of deposit (CDs) in a range of short-term maturities. Non-negotiable CDs cannot be sold.

Negotiable certificates of deposit can be sold. Large denomination (typically more than $1 million) negotiable CDs are an important funding source for banks. They typically have maturities of one year or less and are traded in domestic bond markets as well as in the eurobond market.

Banks may borrow *excess reserves* from other banks in the *central bank funds market*. Rates for these transactions (central bank funds rates) are strongly influenced by the effect of the central bank's open market operations on the money supply and the availability of short-term funds. In the United States, the central bank funds rate is called the *Fed funds rate*.

Other than reserves on deposit with the central bank, funds that are loaned by one bank to another are referred to as *interbank funds*. Interbank funds are loaned between banks for periods of one day to a year. These loans are unsecured and, as with many debt markets, liquidity may decrease severely during times of systemic financial distress.

Repurchase Agreements

In a *repurchase agreement* or *repo*, one party sells a security to a counterparty with a commitment to buy it back at a later date at a specified higher price. The repurchase price is greater than the selling price and the difference is effectively the interest paid to the buyer. In effect, the buyer is lending funds to the seller with the security as collateral. The interest rate implied by the two prices is called the *repo rate*.

A repurchase agreement for one day is called an *overnight repo* and an agreement covering a longer period is called a *term repo*. The interest cost of a repo is customarily less than the rate on bank loans or other short-term borrowing.

A percentage difference between the market value of the security and the amount loaned is called the *repo margin* or the *haircut*. This margin protects the lender in the event that the value of the security decreases over the term of the repo agreement.

Viewed from the standpoint of a bond dealer, a *reverse repo agreement* refers to taking the opposite side of a repurchase transaction, lending funds by buying the collateral security rather than selling the collateral security to borrow funds.

The repo rate is:

- Higher, the longer the repo term.
- Lower, the higher the credit quality of the collateral security.
- Lower when the collateral security is delivered to the lender.
- Higher when the interest rates for alternative sources of funds are higher.

The repo margin is influenced by similar factors. The repo margin is:

- Higher, the longer the repo term.
- Lower, the higher the credit quality of the collateral security.
- Lower, the higher the credit quality of the borrower.
- Lower when the collateral security is in high demand or low supply.

INTRODUCTION TO FIXED-INCOME VALUATION
Cross-Reference to CFA Institute Assigned Reading #54

For an annual-coupon bond with N years to maturity:

$$\text{price} = \frac{\text{coupon}}{(1+\text{YTM})} + \frac{\text{coupon}}{(1+\text{YTM})^2} + ... + \frac{\text{coupon} + \text{principal}}{(1+\text{YTM})^N}$$

For a semiannual-coupon bond with N years to maturity:

$$\text{price} = \frac{\text{coupon}}{\left(1+\dfrac{\text{YTM}}{2}\right)} + \frac{\text{coupon}}{\left(1+\dfrac{\text{YTM}}{2}\right)^2} + \dots + \frac{\text{coupon} + \text{principal}}{\left(1+\dfrac{\text{YTM}}{2}\right)^{N\times2}}$$

A bond's price, YTM, coupon rate, and maturity are related as follows:

- Price and YTM are inversely related. An increase in YTM decreases the price and a decrease in YTM increases the price.
- If a bond's coupon rate is greater than its YTM, its price will be at a premium to par value. If a bond's coupon rate is less than its YTM, its price will be at a discount to par value.
- For a bond valued at a discount or premium, the price will converge to par value as the bond approaches maturity, assuming the issuer does not default.
- The percentage decrease in value when the YTM increases by a given amount is smaller than the increase in value when the YTM decreases by the same amount (the price-yield relationship is convex).
- Other things equal, the price of a bond with a lower coupon rate is more sensitive to a change in yield than is the price of a bond with a higher coupon rate.
- Other things equal, the price of a bond with a longer maturity is more sensitive to a change in yield than is the price of a bond with a shorter maturity.

The *constant-yield price trajectory* is the change in value as time passes for a discount or premium bond. It shows how the bond's price would change as time passes if its yield-to-maturity remained constant. If an investor sells a bond before maturity, a capital gain or loss is measured relative to the bond's constant-yield price trajectory.

Bonds can be valued using *spot rates*, which are market discount rates for a single payment to be received in the future. The discount rates for zero-coupon bonds are spot rates. We sometimes refer to spot rates as *zero-coupon rates* or *zero rates*.

The general equation for calculating a bond's value using spot rates (S_i) is:

$$\text{price} = \frac{\text{coupon}}{(1+S_1)} + \frac{\text{coupon}}{(1+S_2)^2} + \dots + \frac{\text{coupon} + \text{principal}}{(1+S_N)^N}$$

This price calculated using spot rates is sometimes called the *no-arbitrage price* of a bond because if a bond is priced differently, there will be a profit opportunity from arbitrage among bonds.

The *flat price* of a bond does not include interest accrued between coupon dates. The flat price is also known as a bond's *clean price* or *quoted price*. The *full price* of a bond includes interest accrued between coupon dates and is also known as the *dirty price* or *invoice price*.

Accrued interest since the last payment date can be calculated as the coupon payment times the portion of the current coupon period that has passed, based on actual calendar days (typically used for government bonds) or based on 30-day months and 360-day years (typically used for corporate bonds).

Matrix pricing is a method estimating bond YTMs using the YTMs of traded bonds that have credit quality very close to that of the non-traded or infrequently traded bonds of similar maturity and coupon. For example, the YTM for a non-traded six-year bond can be estimated by taking the average of the YTMs of similar seven-year and five-year bonds.

Yield Measures

The *effective yield* for a bond is the compound return.

Yields to maturity for bonds that make semiannual payments are quoted on a *semiannual bond basis*, which is two times the semiannual discount rate.

Yields calculated using the stated coupon payment dates are referred to as following *street convention*. When coupon dates fall on weekends and holidays, coupon payments are made the next business day. A yield calculated using these actual coupon payment dates is the *true yield*, which may be slightly lower than a street convention yield.

Current yield is a bond's annual coupon cash flows divided by the bond's flat price. This yield measure does not account for gains or losses as the bond's price moves toward its par value over time.

Simple yield is the sum of the annual coupon payment plus (minus) the straight-line amortization of a discount (premium), divided by the flat price. This yield measure assumes any discount or premium declines evenly over the remaining years to maturity.

For a callable bond, a *yield-to-call* can be calculated for each possible call date and price. The lowest of yield-to-maturity and the various yields-to-call is termed the *yield-to-worst*.

The *option-adjusted yield* for a callable bond is calculated by adding the value of the call option to the bond's flat price. The value of a callable bond is equal to the value of the bond if it did not have the call option, minus the value of the call option. The option-adjusted yield will be less than the yield-to-maturity for a callable bond.

For an FRN, the coupon rate is the reference rate plus or minus a margin based on the credit risk of the bond. Interest is paid in arrears, with the coupon rate for the next period set using the current reference rate.

The margin used to calculate the bond coupon payments is known as the *quoted margin*. The margin required to return the FRN to its par value is the *required margin* (or *discount margin*). When the credit quality of an FRN is unchanged, the quoted margin is equal to the required margin and the FRN returns to its par value at each reset date. If the credit quality of the issuer decreases, the quoted margin will be less than the required margin and the FRN will sell at a discount. If credit quality has improved, the quoted margin will be greater than the required margin and the FRN will sell at a premium.

Yields on money market securities can be stated as a discount from face value or as add-on yields, and can be based on a 360-day or 365-day basis. These securities should be compared based on their *bond-equivalent yield*, which is an add-on yield based on a 365-day year.

Yield Curves, Spot Rates, and Forward Rates

A *yield curve* shows yields by maturity. The *term structure of interest rates* refers to the yields at different maturities for like securities or interest rates.

A yield curve for coupon bonds shows the YTMs for coupon bonds at various maturities. A spot rate yield curve or *zero curve* shows the YTMs for zero-coupon bonds at various maturities. A par bond yield curve or *par curve* may be constructed from the spot curve to show the coupon rate that a hypothetical coupon bond at each maturity would need to have to be priced at par.

Forward rates are yields for future periods, such as the rate of interest on a three-year loan that would be made two years from now.

An example of forward rate notation is "2y3y." The "2y" refers to the number of years from today when a loan would begin, and the "3y" refers to the tenor (length) of the loan. Thus, 2y3y is the three-year rate two years from today. Forward rates may also be expressed in months. "6m3m" is a three-month rate beginning six months from today.

A *forward yield curve* shows the future rates for bonds or money market securities for the same maturities for annual periods in the future.

Forward rates and spot rates are related because borrowing for N years should have the same cost as borrowing for shorter periods that add up to N years. For example, borrowing for two years at the two-year spot rate should have the same cost as borrowing for the first year at the one-year spot rate and for the second year at the one-year forward rate one year from now. That is, $(1 + S_2)^2 = (1 + S_1)(1 + 1y1y)$. Based on these relationships between spot and forward rates, we can calculate forward rates from spot rates, calculate spot rates from forward rates, or value a bond using forward rates in the same way we valued a bond using spot rates earlier.

Example: Forward rate from spot rates

The two-year spot rate is 5.5% and the three-year spot rate is 6.0%. Calculate the one-year forward rate two years from now (2y1y).

Answer:

$$(1+S_3)^3 = (1 + S_2)^2(1 + 2y1y)$$

$$2y1y = \frac{(1+S_3)^3}{(1+S_2)^2} - 1 = \frac{(1.060)^3}{(1.055)^2} - 1 = 7.01\%$$

A quick way to approximate the forward rate is to ignore compounding:

$$3 \times S_3 \approx 2 \times S_2 + 2y1y$$

$$2y1y \approx 3(6.0\%) - 2(5.5\%)$$
$$18\% - 11\% = 7\%$$

Example: Spot rate from forward rates

The one-year spot rate is 3.5%. One-year forward rates are: 1y1y = 3.8%, 2y1y = 4.2%, and 3y1y = 4.5%. Calculate the four-year spot rate.

Answer:

The cost of borrowing today for four years should be the same as the cost of a sequence of four one-year loans that begin today and in each of the next three years:

$$(1 + S_4)^4 = (1 + S_1)(1 + 1y1y)(1 + 2y1y)(1 + 3y1y)$$

$$S_4 = [(1.035)(1.038)(1.042)(1.045)]^{1/4} - 1 = 3.9993\%$$

Here, too, we can approximate the result if we ignore compounding:

$$4 \times S_4 \approx S_1 + 1y1y + 2y1y + 3y1y$$

$$S_4 \approx (3.5\% + 3.8\% + 4.2\% + 4.5\%) / 4 = 4.0\%$$

Yield Spreads

A yield spread is the difference between the YTMs of two different bonds. Yield spreads are typically quoted in basis points.

A yield spread relative to a benchmark bond is known as a *benchmark spread*. For fixed-coupon bonds, on-the-run government bond yields for the same or nearest maturity are frequently used as benchmarks. A yield spread over a government bond is also known as a *G-spread*.

An alternative to using government bond yields as benchmarks is to use the fixed rates for interest rate swaps in the same currency and with the same tenor as a bond. Yield spreads relative to swap rates are known as *interpolated spreads* or *I-spreads*.

G-spreads and I-spreads are theoretically correct only if the spot yield curve is flat. However, the spot yield curve is not likely to be flat and is typically upward-sloping. A *zero-volatility spread* or *Z-spread* is derived by a method that accounts for the shape of the yield curve. The Z-spread is the single spread that, when added to each spot rate, produces a bond value that is equal to the current market value of a bond.

An *option-adjusted spread (OAS)* is used for bonds with embedded options. The OAS is the spread to the spot rate curve that the bond would have if it were option-free. For a callable bond, the OAS is less than the Z-spread and for a putable bond the OAS is greater than the Z-spread The OAS is the spread that accounts for differences between the liquidity and credit quality of the subject bond and the benchmark, with the effect on yield of any embedded options removed.

INTRODUCTION TO ASSET-BACKED SECURITIES
Cross-Reference to CFA Institute Assigned Reading #55

Securitization refers to a process by which financial assets (e.g., mortgages, accounts receivable, or automobile loans) are purchased by an entity that then issues *asset-backed securities* (ABS) for which the promised payments come from the cash flows from those financial assets.

The primary benefits of the securitization of financial assets are:

1. A reduction in funding costs for firms selling the financial assets to the securitizing entity.

2. An increase in the liquidity of the underlying financial assets.

Compared to a bank serving as a financial intermediary between borrowers and lenders, securitization also provides the following benefits:

- Reduced intermediation costs.
- The investors' legal claim to the underlying financial assets is stronger.
- ABS are often actively traded, increasing the liquidity of the originating bank's assets.
- Banks are able to originate more loans compared to relying only on bank funds.
- Allows investors to better match their preferred risk, maturity, and return characteristics.
- Greater diversification and risk reduction compared to individual loans (whole loans).

Parties to a Securitization Transaction and Their Functions

- The seller (e.g., bank) originates the loans and sells the portfolio of loans to the **special purpose entity** (SPE).

- The **issuer/trust** is the SPE that buys the loans from the seller and issues ABS to investors.
- The **servicer** collects the payments from the underlying loans and may or may not be the issuer.

Figure 1: Structure of Fred Motor Company Asset Securitization

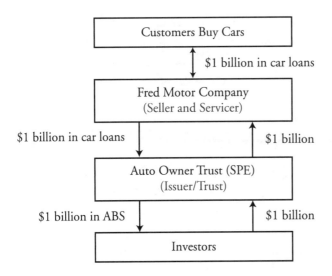

The ABS of a single SPE may have different priority of claims to the cash flow from the underlying assets, so that the most senior class (tranche) receives its promised payments before the next most senior tranche receives any cash flows, and so on. This is referred to as a **waterfall structure.**

Because the SPE is legally separate from the seller, financial distress or even bankruptcy of the seller may not affect the credit quality of the ABS. For this reason, the SPE is referred to as *bankruptcy remote* (from the seller). The credit rating of the ABS may be higher than the credit rating of the seller.

ABS are commonly backed by automobile loans, credit card receivables, mortgage and home equity loans, manufactured housing loans, student loans, Small Business Administration loans, corporate loans, corporate bonds, emerging market bonds, and structured financial products. ABS backed by mortgages are termed mortgage-backed securities (MBS).

Residential Mortgage Loans

Mortgage loans have real estate as collateral and typically have original maturities of 15–30 years in the United States and longer in some other countries.

A **fixed-rate mortgage** has an interest rate that is unchanged over the life of the mortgage.

An **adjustable-rate mortgage** (ARM), or variable-rate mortgage, has an interest rate that can change over the life of the mortgage. An **index-referenced mortgage** has an interest rate that changes based on a market determined reference rate.

A mortgage loan may have a fixed interest rate for some initial period that is adjusted after that. If the loan becomes an adjustable-rate mortgage after the initial fixed-rate period, it is called a **hybrid mortgage.** If the interest rate changes to a different fixed rate after the initial fixed-rate period, it is called a **rollover** or **renegotiable mortgage.**

A **convertible mortgage** is one for which the initial interest rate terms, fixed or adjustable, can be changed at the option of the borrower, to adjustable or fixed, for the remaining loan period.

A **fully amortizing** loan has no outstanding principal after the final payment is made. A **partially amortizing** loan includes some reduction of principal from each payment, but there is a principal payment to be made at maturity as well, called a **balloon** payment. An **interest-only** loan requires the repayment of the entire principal amount of the loan at maturity.

A loan may or may not have a **prepayment penalty**, an extra amount that is due when principal is repaid in greater amounts than scheduled in the loan payments. When there is no prepayment penalty, a decrease in interest rates can allow borrowers to refinance the loan at a lower interest rate and pay off (prepay) the remaining principal on the existing loan.

A prepayment penalty reduces the incentive to repay the loan principal early and protects the lender from receiving additional principal payments when rates are lower and less can be earned from reinvestment of the funds.

With a **non-recourse** loan, the only claim the lender has is to the property, which can be sold and the proceeds up to the amount of the amount owed used to satisfy the loan liability. With a **recourse** loan, the lender has a claim against the assets of the borrower for any excess of the amount owed above the proceeds from the property after it is repossessed and sold.

Residential Mortgage-backed Securities (RMBS)

Agency RMBS are issued by the Government National Mortgage Association (GNMA), the Federal National Mortgage Association (FNMA), and the Federal Home Loan Mortgage Corporation (FHLMC).

GNMA securities are guaranteed and are considered to be backed by the full faith and credit of the U.S. government. FNMA and FHLMC also guarantee the MBS they issue but are **government-sponsored enterprises** (GSE). Credit quality, while high, is considered slightly lower than that of GNMA securities.

Agency RMBS are **mortgage pass-through** securities in that the interest and principal payments received on the pool of mortgages underlying the MBS are passed along to securities holders in proportion to their ownership of the issue. Because of administrative fees, the **pass-through rate** that investors receive is less than the coupon rates on the underlying mortgages.

The mortgages in the pool typically have different maturities and different mortgage rates. The **weighted average maturity** (WAM) of the pool is equal to the principal-weighted average of the final maturities of all the mortgages in the pool. The **weighted average coupon** (WAC) of the pool is the principal-weighted average of the interest rates of all the mortgages in the pool.

To be included in agency MBS pools, mortgages must be **conforming loans**; that is, they meet certain required criteria including a minimum percentage down payment, a maximum loan-to-value (LTV) ratio, maximum size, minimum documentation required, and insurance purchased by the borrower. Loans that do not meet the standards are called **non-conforming loans** and can be securitized by private companies for **non-agency RMBS**.

The mortgages underlying agency RMBS have no prepayment penalties and are subject to **prepayment risk. Extension risk** refers to the risk of receiving principal repayments more slowly than expected, and **contraction risk** refers to the risk of a prepayment rate that is more rapid than expected (principal is returns earlier).

The **conditional prepayment rate** (CPR) is an annualized measure of prepayments. The **Public Securities Association** (PSA) *prepayment benchmark* is expressed as a monthly series of CPRs. A PSA of 50 means that prepayments are 50% of the PSA benchmark CPR, and a PSA of 130 means that prepayments are 130% of the PSA benchmark CPR.

To achieve a credit rating high enough to attract institutional lenders, some form of **credit enhancement** is typically included with ABS. **External credit enhancements** are financial guarantees from third parties that support the performance of the ABS. **Internal credit enhancements** include:

- Reserve funds (either a cash reserve or excess spread of scheduled interest payments from the underlying securities over that promised to ABS holders).
- Overcollateralization (the outstanding principal amount of the ABS is less than that of the underlying securities).
- Senior and subordinated structures (credit risk is shifted from the senior tranche to the subordinated tranche).

Collateralized mortgage obligations (CMOs) are securities that are collateralized by RMBS. Each CMO has multiple tranches, each with a different risk exposure.

With **sequential tranches**, principal repayments flow first to one tranche until its principal balance is repaid and then to the second sequential tranche until its principal value is paid off, and so forth. All tranches receive interest on their beginning-of-period principal values.

A CMO structure can have a **planned amortization class (PAC) tranche** with reduced prepayment risk because **support tranches** take on more prepayment risk. If principal prepayments of the MBS accelerate, the additional payments go to the support tranches and if prepayments are low, principal payments to the support tranches are reduced. Under this structure the PAC tranche can maintain its promised payment schedule within certain bounds of PSA, and these bounds are the PAC's *initial collar*.

Commercial mortgage-backed securities (CMBS) are backed by income-producing real estate [e.g., apartments (multi-family), warehouses (industrial use property), shopping centers, office buildings, health care facilities, senior housing, or hotel/resort property].

Commercial mortgages are non-recourse loans, so the collateral property's value (ability to generate cash flows) is the only source of repayment of the loans. For this reason the credit rating for a CMBS is often focused on two measures: the property's **loan-to value (LTV)** ratio and **debt service coverage** ratio.

$$\text{loan-to-value ratio} = \frac{\text{current mortgage amount}}{\text{current appraised value}}$$

$$\text{debt-to-service coverage ratio} = \frac{\text{net operating income}}{\text{debt service}}$$

Either a lower LTV ratio or a higher debt service coverage ratio can increase the credit rating for a CMBS.

Most CMBS have a senior-subordinated structure so that credit risk is first absorbed by the least senior tranche and then by each more senior tranche in turn as necessary. With this structure, the most senior tranches carry relatively little credit risk, and the lowest priority tranches are quite risky and referred to as the *first-loss tranche* or *equity tranche*.

Call protection (prepayment protection) can be provided for CMBS either at the individual mortgage level or for the CMBS as a whole. Loan level call protection, in various amounts, can be provided by:

- A **prepayment lockout period** of three to five years, during which the loan cannot be prepaid.
- **Defeasance:** any prepayments are used to purchase Treasury securities that will generate cash flows to make future loan payments.
- **Prepayment penalty:** a percentage of the principal amount that must be paid if the loan is paid off early.
- **Yield maintenance (make whole) charges** require an extra payment in the event of an early loan payoff that fully compensates lenders from losses due to early retirement of principal in a lower interest rate environment.

Call protection at the CMBS level is sometimes provided with a senior-subordinated structure so that lower priority tranches receive prepayments first and are first to absorb losses from defaults on the underlying mortgages.

Non-Mortgage ABS

Auto loan ABS are backed by automobile loans, which are typically fully amortizing but with shorter maturities than residential mortgages. Prepayments result when autos are sold or traded in, stolen or wrecked and paid off from insurance proceeds, refinanced, or paid off early by the borrower.

Credit card ABS are backed by credit card receivables, which are revolving debt (non-amortizing). Credit card ABS typically have an initial **lockout period** (of as long as 10 years) during which only interest is paid to investors, and all principal payments on the receivables are used to purchase additional receivables. Credit card ABS can be fixed-rate or floating-rate securities.

Collateralized Debt Obligations

Collateralized debt obligations (CDOs) are structured securities backed by a pool of debt obligations that is managed by a collateral manager. CDOs include:

- Collateralized bond obligations (CBOs) backed by corporate and emerging market debt.
- Collateralized loan obligations (CLOs) backed by leveraged bank loans.
- Structured finance CDOs backed by residential or commercial MBS, ABS, or other CDOs.
- Synthetic CDOs backed by credit default swaps on structured securities.

CDOs issue three classes of bonds (tranches): senior bonds, mezzanine bonds, and subordinated bonds (sometimes called the equity or residual tranche). The subordinated tranche has characteristics more similar to those of equity investments than bond investments.

An investment in the equity or residual tranche can be viewed as a leveraged investment where borrowed funds (raised from selling the senior and mezzanine tranches) are used to purchase the debt securities in the CDO's collateral pool.

The collateral manager may use interest earned on portfolio securities, cash from maturing portfolio securities, and cash from the sale of portfolio securities to cover the promised payments to holders of the CDO's senior and mezzanine bonds. Any excess above that flows to the equity tranche.

In an *arbitrage CDO*, the return promised to the CDO securities is less than the promised return on the underlying securities, so that in the absence of default, this excess return is the cash flow to the residual tranche.

STUDY SESSION 16: FIXED INCOME—ANALYSIS OF RISK

UNDERSTANDING FIXED-INCOME RISK AND RETURN
Cross-Reference to CFA Institute Assigned Reading #56

The three sources of returns from investing in a fixed-rate bond are:

1. Coupon and principal payments.

2. Interest earned on reinvested coupon payments.

3. Capital gain or loss if the bond is sold prior to maturity.

For a bond that does not default, and assuming the rate earned on reinvested coupons is equal to the YTM:

- An investor who holds a fixed-rate bond to maturity will earn an annualized rate of return equal to the YTM of the bond when purchased.
- An investor who sells a bond prior to maturity will earn a rate of return equal to the YTM at purchase if the bond's YTM when sold is equal to the YTM of the bond when purchased.

If the YTM of the bond decreases (increases) shortly after issuance:

- An investor who sells the bond in the short term will have an increased (decreased) return due to the increase (decrease) in the sale price of the bond.
- An investor who holds the bond to maturity (or other suitably long term) will have a decreased (increased) return due to the decreased (increased) reinvestment income earned.

These results illustrate the trade-off between *market price risk* (the uncertainty about price due to uncertainty about market YTM) and *reinvestment risk* (uncertainty about the total of coupon payments and reinvestment income on those payments due to the uncertainty about future reinvestment rates). For an investor with a short investment horizon, market price risk is greater than reinvestment risk. For an investor with a long investment horizon, reinvestment risk is greater than market price risk.

The investment horizon at which these risks just offset is known as a bond's **Macaulay duration**. A bond's annual Macaulay duration is calculated as the weighted average of the number of years until each of the bond's promised cash flows is to be paid, where the weights are the present values of each cash flow as a percentage of the bond's full value. For a semiannual-pay bond, Macaulay duration is calculated as a number of semiannual periods and divided by two to get the annual Macaulay duration.

The difference between a bond's Macaulay duration and the bondholder's investment horizon is referred to as a *duration gap*. A positive duration gap (Macaulay duration greater than the investment horizon) exposes the investor to market price risk from increasing interest rates. A negative duration gap (Macaulay duration less than the investment horizon) exposes the investor to reinvestment risk from decreasing interest rates.

Modified duration is calculated as Macaulay duration divided by one plus the bond's yield to maturity. Modified duration provides an approximate percentage

©2015 Kaplan, Inc.

change in a bond's price for a 1% change in yield to maturity. For a given change in YTM, the price change can be calculated as:

approximate percentage change in bond price = −modified duration × ΔYTM

We can approximate modified duration directly using bond values for an increase and for a decrease in YTM of the same size:

$$\text{approximate modified duration} = \frac{V_- - V_+}{2 \times V_0 \times \Delta\text{YTM}}$$

where:
V_0 = the initial price
V_- = the price of the bond if YTM is decreased by ΔYTM
V_+ = the price of the bond if the YTM is increased by ΔYTM

Modified duration is not appropriate for bonds with embedded options because their future cash flows may change depending on the level and path of interest rates. For these bonds we use **effective duration**, which uses the change in the benchmark yield curve, rather than the change in YTM, to generate V_- and V_+:

$$\text{effective duration} = \frac{V_- - V_+}{2 \times V_0 \times \Delta\text{curve}}$$

Other things equal, a bond's interest rate risk (as measured by duration) is:

- Usually greater with a longer maturity. We must say "usually" because there are instances where an increase in a discount coupon bond's maturity will decrease its Macaulay duration.
- Less with a higher coupon rate. When more of a bond's value will be from payments received sooner, the value of the bond is less sensitive to changes in yield.
- Less with a higher YTM. This is because the price-yield relationship is convex. At lower yields, the price-yield curve has a steeper slope, indicating that price is more sensitive to a given change in yield.
- Less with an embedded call or put option.

The duration concept may be applied to a bond portfolio. There are two approaches to estimating **portfolio duration**:

1. Calculate the weighted average number of periods until the portfolio's cash flows will be received. This approach is theoretically correct but is not often used in practice, and cannot be used if some portfolio bonds have embedded options.

2. Take a weighted average of the durations of the individual bonds in the portfolio, where the weights are the full price of each bond as a proportion of the total portfolio value. A limitation of this approach is that it assumes a parallel shift in the yield curve but the effective duration of bonds with embedded options can be used.

The **money duration** (also called *dollar duration*) of a bond position is expressed in currency units. Multiplying the money duration of a bond times a given change in YTM will provide an estimate of the change in bond value for that change in YTM. Money duration is sometimes expressed as money duration per 100 currency units of bond par value.

Duration is an adequate measure of bond price risk only for parallel shifts in the yield curve. The impact of nonparallel shifts can be measured using **key rate duration**. A key rate duration is the sensitivity of the value of a bond or portfolio to changes in the spot rate for a specific maturity, holding other spot rates constant. A bond or portfolio will have a key rate duration for each maturity range on the spot rate curve.

The **price value of a basis point** (PVBP) is the money change in the full price of a bond when its YTM changes by one *basis point*, or 0.01%. We can calculate the PVBP directly by calculating the average of the decrease in the full value of a bond when its YTM increases by one basis point and the increase in the full value when its YTM decreases by one basis point.

Because modified duration is a linear approximation of the relationship between yield and price, duration-based estimates of a bond's full price become increasingly poor for larger changes in YTM. Estimates of the price impact of a change in yield can be improved by including **convexity**, a measure of the curvature of the price-yield relation. A bond's convexity can be estimated as:

$$\text{approximate convexity} = \frac{V_- + V_+ - 2V_0}{(\Delta YTM)^2 \times V_0}$$

Effective convexity, like effective duration, must be used for bonds with embedded options.

$$\text{effective convexity} = \frac{V_- + V_+ - 2V_0}{(\Delta curve)^2 \times V_0}$$

The estimated price change including the convexity adjustment is:

$$\text{change in full bond price} = -(\text{annual modified duration})(\Delta YTM) + (1/2)(\text{annual convexity})(\Delta YTM)^2$$

While the convexity of any option-free bond is positive, the convexity of a callable bond can be negative at low yields. The call price puts an effective limit on increases in bond value because at low yields the bond is likely to be called. For a bond with negative convexity, the price increase from a decrease in YTM is smaller than the price decrease from an increase in YTM.

Bondholders prefer greater convexity, other things equal. A bond with greater convexity is more price-sensitive to decreases in YTM, and less price-sensitive to increases in YTM, than a bond with less convexity. That is, with greater convexity a bond's price will increase more, and decrease less, in response to a given change in YTM.

In calculating duration and convexity, we implicitly assume the yield curve shifts in a parallel manner. In practice, this is often not the case. A shorter term bond can have more price volatility than a longer term bond with a greater duration if the volatility of the shorter term yield is greater. The *term structure of yield volatility* refers to the relation between the volatility of bond yields and their times to maturity.

FUNDAMENTALS OF CREDIT ANALYSIS
Cross-Reference to CFA Institute Assigned Reading #57

Credit risk refers to potential losses from the failure of a borrower to make promised payments and has two components: default risk and loss severity. **Default risk** is the probability that a borrower will fail to pay interest or principal when due. **Loss severity** refers to the value (in money or as a percentage) that a bond investor will lose if the issuer defaults.

The **expected loss** is equal to the default risk multiplied by the loss severity. Percentage loss severity is equal to one minus the **recovery rate**, the percentage of a bond's value an investor will receive if the issuer defaults.

Bonds with greater credit risk trade at higher yields than bonds thought to be free of credit risk. The difference in yield between a credit-risky bond and a credit-risk-free bond of similar maturity is called its **yield spread**. Bond prices decrease when their yield spreads increase.

The yield spread also compensates investors for liquidity risk. **Market liquidity risk** is the risk of receiving less than market value when selling bonds and is reflected in their bid-ask spreads. **Downgrade risk** refers to the risk that spreads will increase because the issuer has become less creditworthy so its credit rating is lowered.

The priority of a bond's claim to the issuer's assets and cash flows is referred to as its **seniority ranking**. Secured debt is backed by collateral, while unsecured debt (debentures) is a general claim against the issuer.

The seniority (and recovery rate) rankings for various types of debt securities (highest priority to lowest) are:

1. First lien or first mortgage.

2. Senior secured debt.

3. Junior secured debt.

4. Senior unsecured debt.

5. Senior subordinated debt.

6. Subordinated debt.

7. Junior subordinated debt.

All debt securities in the same category have the same priority and are said to rank **pari passu**. Strict priority of claims is not always applied in practice. In a bankruptcy, the court may approve a reorganization plan that does not strictly conform to the priority of claims.

Credit Ratings

Credit rating agencies assign ratings to corporate issuers based on the creditworthiness of their senior unsecured debt ratings, referred to as **corporate family ratings** (CFR), and to individual debt securities, referred to as **corporate credit ratings** (CCR). Higher ratings indicate a lower expected default rate. **Notching** is the practice of assigning different ratings to bonds of the same issuer.

Figure 2 shows ratings scales used by Standard & Poor's, Moody's, and Fitch. Bonds with ratings of Baa3/BBB– or higher are considered **investment grade**. Bonds rated Ba1/BB+ or lower are considered non-investment grade and are often called **high yield bonds** or **junk bonds**.

Figure 2: Credit Rating Categories

(a) Investment grade ratings		(b) Non-investment grade ratings	
Moody's	*Standard &Poor's, Fitch*	*Moody's*	*Standard &Poor's, Fitch*
Aaa	AAA	Ba1	BB+
Aa1	AA+	Ba2	BB
Aa2	AA	Ba3	BB–
Aa3	AA–	B1	B+
A1	A+	B2	B
A2	A	B3	B–
A3	A–	Caa1	CCC+
Baa1	BBB+	Caa2	CCC
Baa2	BBB	Caa3	CCC–
Baa3	BBB–	Ca	CC
		C	C
		C	D

In a holding company structure, a subsidiary's debt covenants may prohibit the transfer of cash or assets to the parent until after the subsidiary's debt is serviced. The parent company's bonds are thus effectively subordinated to the subsidiary's bonds. This is referred to as **structural subordination** and is considered by rating agencies when notching an issue credit rating.

Relying on ratings from credit rating agencies has risks. Credit ratings change over time and ratings mistakes happen. Event risks specific to a company or industry such as natural disasters, acquisitions, and equity buybacks using debt, are difficult to anticipate and therefore not easily captured in credit ratings. Finally, changes in yield spreads and bond prices anticipate ratings changes and reflect expected losses, while ratings are based solely on default risk.

Credit Analysis

One way to represent the key components of credit analysis is by the **four Cs** of credit analysis: **capacity, collateral, covenants**, and **character**. *Capacity* refers to a corporate borrower's ability repay its debt obligations on time. *Collateral* refers to the value of a borrower's assets. *Covenants* are the terms and conditions the borrowers and lenders have agreed to as part of a bond issue. *Character* refers to management's integrity and its commitment to repay.

Capacity to repay is assessed by examining: (1) industry structure, (2) industry fundamentals, and (3) company fundamentals. Industry structure can be described by Porter's five forces: rivalry among existing competitors, threat of new entrants, threat of substitute products, bargaining power of buyers, and bargaining power of suppliers. Analysis of industry fundamentals focuses on industry cyclicality (more cyclicality indicates greater credit risk) and growth prospects (earnings growth indicates less credit risk). Company fundamentals include competitive position, operating history, management's strategy and execution, and leverage and coverage ratios.

Collateral analysis is more important for less creditworthy companies. The market value of a company's assets can be difficult to observe directly. High depreciation expense relative to capital expenditures may signal that management is not investing sufficiently and the quality of the company's assets may be poor. Some intangible assets that can be sold to generate cash flows, such as patents, are considered high-quality collateral, whereas goodwill is not considered a high-quality, intangible asset.

Bond covenants protect lenders while leaving some operating flexibility to the borrowers to run the company.

Character analysis includes an assessment of management's ability to develop a sound strategy; management's past performance in operating the company without bankruptcies or restructurings; accounting policies and tax strategies that may be hiding problems, such as revenue recognition issues, frequent restatements, and frequently changing auditors; any record of fraud or other legal and regulatory problems; and prior treatment of bondholders, such as benefits to equity holders at the expense of debt holders through debt-financed acquisitions and special dividends.

Financial ratios used in credit analysis

Profit and cash flow metrics commonly used in ratio analysis include earnings before interest, taxes, depreciation, and amortization (EBITDA); funds from operations (FFO), which is net income from continuing operations plus depreciation, amortization, deferred taxes, and noncash items; free cash flow before dividends; and free cash flow after dividends.

Two primary categories of ratios for credit analysis are leverage ratios and coverage ratios. The most common measures of leverage used by credit analysts are the debt-to-capital ratio, the debt-to-EBITDA ratio, the FFO-to-debt ratio, and the FCF after dividends-to-debt ratio. The most commonly used coverage ratios are EBITDA-to-interest and EBIT-to-interest. When calculating ratios, analysts should adjust debt reported on the financial statements by including the firm's obligations, such as underfunded pension plans (net pension liabilities), and off-balance-sheet liabilities, such as operating leases. In general, higher coverage ratios and lower leverage ratios are associated with higher credit quality. A firm's ratios are compared to benchmark ratios in determining its overall credit rating.

Yield Spreads

A bond's yield spread is primarily affected by five interrelated factors: the credit cycle, economic conditions, financial market performance, broker-dealer capital, and general market demand and supply. Yield spreads on lower-quality issues tend to be more volatile than spreads on higher-quality issues.

High Yield Debt

Reasons for non-investment grade ratings may include high leverage; unproven operating history; low or negative free cash flow; high sensitivity to business cycles; low confidence in management; unclear competitive advantages; large off-balance-sheet liabilities; or an industry in decline.

Special considerations for high yield bonds include their liquidity, projections of earnings and cash flow, debt structure, corporate structure, and covenants.

Sources of liquidity (in order of reliability) include:

1. Balance sheet cash.

2. Working capital.

3. Operating cash flow.

4. Bank credit.

5. Issuing equity.

6. Sales of assets.

To understand difficulties firms may have in meeting their debt payments, analysts should include stress scenarios when forecasting future earnings and cash flows and consider the effects of possible changes in capital expenditures and working capital investment.

High yield issuers' capital structures often include different types of debt with several levels of seniority and hence varying levels of potential loss severity.

Companies for which secured bank debt is a high proportion of the capital structure are said to be *top heavy* and have less capacity to borrow from banks in financially stressful periods. When an issuer has multiple layers of debt with a variety of expected recovery rates, a credit analyst should calculate leverage for each level of the debt structure.

Many high-yield companies use a holding company structure so that structural subordination can lead to lower recovery rates for the parent company's debt.

Important covenants for high yield debt may include a **change of control put** that gives debt holders the right to require the issuer to buy back debt in the event of an acquisition; restricted payments to equity holders; limitations on liens; and **restricted subsidiaries**. Restricted subsidiaries' cash flows and assets are designated to service the debt of the parent holding company. This benefits creditors of holding companies because their debt is pari passu with the debt of restricted subsidiaries, rather than structurally subordinated.

Sovereign and Non-Sovereign Government Debt

Sovereign debt is issued by national governments. Sovereign credit analysis must assess both the government's *ability* to service debt and its *willingness* to do so. Willingness is important because bondholders usually have no legal recourse if a national government refuses to pay its debts.

A basic framework for evaluating and assigning a credit rating to sovereign debt includes five key areas:

1. *Institutional effectiveness*: Successful policymaking, absence of corruption, and commitment to honor debts.

2. *Economic prospects*: Growth trends, demographics, income per capita, and size of government relative to the private economy.

3. *International investment position*: Foreign reserves, external debt, and the status of the country's currency in international markets.

4. *Fiscal flexibility*: Willingness and ability to increase revenue or cut expenditures to ensure debt service, and trends in debt as a percentage of GDP.

5. *Monetary flexibility*: Ability to use monetary policy for domestic economic objectives (this might be lacking with exchange rate targeting or membership in a monetary union) and credibility and effectiveness of monetary policy.

Credit rating agencies assign each national government a **local currency debt rating** and a **foreign currency debt rating**. Foreign currency debt typically has a higher default rate and a lower credit rating because the government must purchase foreign currency in the open market to make payments. In contrast, local currency debt can be repaid by simply printing more currency. Ratings can differ as much as two notches for local currency and foreign currency bonds.

Municipal bonds are issued by state and local governments or their agencies. Municipal bonds usually have lower default rates than corporate bonds with same credit ratings. Most municipal bonds can be classified as general obligation bonds or revenue bonds. **General obligation** (GO) **bonds** are unsecured bonds backed by the full faith and credit (taxing power) of the issuer. **Revenue bonds** finance specific projects. Revenue bonds often have higher credit risk than GO bonds because the project is the sole source of funds to service the debt.

Municipal governments' ability to service their general obligation debt depends ultimately on the local economy. Economic factors to assess include employment, trends in per capita income and per capita debt, tax base, demographics, and ability to attract new jobs. Credit analysts must also observe revenue variability through economic cycles. Relying on tax revenues that are highly variable over an economic cycles indicate higher credit risk. Municipalities may have underfunded long-term obligations such as pension and other post-retirement benefits.

Analysis of revenue bonds requires both analysis of the project and analysis of the financing structure of the project. A key metric for revenue bonds is the **debt service coverage ratio**, which is the ratio of the project's net revenue to the required interest and principal payments on the bonds.

DERIVATIVES

Weight on Exam	5%
SchweserNotes™ Reference	Book 5, Pages 154–201

DERIVATIVE MARKETS AND INSTRUMENTS
Cross-Reference to CFA Institute Assigned Reading #58

Overview of Derivative Contracts

A *derivative* is a security that *derives* its value from the value of, or return on, another asset or security. A physical exchange exists for many options contracts and futures contracts. Exchange-traded derivatives are standardized and backed by a clearinghouse.

Forwards and *swaps* are custom instruments traded/created by dealers in a market with no central location. A dealer market with no central location is referred to as an over-the-counter market. They are largely unregulated markets, and each contract is with a counterparty, which exposes the owner of a derivative to default risk (when the counterparty does not honor their commitment).

Some *options* trade in the over-the-counter market, notably bond options.

A **forward commitment** is a legally binding promise to perform some action in the future. Forward commitments include forward contracts, futures contracts, and swaps. Forward contracts and futures contracts can be written on equities, indexes, bonds, foreign currencies, physical assets, or interest rates.

A **contingent claim** is a claim (to a payoff) that depends on a particular event. Options are contingent claims that depend on a stock price at some future date.

Credit derivatives are contingent claims that depend on a credit event such as a default or ratings downgrade.

The criticism of derivatives is that they are "too risky," especially to investors with limited knowledge of sometimes complex instruments. Because of the high leverage involved in derivatives payoffs, they are sometimes likened to gambling.

The benefits of derivatives markets are that they:

- Provide price information.
- Allow risk to be managed and shifted among market participants.
- Reduce transactions costs.

Forward Contracts

In a forward contract, one party agrees to buy and the counterparty to sell a physical or financial asset at a specific price on a specific date in the future. A forward contract can be used to reduce or eliminate uncertainty about the future price of an asset (hedge) or to speculate on movements in asset prices.

Typically, neither party to the contract makes a payment at the initiation of a forward contract. If the expected future price of the asset increases over the life of the contract, the right to buy at the forward price (the long) will have positive value, and the obligation to sell (the short) will have an equal negative value.

If the expected future price of the asset falls below the forward price, the result is opposite and the right to sell (at an above-market price) will have a positive value.

A deliverable forward contract is settled by the short delivering the underlying asset to the long. Other forward contracts are settled in cash. In a cash-settled forward contract, one party pays cash to the other when the contract expires based on the difference between the forward price and the market price of the underlying asset at the settlement date.

Futures Contracts

Futures contracts are similar to forward contracts in that both:

- Can be either deliverable or cash-settled contracts.
- Have contract prices set so each side of the contract has a value of zero at the initiation of the contract.

Futures contracts differ from forward contracts in the following ways:

- Futures contracts trade on organized exchanges. Forwards are private contracts and typically do not trade.
- Futures contracts are standardized. Forwards are customized contracts satisfying the specific needs of the parties involved.
- A clearinghouse is the counterparty to all futures contracts. Forwards are contracts with the originating counterparty and, therefore, have counterparty (credit) risk.
- The government regulates futures markets. Forward contracts are usually not regulated and do not trade in organized markets.

The **settlement price** is an average of the prices of the trades during the last period of trading, called the closing period, which is set by the exchange. It is used to calculate the daily gain or loss at the end of each trading day. On its final day of trading, the settlement price is equal to the spot price of the underlying asset.

As with forwards, the buyer of a futures contract has a long position, while the seller of a futures contract has a short position. For each contract traded, there is a buyer (long) and a seller (short).

Open interest is the number of futures contracts of a specific kind outstanding at any given time. Open interest increases when traders enter new long and short positions and decreases when traders exit existing positions.

Speculators use futures contracts to gain exposure to changes in the price of the asset underlying a futures contract. In contrast, **hedgers** use futures contracts to reduce an existing exposure to price changes in the asset.

Each futures exchange has a **clearinghouse**. It guarantees traders in the futures market will honor their obligations by acting as the buyer to every seller and the seller to every buyer. By doing this, the clearinghouse allows either side of the trade to reverse positions at a future date without having to contact the other side of the initial trade. The guarantee of the clearinghouse removes counterparty risk from futures contracts.

In the futures markets, margin must be deposited by both the long and the short as a performance guarantee prior to entering into a futures contract. This provides protection for the clearinghouse. Each day, the margin balance in a futures account is marked to market; that is, gains are added to the margin account and losses deducted.

Initial margin is the amount that must be deposited in a futures account before a trade may be made.

Maintenance margin is the minimum amount of margin that must be maintained. If the margin balance in the account falls below the maintenance margin, additional funds must be deposited to bring the margin balance back up to the initial margin amount. Margin requirements are set by the clearinghouse.

Exchange members are prohibited from executing trades at prices outside set price limits. If the equilibrium price at which traders would willingly trade is above the upper limit or below the lower limit, trades cannot take place.

Swaps

Swaps are agreements to exchange a series of payments on periodic *settlement dates* over a certain time period. At each settlement date, the two payments are *netted* so that only one (net) payment is made. The party with the greater liability makes a payment to the other party. The length of the swap is termed the *tenor* of the swap, and the contract ends on the termination date.

Swaps are similar to forwards in several ways:

- Swaps typically require no payment by either party at initiation.
- Swaps are custom instruments.
- Swaps are not traded in any organized secondary market.
- Swaps are largely unregulated.
- Default risk is an important aspect of the contracts.
- Most participants in the swaps market are large institutions.

In a **plain vanilla interest rate swap**:

- One party makes fixed-rate interest payments on a notional principal amount specified in the swap in return for floating-rate payments from the other party.
- The party who wants floating-rate interest payments agrees to pay fixed-rate interest and has the *pay-fixed* side of the swap. The other party is known as the *pay-floating* side.
- The payments owed by one party to the other are based on a notional principal that is stated in the swap contract.

In a **basis swap**, one set of floating-rate payments is swapped for another.

Options

An option contract gives its owner the right, but not the obligation, to either buy or sell an underlying asset at a given price (the exercise price or strike price). The option buyer can choose whether to exercise an option, whereas the seller is obligated to perform if the buyer exercises the option. There are four possible options positions:

1. Long call: the buyer of a call option—has the right to buy an underlying asset.

2. Short call: the writer (seller) of a call option—has the obligation to sell the underlying asset.

3. Long put: the buyer of a put option—has the right to sell the underlying asset.

4. Short put: the writer (seller) of a put option—has the obligation to buy the underlying asset.

The price of an option is also referred to as the option premium.

American options may be exercised at any time up to and including the contract's expiration date.

European options can be exercised only on the contract's expiration date.

Credit Derivatives

A credit derivative is a contract that provides a bondholder (lender) with protection against a downgrade or a default by the borrower.

A **credit default swap** (CDS) is an insurance contract against default. A bondholder pays a series of cash flows to a credit protection seller and receives a payment if the bond issuer defaults.

A **credit spread option** is typically a call option that is based on a bond's yield spread relative to a benchmark. If the bond's credit quality decreases, its yield spread will increase and the bondholder will collect a payoff on the option.

Arbitrage

Arbitrage opportunities arise when assets are mispriced. Trading by arbitrageurs will continue until they affect supply and demand enough to bring asset prices to efficient (no-arbitrage) levels.

There are two arbitrage arguments that are particularly useful in the study and use of derivatives:

1. The first is based on the "law of one price." Two securities or portfolios that have identical cash flows in the future, regardless of future events, should have the same price. If A and B have identical future payoffs, and A is priced lower than B, buy A and sell B.

2. The second type of arbitrage is used when two securities with uncertain returns can be combined in a portfolio that will have a certain payoff. If a portfolio consisting of A and B has a certain payoff, the portfolio should yield the risk-free rate.

BASICS OF DERIVATIVE PRICING AND VALUATION
Cross-Reference to CFA Institute Assigned Reading #59

No-Arbitrage Valuation

Typically, we value a risky asset by calculating the present value of its expected future cash flows using a discount rate that depends on the risk of the expected cash flows and the risk aversion of investors.

In contrast, we value **derivative securities** based on a no-arbitrage condition. We can **replicate** the cash flows from a risky asset with a portfolio that includes a derivative security. Unless the asset and the portfolio that replicates its cash flows sell at the same price, there is an **arbitrage opportunity** to sell the one with the higher price and buy the one with the lower price. Arbitrage opportunities will be rapidly exploited so the prices of derivative securities are driven to their **no-arbitrage values**. In practice, arbitrage will ensure that derivatives prices deviate from their no-arbitrage values by no more than the transaction costs of executing the arbitrage strategy.

With a long and short position in an asset and a replicating portfolio, the payoffs on this *hedged* portfolio are certain, so investor risk aversion does not affect the value of the hedged portfolio or the value of the derivative. Because of this, we sometimes refer to this method as **risk-neutral pricing**.

As a simple example of a hedged portfolio, consider a long position in a risky asset selling for S_0 and a short forward contract on the asset at a forward price of $F_0(T)$. If there are no costs or benefits to holding the asset, the cost of buying the asset and holding it until settlement of the forward contract at time T is simply S_0 plus the opportunity cost of the funds for the period, $S_0 (1 + Rf)^T$.

The forward hedge requires the asset be sold for $F_0(T)$ at time T so there is no arbitrage opportunity if the forward contract is priced so that $F_0(T) = S_0 (1 + Rf)^T$, the opportunity cost of buying and holding the asset until time T.

If the equality holds, the derivative is currently at its no-arbitrage price. As the spot price, risk-free rate, and certain payoff at time T are all known, the equation can be used to solve for the no-arbitrage price of the derivative.

In general, with "+" a long position and "−" a short position, we have:

> risky asset + derivative = risk free asset

so that

risky asset – risk free asset = – derivative position

derivative position – risk free asset = – risky asset

Pricing and Valuing Derivatives

The *price* of a derivative is the price or interest rate specified in the contract. At initiation, the derivative price is typically set so that the *value* of the derivative is zero. During the life of the derivative contract, increases in the spot price of the underlying asset increase the value of a long derivative position, and decreases in the spot price of the asset decrease the value of a long derivative position.

Previously, we explained the no-arbitrage relation for a forward contract on an asset with no storage costs or benefits to holding it. In this case, the *net cost of carry* is the opportunity cost of invested funds, which we assume to be the risk-free rate, Rf. Based on the condition of no-arbitrage, the forward price at contract initiation must be:

$$F_0(T) = S_0(1 + Rf)^T$$

If the forward price were $F_0(T)+ > S_0(1 + Rf)^T$, an arbitrageur could:

- Take a short position in (sell) the forward contract.
- Buy the asset at S_0, with funds borrowed at Rf.

At time T, the arbitrageur would deliver the asset and receive $F_0(T)+$, repay the loan at a cost of $S_0(1 + Rf)^T$, and keep the difference between $F_0(T)+$ and $S_0(1 + Rf)^T$.

If the forward price were $F_0(T)- < S_0(1 + Rf)^T$, an arbitrageur could:

- Take a long position in (buy) the forward contract.
- Short sell the asset and invest the proceeds at Rf.

At time T, the arbitrageur would receive $S_0(1 + Rf)^T$ from investing the proceeds of the short sale, pay $F_0(T)$ to purchase the asset (to cover the short position), and keep the difference between $S_0(1 + Rf)^T$ and $F_0(T)-$.

This process is the mechanism that ensures $F_0(T)$ is the (no-arbitrage) price in a forward contract that has zero value at t = 0.

Valuing a forward contract. At initiation:

$$V_0(T) = S_0 - \frac{F_0(T)}{(1+Rf)^T} = 0, \text{ because } S_0 = \frac{F_0(T)}{(1+Rf)^T}$$

At any time = t prior to settlement, t < T, the value of the forward is the spot price of the asset minus the present value of the forward price:

$$V_t(T) = S_t - \frac{F_0(T)}{(1+Rf)^{T-t}}$$

At settlement, the payoff to a long forward position is:

$$S_T - F_0(T)$$

Holding Costs and Benefits

In addition to the opportunity cost of the funds, Rf, there may be costs of holding an asset such as storage and insurance costs, especially with physical assets.

There also may be benefits to holding the asset. These benefits may be *monetary* if the asset makes cash payments (e.g., interest, dividends) over the life of the derivative. There may also be *nonmonetary* benefits to owning an asset (e.g., ability to sell it) that we refer to as the asset's **convenience yield.**

Denoting the present value of any costs of holding the asset as PV_0(cost) and the present value of cash flows and convenience yield as PV_0(benefit), the no-arbitrage price becomes:

$$F_0(T) = [S_0 + PV_0(\text{cost}) - PV_0(\text{benefit})](1 + Rf)^T$$

Here we have replaced the spot price of the asset with its cost adjusted for the present value of the costs and benefits of holding it until time = T.

Note that, for a given spot price, greater benefits of owning the asset decrease the no-arbitrage forward price and greater costs of holding the asset increase the no-arbitrage forward price.

The value of the forward at any point in time t < T becomes:

$$V_t(T) = S_t + PV_t(\text{cost}) - PV_t(\text{benefit}) - \frac{F_0(T)}{(1+Rf)^{T-t}}$$

At settlement there are no further costs or benefits, so once again the value at time = T is:

$$V_t(T) = S_T - F_0(T)$$

Forward Rate Agreements

A **forward rate agreement** (FRA) is a derivative contract that has an interest rate, rather than an asset price, as its underlying. An FRA permits an investor to lock in a certain interest rate for borrowing or lending at some future date. One party will pay the other party the difference (based on an agreed-upon notional contract value) between the interest rate specified in the FRA and the market interest rate at contract settlement.

LIBOR is most often used as the underlying rate. U.S. dollar LIBOR refers to the rates on Eurodollar time deposits, interbank U.S. dollar loans in London.

Consider an FRA that will, in 30 days, pay the difference between 90-day LIBOR and the 90-day rate specified in the FRA (the contract rate).

- A company that expects to borrow 90-day funds in 30 days will have higher interest costs if 90-day LIBOR increases over the next 30 days.
- A long position in an FRA (to "borrow" at the fixed rate) will receive a payment at settlement that will offset the increase in borrowing costs from the increase in 90-day LIBOR.
- Conversely, if 90-day LIBOR decreases over the next 30 days, the long position in the FRA will make a payment to the short in the amount that the company's borrowing costs have decreased relative to the FRA contract rate.

Firms can, therefore, reduce or eliminate the risk of (uncertainty about) future borrowing costs using an FRA.

Similarly, a firm that expects to lend (deposit) funds for 90 days, 30 days from now, can take a short position in an FRA. If the future 90-day LIBOR decreases, the return on the loan decreases, but this is offset by a payment received from the long FRA position.

Rather than enter into an FRA, a bank can create the same payment structure (a **synthetic FRA**) with two LIBOR loans (e.g., by borrowing money for 120 days and lending that amount for 30 days). By these transactions, the bank receives the funds from the repayment of the 30-day loan and has use of these funds for the next 90 days at an effective rate determined by the original transactions. The effective rate of interest on this 90-day loan depends on both 30-day LIBOR and 120-day LIBOR at the time the money is borrowed and loaned. This rate is the contract rate on a 30-day FRA on 90-day LIBOR. The resulting cash flows will be the same with either an FRA or its synthetic equivalent.

Forward versus Futures Prices

Futures contracts are standardized, traded, liquid contracts that are marked to market at the end of each trading day. Based on the change in the futures price from the previous day, gains are added to, and losses subtracted from, the balance in the investor's margin account. If losses reduce the margin balance below the minimum margin level, funds must be deposited to bring the margin balance back to its initial required level or the position will be closed out.

Forward contracts typically are not marked to market during their lives. This difference in valuation is only relevant in practice if futures prices are correlated with interest rates.

If the price of the underlying asset is positively correlated with interest rates, long futures positions will generate cash when rates are higher and require funds when rates are lower, with a net positive effect on the value of a futures position, so that futures prices will be higher than forward prices. Futures prices will be lower when asset prices and interest rates have negative correlation.

If rates are uncorrelated with futures prices, or rates are constant, forward and futures prices will be the same.

Swaps

In a simple interest-rate swap, one party pays a floating rate (LIBOR) and the other pays a fixed rate on a notional principal amount. For example, on a one-year swap with quarterly settlement dates, the difference between the swap fixed rate and LIBOR (for the *prior* 90 days) is paid by the party who owes more at each settlement date.

We can replicate each of these payments to (or from) the fixed-rate payer in the swap with a forward contract. A long position in an FRA will replicate the position of the fixed-rate payer: the long will receive a payment when LIBOR is above the forward rate and pay when LIBOR is below the forward rate.

An interest rate swap is, therefore, equivalent to a series of forward rate agreements, each with a forward contract rate equal to the swap fixed rate. However, there is one important difference. Because the forward contract rates are all equal in the FRAs that are equivalent to the swap, these would not be zero-value forward contracts at the initiation of the swap.

When a forward contract is created with a contract rate that gives it a non-zero value at initiation, it is called an **off-market forward**. Some, if not all, of the forward contracts that comprise a swap will almost certainly be off-market forwards. Because a swap has zero value to both parties at initiation, the values of the individual off-market forwards must sum to zero.

The swap fixed rate (which is also the contract rate for the off-market forwards) that gives the swap a zero value at initiation can be found using the principle of no-arbitrage pricing.

The fixed-rate payer in a swap can replicate that derivative position by borrowing at a fixed rate and lending the proceeds at a variable (floating) rate.

As with forward rate agreements, the price of a swap is the fixed rate of interest specified in the swap contract (the contract rate), and the value depends on how expected future floating rates change over time.

At initiation, a swap has zero value because the present value of the fixed-rate payments equals the present value of the expected floating-rate payments. An increase in expected short-term future rates will produce a positive value for the fixed-rate payer in an interest rate swap, and a decrease in expected future rates will produce a negative value because the promised fixed-rate payments have more value than the expected floating-rate payments over the life of the swap.

Options: Moneyness, Intrinsic Value, Time Value

An option that would provide a positive payoff if exercised is said to be **in the money**. The **intrinsic value** of an option is the amount that it is in the money or zero if the option is at- or out-of-the-money. The difference between the price of an option (called its premium) and its intrinsic value is termed its **time value**. Hence:

option premium = intrinsic value + time value

The following table summarizes the moneyness of options based on the stock's current price, S, and the option's exercise price, X.

Moneyness	Call Option	Put Option
In the money	$S > X$	$S < X$
At the money	$S = X$	$S = X$
Out of the money	$S < X$	$S > X$

Factors Determining European Option Values

Price of the Underlying Asset

An increase in the price of the underlying asset will increase the value of a call option, and a decrease in the price of the underlying asset will decrease the value of a call option.

An increase in the price of the underlying asset will decrease the value of a put option, and a decrease in the price of the underlying asset will increase the value of a put option.

The Exercise Price

A higher exercise price decreases the values of call options, and a lower exercise price increases the values of call options.

A higher exercise price increases the values of put options, and a lower exercise price decreases the values of put options.

The Risk-Free Rate of Interest

For options on assets other than bonds, an increase in the risk-free rate will increase call values, and a decrease in the risk-free rate will decrease call values.

An increase in the risk-free rate will decrease put option values, and a decrease in the risk-free rate will increase put option values.

Volatility of the Underlying

An increase in the volatility of the price of the underlying asset increases the values of both put and call options and a decrease in volatility of the price of the underlying decreases both put values and call values.

Time to Expiration

Longer time to expiration increases expected volatility of the asset price over the option's life and increases the value of call options. Less time to expiration decreases the value of call options.

For most put options, longer time to expiration will increase option values because expected volatility is greater with longer time to expiration. For some European put options, however, extending the time to expiration can decrease the value of the put because the intrinsic value will be paid in the future and its present value decreases with longer time to expiration.

In general, the deeper a put option is in the money, the higher the risk-free rate; the longer the current time to expiration, the more likely that extending a put option's time to expiration will decrease its value.

Costs and Benefits of Holding the Asset

If there are benefits of holding the underlying asset (dividend or interest payments on securities or a convenience yield on commodities), call values are decreased and put values are increased.

An increase in storage costs for an asset has the opposite effect: increasing call values and decreasing put values. Call values increase because owning a call option becomes relatively more attractive than holding the asset itself when storage costs increase. Put values fall because buying and holding the asset for future delivery at the put price becomes more expensive.

Put-Call Parity for European Options

Put-call parity is based on the no-arbitrage principle that portfolios with identical payoffs must sell for the same price. A **fiduciary call** (composed of a European call option and a risk-free bond that will pay X at expiration) and a **protective put** (composed of a share of stock and a long put) both have identical payoffs at maturity regardless of value of the underlying asset at expiration. Based on this fact and the law of one price, we can state that, for European options:

$$c + X / (1 + Rf)^T = S + p$$

That is, the value of a call at X and the present value of the exercise price must equal the current asset price plus the value of a put or there would be an opportunity for profitable arbitrage. Using just a bit of algebra, we can also state that:

$$S = c - p + X / (1 + Rf)^T$$

$$p = c - S + X / (1 + Rf)^T$$

$$c = S + p - X / (1 + Rf)^T$$

$$X / (1 + Rf)^T = S + p - c$$

The single securities on the left-hand side of the equations all have exactly the same payoffs at expiration as the portfolios on the right-hand side. The portfolios on the right-hand side are the "synthetic" equivalents of the securities on the left. Note that the options must be European-style, and the puts and calls must have the same exercise price, X, for these relations to hold.

If these equalities do not hold, buying the "cheap" side of the equation and selling the other "expensive" side will produce an immediate riskless arbitrage profit.

Put-Call Forward Parity for European Options

Put-call forward parity is derived with a forward contract rather than the underlying asset itself. A forward contract on an asset at time T has zero value at initiation; therefore, a long forward at a price of $F_0(T)$, combined with a bond that pays the forward price, $F_0(T)$, at the settlement date is equivalent to owning the asset at settlement. The cost of this position is simply the present value of $F_0(T)$, or $F_0(T) / (1 + Rf)^T$. Because this is a way to own the asset at expiration, we can substitute this value for the current price of the asset in put-call parity for European options and get:

$$F_0(T) / (1 + Rf)^T + p_0 = c_0 + X / (1 + Rf)^T$$

which is put-call forward parity at time 0, the initiation of the forward contract, based on the principle of no arbitrage. By rearranging the terms, put-call forward parity can also be expressed as:

$$p_0 - c_0 = [X - F_0(T)] / (1 + Rf)^T$$

Binomial Model

In a binomial model, an asset price will change to one of two possible values (a movement either up or down) over the next period. The inputs required are:

- Beginning asset value.
- Size of up and down movements.
- Risk-neutral probabilities of up and down movements.

The risk-neutral probabilities of an up and down move are calculated as:

$$\pi_U = \text{risk-neutral probability of an up-move} = \frac{1 + R_f - D}{}$$

$$\pi_U = \text{risk-neutral probability of aa down-move} = 1 - \pi_U$$

where:
R_f = risk-free rate
U = size of an up-move
D = size of a down-move

Note that these are not the actual probabilities of an up-move or a down-move but the probabilities that apply if we are to discount the expected payoff on the asset at the risk-free rate. Determining the value of an option using a binomial model requires that we:

- Calculate the payoffs of the option at the end of the period for both an up-move and down-move.
- Calculate the expected value of the option in one year as the probability-weighted average of the payoffs in each state.
- Discount this expected value back to today at the risk-free rate.

European versus American Option Values

The only difference between European and American options is that a holder of an American option has the right to exercise prior to expiration, while European options can only be exercised at expiration.

For a call option on an asset that has no cash flows during the life of the option, there is no advantage to early exercise. Thus, otherwise identical American and European call options on assets with no cash flows will have the same value.

If the underlying asset makes cash payments (e.g., pays a dividend) during the life of a call option, the price of an American call option will be greater than the price of otherwise identical European call options. A cash payment will decrease the value of the asset and reduce the value of a European call. Early exercise of an American option may be valuable as it allows exercise of the call before the cash distribution is made.

For put options, cash flows on the underlying do not make early exercise valuable because a decrease in the price of the underlying asset when it makes a cash distribution would increase the value of a put option. In the case of a put option that is deep in the money, however, early exercise may be advantageous. Consider the extreme case of a put option on a stock that has fallen in value to zero. Exercising the put will result in an immediate payment of the exercise price. For a European put option, this payment cannot be received until option expiration, so its value now is the present value of that exercise price. Given the potential positive value of early exercise for put options, American put options can be priced higher than otherwise identical European put options.

RISK MANAGEMENT APPLICATIONS OF OPTION STRATEGIES
Cross-Reference to CFA Institute Assigned Reading #60

The key here is your ability to interpret option payoff diagrams. It is absolutely critical that you understand each option payoff diagram and be able to make the appropriate computations for option payoffs and the payoffs for the included option strategies (e.g., a covered call).

* Buyer of a call option—long position.
* Writer (seller) of a call option—short position.
* Buyer of a put option—long position.
* Writer (seller) of a put option—short position.

Call Option Payoff Diagrams

The following graph illustrates the payoff at expiration for a call option as a function of the stock price, for both buyers and writers. Note that this differs from the *profit diagram* that follows in that the profit diagram reflects the initial cost of the option (the *premium*). Remember that the option buyer pays the premium to the option seller and if the option finishes out of the money, the writer keeps the premium and the buyer loses the premium. Options are considered a *zero-sum game* because whatever amount the buyer gains, the seller loses, and vice versa.

> intrinsic value of a call option = max[0, S – X]
> intrinsic value of a put option = max[0, X – S]

Figure 1: Call Option Payoff Diagram

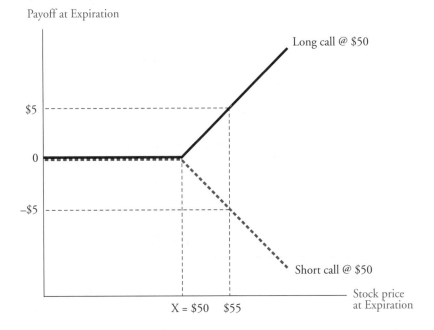

Figure 2: Profit/Loss Diagram for a Call Option

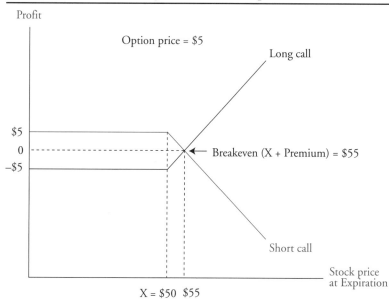

For a *call option:*

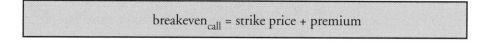

$$\text{breakeven}_{call} = \text{strike price} + \text{premium}$$

	Call Option	
	Maximum Loss	*Maximum Gain*
Buyer (long)	Premium	Unlimited
Seller (short)	Unlimited	Premium
Breakeven	X + premium	

Put Option Diagrams

The following graph illustrates the payoff at expiration for a put option as a function of stock price, for both buyers and writers.

Figure 3: Put Option Payoff Diagram

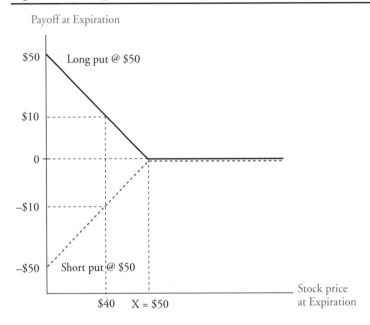

Note that in the *profit diagram* that follows, the cost of the option (the *premium*) is included.

Figure 4: Profit/Loss Diagram for a Put Option

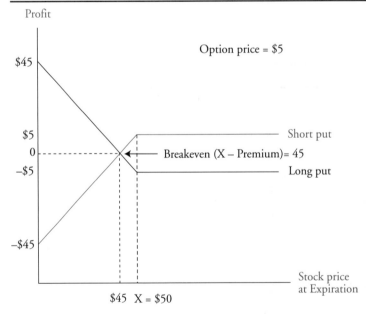

For a *put option:*

	Put Option	
	Maximum Loss	*Maximum Gain*
Buyer (long)	Premium	X – premium
Seller (short)	X – premium	Premium
Breakeven	X – premium	

Covered Calls, Protective Puts

A *covered call* is the combination of a long stock and a short call. The term *covered* means that the stock covers the inherent obligation assumed in writing the call. Why would you write a covered call? You feel the stock's price will not go up any time soon, and you want to increase your income by collecting some call option premiums. This strategy for enhancing income is not without risk. The call writer is trading the stock's upside potential above the strike price for the call premium.

A *protective put* is an investment management technique designed to protect a stock from a decline in value. It is constructed by buying a stock and put option on that stock. Any gain on the stock at option expiration is reduced by the put premium paid. The combined (protective put) position will produce profits at option expiration only if the stock price exceeds the sum of the purchase prices of the stock and the put. If the stock price at option expiration is below the put's strike price, the put payoff will limit the maximum loss to the difference between the cost of the position and the strike price of the put.

ALTERNATIVE INVESTMENTS

Weight on Exam	4%
SchweserNotes™ Reference	Book 5, Pages 202–230

INTRODUCTION TO ALTERNATIVE INVESTMENTS
Cross-reference to CFA Institute Assigned Reading #61

Alternative investments differ from traditional investments in the types of assets and securities included in this asset class and in the structure of the investment vehicles in which these assets are held. Managers of alternative investment portfolios may use derivatives and leverage, invest in illiquid assets, and short securities. Many types of real estate investment are considered alternative investments as well. (For the exam, alternative investments are what the CFA Curriculum says they are.)

Compared to traditional investments, alternative investments generally can be characterized as having **less liquidity** of assets held, **more specialization by investment managers, less regulation and transparency**, more problematic and **less available historical return and volatility data**, and **different legal issues and tax treatments**. Types of alternative investment structures include hedge funds, private equity funds, real estate, and commodities.

- **Hedge funds** may use leverage, hold long and short positions, use derivatives, and invest in illiquid assets. Managers of hedge funds use many different strategies in attempting to generate investment gains. They do not necessarily hedge risk.
- **Private equity funds** invest in the equity of companies that are not publicly traded or in the equity of publicly traded firms that the fund intends to take private. **Leveraged buyout (LBO) funds** use borrowed money to purchase equity in established companies and comprise the majority of private equity investment funds. **Venture capital funds** invest in companies early in their existence.
- **Real estate** investments include residential or commercial properties as well as real estate backed debt. These investments are held in a variety of structures including full or leveraged ownership of individual properties, individual real estate backed loans, private and publicly traded securities backed by pools of properties or mortgages, and limited partnerships.

- **Commodities** investors can own physical commodities, commodities derivatives, or the equity of commodity producing firms. Some funds seek exposure to the returns on various commodity indices, often by holding derivatives contracts that are expected to track a specific commodity index.
- **Infrastructure** refers to long-lived assets that provide public services. These include economic infrastructure assets such as roads, airports, and utility grids, and social infrastructure assets such as schools and hospitals.
- Other alternative investments include patents and collectible assets such as fine wines, stamps, automobiles, antique furniture, and art.

The primary motivation for holding alternative investments is their historically low correlation of returns with those of traditional investments, which can reduce an investor's overall portfolio risk. However, the risk measures we use for traditional assets may not be adequate to capture the risk characteristics of alternative investments.

Historical returns for alternative investments have been higher on average than for traditional investments, so adding alternative investments to a traditional portfolio may increase expected returns. The reasons for these higher returns are thought to be that some alternative investments are less efficiently priced than traditional assets; that alternative investments may offer extra returns for being illiquid; and that alternative investments often use leverage.

There are potential problems with historical returns data and traditional risk measures. **Survivorship bias** refers to the upward bias of returns if data only for currently existing firms is included. Since surviving firms tend to be those that had better-than-average returns, excluding the returns data for failed firms results in average returns that are biased upward. **Backfill bias** is introduced by including the previous performance data for firms recently added to a benchmark index. Since firms that are newly added to an index must be those that have survived and done better than average, including their returns for prior years tends to bias average returns upward.

Hedge Funds

Hedge funds are typically set up as limited partnerships, with the investors as the limited partners. Investors must have sufficient wealth, liquidity, and investment sophistication. The management firm is the general partner and typically receives both a management fee based on the value of assets managed and an incentive fee based on fund returns. The most common fee structure for a hedge fund is "2 and 20," or 2% of the value of the assets under management plus an incentive fee of 20% of profits.

Hedge fund investments are less liquid than traditional, publicly traded investments. Restrictions on redemptions may include a lockup period and/or a notice period. A **lockup period** is a time after initial investment during which withdrawals are not allowed. A **notice period** is the amount of time a fund has after receiving a redemption request to fulfill the request. Additional fees may be charged at redemption.

A **fund of funds** is an investment company that invests in hedge funds, giving investors diversification among hedge fund strategies and allowing smaller investors to access hedge funds in which they may not be able to invest directly. Investors in funds of funds incur additional fees from the managers of the funds of funds. A common fee structure from funds of funds is "1 and 10" in addition to any fees charged by the individual hedge funds within the fund-of-funds structure.

According to Hedge Fund Research, Inc., there are four main classifications of hedge fund strategies: event-driven, relative value, macro, and equity hedge fund.

- **Event-driven strategies** are typically based on a corporate restructuring or acquisition that creates profit opportunities for long or short positions in common equity, preferred equity, or debt of a specific corporation. Subcategories are merger arbitrage, distressed/restructuring, activist shareholder, and special situations.
- **Relative value strategies** involve buying a security and selling short a related security with the goal of profiting when a perceived pricing discrepancy between the two is resolved. Subcategories include convertible arbitrage fixed income, asset-backed fixed income, general fixed income, volatility, and multi-strategy.
- **Macro strategies** are based on global economic trends and events and may involve long or short positions in equities, fixed income, currencies, or commodities.
- **Equity hedge fund strategies** seek to profit from long or short positions in publicly traded equities and derivatives with equities as their underlying assets. Subcategories include market neutral, fundamental growth, fundamental value, quantitative directional, and short bias.

Hedge fund values are based on market values for traded securities in their portfolios, but must use estimated values for non-traded securities. For traded securities it is most conservative to use the prices at which a position could be closed: bid prices for long positions and ask prices for short positions. Some funds use the average of the bid and ask prices instead. For illiquid securities, market prices may be reduced for the degree of illiquidity. Some funds calculate a **trading NAV** in addition to the accounting NAV, by reducing asset values for their lack of liquidity.

Due diligence of available hedge funds may be somewhat hampered by a lack of transparency by funds that consider their strategies and systems to be proprietary information. Regulatory requirements for hedge fund disclosures are minimal.

The total fee paid by investors in a hedge fund consists of a management fee and an incentive fee. The **management fee** is earned regardless of investment performance and **incentive fees** are a portion of profits. Profits can be (1) any gains in value, (2) any gains in value in excess of the management fee, or (3) gains in excess of a **hurdle rate**. A hurdle rate can be a **hard hurdle rate** with incentive fees earned only on returns in excess of the benchmark, or a **soft hurdle rate** with incentive fees paid on all profits, but only if the hurdle rate is met.

A **high water mark** means incentive fees are only paid to the extent that the current value of an investor's account is above the highest value previously recorded. This feature ensures that investors will not be charged incentive fees twice on the same gains.

Management fees may be calculated on either the beginning-of-period or end-of-period values of assets under management. Incentive fees may be calculated net of management fees or independent of management fees.

Private Equity

Most private equity funds are **leveraged buyout funds** that invest either in private companies or in public companies they intend to take private, or **venture capital funds** that invest in early stage companies. Two smaller categories of private equity funds are *distressed investment funds and developmental capital funds.*

There is evidence that returns on private equity funds have been higher on average than those of traditional equity investments. There may also be portfolio diversification benefits from including private equity in portfolios. The standard deviation of private equity returns has been higher than the standard deviation of equity index returns, suggesting greater risk. As with hedge fund returns data, private equity returns data may suffer from survivorship bias and backfill bias.

Similar to hedge funds, private equity funds are typically structured as limited partnerships. **Committed capital** is the amount of capital provided to the fund by investors. The committed capital amount is typically not all invested immediately but is "**drawn down**" (invested), usually over three to five years, as securities are identified and added to the portfolio. Management fees are typically 1% to 3% of committed, rather than invested, capital.

Incentive fees for private equity funds are typically 20% of profits, but these fees are not earned until after the fund has returned investors' initial capital. A **clawback provision** requires the manager to return any incentive fees that would result in investors receiving less than 80% of the profits generated by portfolio investments as a whole. This situation can arise when returns on portfolio companies are high early and decline later.

Leveraged buyouts (LBOs) are the most common type of private equity fund investment. "Leveraged" refers to the fact that the fund's purchase of the portfolio company is funded primarily by debt. This may be bank debt, high-yield bonds, or **mezzanine financing**, which refers to debt or preferred shares that are subordinate to the high-yield bonds issued and carry warrants or conversion features.

Two types of LBOs are **management buyouts** (MBOs), in which the existing management team is involved in the purchase, and **management buy-ins** (MBIs), in which an external management team will replace the existing management team.

In an LBO, the private equity firm seeks to increase the value of the firm through management incentives, restructuring, cost reduction, revenue enhancement, or new management. Firms with high cash flow are attractive LBO candidates because their cash flow can be used to service the debt taken on for acquisition.

Venture capital funds invest in companies in the early stages of their development. Venture capital fund managers are closely involved in the development of portfolio companies, often sitting on their boards or filling key management roles.

Venture capital investment at different stages of the company's life includes the following:

- **Formative stage** investment refers to investments made during a firm's earliest period, including:
  - **angel investing stage** (individuals; idea stage and business plan)
  - **seed stage** (VC investors; product development and marketing)
  - **early stage** (VC investors; initial commercial production and sales)
- **Later stage investment** (company is operating; expansion of production, and marketing)
- **Mezzanine-stage financing** (capital provided to prepare the firm for an IPO, refers to the timing of the financing rather than the type of financing)

Other private equity strategies include **developmental capital** or **minority equity investing**, which refer to providing capital for business growth or restructuring. If the firms financed are public, such financing is referred to as **private investment in public equities** (PIPEs).

Distressed investing involves buying debt of a firm that is potentially or currently in default, or in bankruptcy proceedings. Investors in distressed debt often take an active role in the turnaround by working with management on reorganization or to determine the direction the company should take. Distressed debt investors are sometimes referred to as **vulture investors**.

Real Estate

Real estate as an asset class can provide diversification benefits to an investor's portfolio and a potential inflation hedge because rents and real estate values tend to increase with inflation. Assets included under the heading of real estate investments include residential property, commercial property, and loans with residential or commercial property as collateral.

Residential property is considered a direct investment in real estate. Most buyers take on a mortgage to purchase. The mortgage lender has a direct investment in a whole loan and is said to hold the mortgage. Mortgages are often pooled into mortgage-backed securities (MBS), which represent an indirect investment in the mortgage loan pool.

Commercial real estate properties generate income from rents. Homes purchased for rental income are considered investment in commercial property. Long time horizons, illiquidity, the large size of investment needed, and the complexity of the investments make commercial real estate inappropriate for many investors. As with residential mortgages, commercial property mortgages can be pooled into commercial mortgage-backed securities.

Real estate investment trusts (REITs) issue shares that trade publicly like shares of stock. REITs are often identified by the type of real estate assets they hold: mortgages, hotel properties, malls, office buildings, or other commercial property. Typically, 90% of income must be distributed to shareholders to avoid taxes on this income that would have to be paid by the REIT.

Two additional assets considered as real estate investments are **timberland** and **farmland**, for which one component of returns is the proceeds of timber or agricultural product sales. Timberland returns also include price changes on timberland, which depend on expectations of lumber prices. Farmland returns include land price changes and are affected by price changes in agricultural commodities, as well as the quality and quantity of the crops produced.

Three methods are commonly used to value real estate:

1. The **comparable sales approach** bases valuation on recent sales of similar properties. Values for individual properties include adjustments for differences between the characteristics of the specific property and those of the comparable properties, such as age, location, condition, and size.

2. The **income approach** estimates property values by calculating the present value of expected future cash flows from property ownership or by dividing the net operating income (NOI) for a property by a capitalization rate.

3. The **cost approach** estimates the replacement cost of a property. The value of the land included and the cost of rebuilding at current construction costs are summed to estimate replacement cost.

Commodities

The most commonly used instruments to gain exposure to commodity prices are derivatives. Futures, forwards, options, and swaps are all available forms of commodity derivatives. Other methods of gaining exposure to commodities returns include exchange-traded funds, equities that are linked to a commodity, managed futures funds, individual managed accounts, and commodity funds in specific sectors.

Returns on commodities over time have been less than returns on global stocks or bonds. Correlations of commodity returns with those of global equities and global bonds have been low, so that adding commodities to a traditional portfolio has provided diversification benefits. Because commodity prices tend to move with inflation rates, holding commodities can hedge inflation risk.

A commodity today and a commodity in the future are different products. Purchasing a commodity today gives the buyer use of it if needed, while contracting for it to be delivered six months from today avoids storage costs and interest costs on invested cash. An equation that considers these aspects is:

$$\text{futures price} \approx \text{spot price } (1 + \text{risk-free rate}) + \text{storage costs} - \text{convenience yield}$$

Convenience yield is the value of having the physical commodity for use over the period of the futures contract. If there is little or no convenience yield, futures prices will be higher than spot prices, a situation termed **contango**. When the convenience yield is high, futures prices will be less than spot prices, a situation referred to as **backwardation**.

The return on a commodity investment includes:

- *Collateral yield:* the return on the collateral posted to satisfy margin requirements.
- *Price return:* the gain or loss due to changes in the spot price.
- *Roll yield:* the gain or loss resulting from re-establishing positions as contracts expire.

Note that *roll yield* is positive if the futures market is in backwardation and negative if the market is in contango.

Infrastructure

Infrastructure investments include transportation assets such as roads, airports, ports, and railways, as well as utility assets, such as gas distribution facilities, electric generation and distribution facilities, and waste disposal and treatment facilities. Other categories of infrastructure investments are communications (e.g., broadcast assets and cable systems) and social (e.g., prisons, schools, and health care facilities).

Investments in infrastructure assets that are already constructed are referred to as **brownfield investments**. In general, investing in brownfield investments provides stable cash flows and relatively high yields but offers little potential for growth.

Investments in infrastructure assets that are to be constructed are referred to as **greenfield investments**. Investing in greenfield investments is subject to more uncertainty and may provide relatively lower yields but offers greater growth potential.

Infrastructure assets typically have long lives and are quite large in cost and scale, so direct investments in them are not liquid. ETFs, mutual funds, private equity funds, or master limited partnerships that invest in infrastructure assets can provide greater liquidity.

Essential Exam Strategies

The level of review contained in this section is different from our other CFA review materials. As always, our objective is to enhance your chances of passing the CFA exam. Unlike the previous part of this book, which covers *what* you need to know to pass the Level I CFA exam, this section provides you important guidance on *how* to pass the exam. By this time, you have likely studied the entire Level I curriculum and have a solid grasp on the content, so we won't spend any time here reviewing or quizzing you on material you already know. Instead, we provide insights about how to successfully apply your hard-earned knowledge on exam day.

First, we provide some proven approaches to mastering the Level I CFA curriculum. Next, we present a structured plan for the last week before the exam. Following this plan assures that you will be sharp on exam day, and your performance will not be adversely affected by your nerves. We will also spend some time discussing general exam-taking strategies and how to approach individual questions.

A Formidable Task

Over the past few months, you have studied an enormous amount of material. CFA Institute's assigned readings for the Level I curriculum include more than 3,000 pages. There are more than 500 learning outcome statements. This is a huge amount of material. Realistically speaking, it is virtually impossible to remember every detail within the curriculum. The good news is you don't have to know every detail. From this guide, you will learn how to get the most benefit from the short time remaining until the exam.

As you prepare for the CFA exam, try to focus on the exam itself. Don't add to your stress level by worrying about whether you'll pass or what might happen if you don't. If you must, you can worry about all of that after the exam. If you worry about it before the exam, or especially during the exam, your performance will likely suffer. There is ample stress in remembering the material, let alone worrying whether you'll pass. Many of the tips we provide are proven stress reducers on exam day. Your grasp of the content, combined with the tips we provide, will have you well prepared for the exam experience.

All of the faculty at Kaplan Schweser have earned CFA charters and have extensive experience in teaching the topics covered in the CFA curriculum. As such, we know what you are going through from our own personal experiences, and we have helped tens of thousands of candidates earn the right to use the CFA designation. We've been there and done that! We know the agony and anxiety you are experiencing. Now, we want to share with you the time-honored strategies that we have personally seen lead to success on the Level I CFA exam.

Let's start with some overall thoughts. There are two basic strategies you should follow in learning the CFA curriculum: Focus on the big picture, and know the main concepts.

The Big Picture

Focusing on the big picture means you should know at least a little about every concept. When we took the exam, some of us were not overly comfortable with debt securities. We just didn't deal with bonds on a regular basis. Still, we knew that we had to learn some of the basics for the exam. For example, even if you don't know the formula for effective duration, at least know that effective duration is a measure of interest rate risk. By remembering some basic information on exam day, you will be able to narrow your answer choices. You probably won't answer many questions correctly with only a basic grasp of the concept, but you can improve your odds on a multiple choice question from 33% to 50%. You also will be able to better distinguish between the relevant and irrelevant information in a question. Continuing with our duration theme, you would know that bond rating information provided in a duration question is not relevant, since bond ratings reflect credit risk, not interest rate risk.

Even if you don't currently work with, for example, futures, and you know you never will, try to at least get a basic grasp of the important concepts within the topic. It is simply a poor exam strategy to completely blow off significant pieces of the curriculum. We have known people in the CFA program who thought that as long as they knew a few of the assigned topics really well, they could bluff their way through the rest of the exam. These were smart individuals, but they had poor exam strategies. So far, none of them have earned their charters.

Know the Main Concepts

It is important to identify those concepts that can be considered core knowledge for a financial analyst. In any given year, some concepts might be emphasized more than others, but if you can answer most of the questions concerning the main concepts, you will dramatically increase your chance of passing. Generally, the idea is to be correct on most of the questions dealing with the core concepts, and then rely on your "big picture" knowledge to get points on the remaining material.

Topic Weighting

In preparing for the exam, you must pay attention to the weights assigned to each topic within the curriculum. The Level I topic weights are as follows:

Topic	Exam Weight	Number of LOS	Points per LOS
Ethical and Professional Standards	15%	13	4.15
Quantitative Methods	12%	88	0.49
Economics	10%	103	0.35
Financial Reporting and Analysis	20%	123	0.59
Corporate Finance	7%	43	0.59
Portfolio Management	7%	35	0.72
Equity Investments	10%	60	0.60
Fixed Income Investments	10%	55	0.65
Derivatives	5%	22	0.82
Alternative Investments	4%	7	2.06
Totals	**100%**	**549**	**0.66**

Notice how the LOS counts are not consistent with the exam weights. In fact, some topic areas with a relatively high number of LOS are frequently not covered very heavily on the exam, so allocating your preparation time based on the number of LOS will most likely lead to over-preparation in some areas (e.g., Economics) and under-preparation in others (especially Ethics).

Formulas

You may be surprised to know that the Level I CFA examination is quite conceptual and is not heavily weighted toward computations based on memorized formulas. It is nothing like what my undergraduate students used to refer to as "plug and chug" problems. Certainly, some formulas are required, but you will find that you need to use your calculator much less often than you might imagine after reading the required material. Examples of the types of formulas that you need to commit to memory are the constant growth dividend discount model, the security market line, the correlation coefficient, and both the traditional and expanded DuPont formulas for decomposing ROE.

Many times you will be given questions where the answer can be obtained by using a formula and a fairly lengthy calculation but where you can also identify the correct answer without calculation, if you truly understand the concept or relationship being tested. With any formula you encounter in the required readings, you should try to gain a clear understanding of what it is telling you (when it is appropriate to use it) and of the relationship among the various input variables.

One example of this sort of understanding is the holding period return or holding period yield. It is simply the percentage increase in the value of an investment over the holding period. If you buy a stock for $100, receive a $5 dividend, and sell it for $103 at the end of the period, the value increased from $100 to $108, an increase of 8% (which is the holding period return or yield). If you understand that the harmonic mean is used to get the average price per share when the same amount is invested over multiple periods, you can easily calculate the harmonic mean of $1, $2, and $3. If you invested a total of $6 at each of these three prices, you would buy 6/1 + 6/2 + 6/3 = 11 shares and spend a total of $6 × 3 = $18. The average price per share (and the harmonic mean) is 18/11 = $1.636.

Think of the formula as just a shorthand way of expressing a relation or concept you need to understand. For example, the formula tells you that the population variance is the average squared deviation from the mean. Approaching formulas in this way will reduce your chances of missing a problem because your memory fails you under the stress of the exam. I can never remember the formula for an updated probability using Bayes' Theorem, but ever since I understood it as presented in a tree diagram, I can calculate updated probabilities without a problem and without worrying whether I "remembered" the precise formula correctly.

"Characteristic" Lists

Another common source of specific questions is identifying the characteristics of various securities, models, and valuation methods. A typical question format would be "Which of the following most accurately describes…?" Here, the big-picture approach can help you weed out wrong answers. Also, some candidates use mnemonics to help them remember lists of characteristics or lists of pros and cons.

Essential Exam Strategies

Acronyms

Exam questions may include common abbreviations and acronyms that appear in the Level I curriculum. You should be able to recognize all the abbreviations in the following list:

Abbreviation	Full name
CAPM	Capital Asset Pricing Model
CML	Capital Market Line
D/E	Debt-to-equity ratio
DDM	Dividend Discount Model
EBIT	Earnings before interest and taxes
EBITDA	Earnings before interest, taxes, depreciation, and amortization
EPS	Earnings per share
ETF	Exchange Traded Funds
EUR	Euro (currency)
FCFE	Free cash flow to equity
FCFF	Free cash flow to the firm
FIFO	First-in, first-out
FOF	Fund-of-funds
GBP	British pound
GIPS	Global Investment Performance Standards
IFRS	International Financial Reporting Standards
IPO	Initial public offering
IPS	Investment Policy Statement
IRR	Internal rate of return
JPY	Japanese yen
LIBOR	London Interbank Offer Rate
LIFO	Last-in, first-out
NAV	Net asset value
NPV	Net present value
OAS	Option-adjusted spread
P/B	Price-to-book ratio
P/CF	Price-to-cash-flow ratio
P/E	Price-to-earnings ratio
PPE or PP&E	Property, plant, and equipment
REIT	Real Estate Investment Trust
ROA	Return on assets
ROE	Return on equity
SML	Security Market Line
U.S. GAAP	U.S. Generally Accepted Accounting Principles
USD	U.S. dollar
WACC	Weighted average cost of capital

Know Your Strengths

We each have our own style of learning. Some of us can sit down and study for hours at a time, while some of us learn better in small doses each day. Be aware of your study habits, and do not place unrealistic burdens on yourself. Be especially aware of problems with certain topics. For example, if you have always struggled with accounting, look at ways to improve your grasp of the accounting material—spend more time with it, attend a review course, or join a study group. *Do not* expect that you can ignore a topic and make up for the lost points by excelling in another area. Similarly, do not skip an area just because you think you already know it. There are CPAs who fail the accounting section and PhDs in Economics who fail the economics section. You need to review the specific material in the assigned CFA curriculum to pass the CFA exam.

The Rules

At some point in your studies, it would be a good idea to review the Testing Policies section of the CFA Institute web site. Believe it or not, you will probably find this to be a nice break from accounting or derivatives! Be sure that you have a passport that will not expire before exam day. Select an approved calculator and learn how to use it proficiently. You should also read the CFA Program Errata that are issued in the months before the exam.

Be aware of items you can and cannot take to the exam. CFA Institute strictly prohibits taking any of the following into the testing room:

- Backpacks, briefcases, luggage of any kind.
- *Any* study materials.
- Scratch paper, calculator manuals.
- Highlighters, rulers, correction fluid (white-out).
- Cell phones, any personal electronics.

Do not expect that these policies do not apply to you. Every year numerous candidates have problems on exam day because they assumed their cases would be legitimate exceptions. There is no such thing. We have stories of people sprinting back to their cars to put stuff away and get back in time to start the exam. If you read the rules and follow them, you reduce the potential for unexpected stress on the day of the exam. That's a good thing!

Final Preparation

Have a well-defined strategy for the last week before the exam. If at all possible, it is best to take at least some leave from your job. You should save at least one practice exam for the last week. To simulate the real exam, you should avoid looking at this exam or studying questions from it until you are ready to sit down and take it for the first time. Take this exam early in the final week. Take the first half of the exam in a 3-hour period, take a 90-minute break, then take the other half in a second 3-hour period. Time yourself so you can get a feel for the time constraints and pressure of exam day. Remember, you have an average of 90 seconds per question. When you have completed the entire exam, grade your answers and use these results to identify areas where you need to focus your study efforts over the last few days. You should devote most of your time to areas where you performed poorly, but you should also spend enough time keeping your stronger topics fresh in your mind.

At some point during the week before the exam, it is a good idea to visit the actual exam center. Figure out how long it will take to get to your test center and where you can park. It might even be helpful to locate a lunch destination in the area. If you are relying on public transportation, make sure it runs on weekends. The fewer surprises and distractions on exam day, the better.

Expect problems on exam day. Not major ones, but be prepared for things like cold/hot rooms, noise, lines, etc. Some of these problems you cannot control, but if you are prepared for them, they are less likely to affect your exam performance.

The evening before the exam, it is best to avoid studying. Try to relax and make a concerted effort to get a good night's sleep. Tired candidates make silly mistakes on the exam. If you are not rested, you will more than likely miss easy points. This seems like an obvious and trite point, but it is difficult to overemphasize the importance of going into the exam well rested. If for some unfortunate reason you do not sleep well the night before, do not panic! It happens to the best of us. Sometimes your brain cannot stop thinking about the pressure of the upcoming day. Keep in mind that you can still function and you can still give a solid effort on exam day with just a little sleep (even though it is not recommended). If you're one of those candidates who has difficulty sleeping before an important event, plan accordingly and go to bed early.

Exam Day

Answering Level I Multiple-Choice Questions

Read the full question carefully! Watch for double negatives like "Which of the following is least likely a disadvantage..." It is very important not to miss words, or parts of words, by reading too quickly (e.g., reading "most likely" instead of "least likely," or "advantages" instead of "disadvantages").

For non-numerical questions, read *all* answer choices. Don't just stop when you get to one that sounds right. There may be a better choice.

For long questions, dissect the bits of information that are provided. What information is relevant? What is most specifically related to the question? Often a wrong answer looks good because it is consistent with information in the question that is actually irrelevant.

After you read the question, determine what you think the question is asking. This can help you filter out extraneous information and focus quickly on appropriate answer choices.

Similarly, after you read the question, it is a good idea to formulate your own answer before reading the answer choices. Develop an expectation of what the answer should be. This may make the correct answer sound better to you when you read it.

On calculation problems, after you have selected an answer choice, pause for a moment and think about whether the answer makes sense. Is the sign of the result correct, or does the direction of change make sense?

Do not look for patterns in answers. Just because the last three questions all had "C" for an answer, do not expect the next answer not to be "C." There is no reason to expect that CFA Institute has a preference for how many questions are answered with the same letter.

Be *very* sure that you are marking your answer in the right place on the answer sheet. If you skip questions or do the topics out of order, be especially careful to check yourself. Obviously, mis-marking can be devastating if you do not catch it right away.

Trust your first impressions. You will find that you are often correct. It is okay to change an answer, but only do so if you have a *good* reason. Over the years, we have heard many stories of how candidates talk themselves out of the correct answer. We have all done this. When you come back to a question, be sure you can justify any change before you make it.

Finally, and probably *most* importantly, *do not lose confidence*. No one has ever received a perfect score on the CFA exam. It just does not happen. Remember, historically 70% has always been a passing score. This means you can miss 30% (roughly 72 questions) and still pass. Even if you have struggled on a few questions, maybe even five or six in a row, do not lose confidence. The worst thing you can do is second-guess yourself—you will take longer on every question and start changing correct answers.

What To Do With a Difficult Question

There will undoubtedly be questions that give you trouble. You might not understand the question, may think that none of the answers make sense, or simply may not know the concept being tested. The following tips will likely prove to be useful if you find yourself facing a difficult question.

- If the question does not make sense or if none of the answers look remotely correct, reread the question to see if you missed something. If you are still unsure, mark an answer choice and move on. Don't agonize over it and waste precious time that can be allocated to questions you can nail.
- *Never leave an answer blank.* A blank answer has a maximum point value of zero. A randomly marked answer has an expected value of $0.33 \times 1.5 = 0.5$ points, and if you can eliminate one bad answer, this value increases to $0.5 \times 1.5 = 0.75$. You are not penalized for wrong answers.
- If you are unable to determine the "best" answer, you still should be able to help your odds. Try to eliminate one answer choice and then just guess.
- Take some comfort in the fact that the CFA exams are graded on a curve. If a question gave you trouble, it is quite possible that it was troublesome for many other candidates as well.
- Do not lose your confidence over one, or even several, tough questions. You can miss 72 questions (or a few more) and still pass.

Time Management

Candidates who fail to pass CFA exams cite time management as their biggest downfall. Do not let poor time management determine your exam results. The following are some tips to help you manage your time wisely.

Take at least one practice exam where you time yourself. This will give you some indication of whether you will have problems on exam day. However, do not let your positive results on practice exams lull you into overconfidence. The stress of exam day, plus possible distractions like noise or a cold exam room, can make a big difference in how fast you work.

Monitor your progress. Keep an eye on the time as you work through the exam. There will be 120 questions in each 3-hour exam session, which means 40 questions per hour or 10 questions every 15 minutes. You may deviate some as you work through easier or more difficult questions, but be careful not to let yourself fall too far behind. Note that some test centers will not have clocks, but you will be notified of how much time is remaining in increments of 15 to 30 minutes.

One way to alleviate time pressure is to bank a few minutes by doing an easy topic first. Select a topic you feel comfortable with and start there. If you begin to struggle, move to a different topic. This strategy will help you gain confidence as you progress through the exam, and will also allow you to get a little ahead with your time allocation. Historically, the length and difficulty of ethics questions have made this topic a bad one to start with, even though it will be first during both sessions. Also, the gray areas covered by ethics questions often make you start to second-guess yourself, which is a bad precedent to set early in the exam. Be *very* careful if you jump around between topics to make sure you are marking the correct blanks on the answer sheet.

Have a game plan before you walk into the exam. We like the idea of doing an easy topic first to get going, but we do not recommend skipping around as you work through the exam. Do an easy topic, and then go back and do the remaining questions in order. Skipping back and forth may break your concentration and consume valuable time as you try to figure out what you have and have not done. Skipping around also increases the chance of marking the wrong blank on the answer sheet.

Never panic! Even if you fall behind, panicking will only make things worse. You won't think clearly and you'll miss easy questions. If you need a short break, put your pencil down and take a few deep breaths. The 30 seconds or so that this takes may very well help you think clearly enough to answer several additional questions correctly.

Catch your breath at lunch. As we mentioned before, it is a good idea to have a lunch destination planned beforehand. You may or may not want to join other candidates for lunch. If you do talk to other candidates, do not let their comments influence you. They may say the exam is easier or more difficult than they expected, but they might not be correct about how well they are doing. If you want, you can review a little at lunch. That's fine. But if you need to relax for a few minutes, that may do you just as much good as an additional 30-minute cram session. Do what you are most comfortable with.

Question Formats at Level I

Here are some guidelines CFA Institute adheres to in constructing questions for the Level I exam:

- Each question draws on one or more Learning Outcome Statements.
- Terminology and symbols will be consistent with those used in the readings (and, therefore, the SchweserNotes).
- Candidates do not need to know the numbers for specific Standards of Practice.
- Empirical results cited in the readings are not tested.
- The exam does not reuse old questions. All questions are new.
- Distractors (the incorrect choices) are written to capture the most common mistakes a candidate is likely to make on a question.
- Each question has three answer choices.
- "None of the above," "all of the above," and "not enough information" are not used.
- The words "true," "false," and "except" do not appear in the question stems. Instead, the questions use phrases like "most accurate," "least likely," or "closest to."
- Every question has its own stem and answer choices. The Level I exam does not have any multiple-part questions.
- Written answer choices are arranged from shortest to longest.
- Numeric answer choices are arranged from lowest to highest.

As to the format of Level I questions, you can expect two main varieties.

1. Sentence completion with three choices, such as the following:

   When yields increase, bond prices:
   A. fall.
   B. rise.
   C. are unaffected.

2. A complete question with three answer choices:

   If the U.S. Federal Reserve decreases its fed funds target rate by 1% and nominal long-term interest rates increase, which of the following is the *most likely* reason?
   A. The Fed also increased its target for long-term rates.
   B. Changes in long-term rates always are opposite to changes in the fed funds target rate.
   C. The expansionary monetary policy action caused an increase in expected future inflation.

Some questions may employ a two-column format. This type often tests two separate questions that each have only two possible answers: true/false or up/down. These may be either in the sentence-completion format or in the question-answer format with yes/no choices:

If a company chooses to capitalize significant advertising costs in the current period, how will this affect CFO and CFI, respectively?

	CFO	CFI
A.	Increase	Decrease
B.	Decrease	Decrease
C.	Decrease	Increase

With respect to the use of the CFA designation, do the Standards allow the initials CFA to be:

	used as a noun?	in larger type than the charterholder's name?
A.	No	No
B.	No	Yes
C.	Yes	Yes

No matter which format you encounter, the advice is the same—read the question carefully, and make sure you answer what is being asked. Two-column questions not only allow the testing of yes/no and up/down types of questions, they can also effectively lengthen the exam and allow more material to be tested.

Specific Types of Questions You Should Expect

It is very difficult to generalize Level I questions. Some are straightforward, some look straightforward but have a trick to them, and some are just confusing. CFA Institute's objective is to evaluate your grasp of the Level I Candidate Body of Knowledge. They do not set out to confuse or frustrate you, although that *is* a common result.

Following are some general types of questions and answers to expect.

Cause and Effect Problems

Part of the reason Level I CFA questions seem so difficult is because they ask you to apply your knowledge in ways you may not expect. Many questions combine more than one LOS or ask you to reason out the results and implications of a given series of events. These questions require some thought and will definitely be more difficult if you are not well-rested, or if you are stressed out.

Essential Exam Strategies

Long Questions

Look out for these. They are major time-burners. The worst areas are Ethics and Financial Reporting and Analysis. In both areas, you get a lot of irrelevant information, so try to weed out the confusion factors and focus on what's important. It often helps to *read the end of the question first* and then know what information is relevant as you read the body of the question.

Two-Column Questions

Keep a few things in mind with these types of questions:

- Two concepts are being tested in one question.
- These questions often test a calculation with a qualitative question rather than a quantitative one (but you still need to know the formulas).
- If you can get one column right, you will either be able to choose the correct letter answer or at least eliminate one of the choices.

In questions like these, if you can answer one but not the other, eliminate the wrong choice, make a guess, and go on. Don't let these types of questions take more than a minute and a half.

Tempting but Unnecessary Calculations

CFA Institute is interested in testing your grasp of the Level I curriculum. They are not particularly interested in whether or not you can use your calculator. CFA Institute has always emphasized the qualitative grasp of a concept over the quantitative "number crunching" type question. You will see questions that appear to call for long, complex calculations. Before you start wearing down your calculator battery, spend a moment to see if there is a short cut. Here is a question on debt securities to emphasize this point.

1. Given the spot rates in the table, the 1-year forward rate two years from now is:

Time (years)	Annual Spot Rate
1	15.0%
2	12.5%
3	10.0%
4	7.5%

A. −3.21%.
B. 5.17%.
C. 10.00%.

The correct answer is B. This is an example of a calculation question where you can look at the answer choices and reason out a correct answer without doing any calculations. Think about this question for a minute. The spot yield curve is declining. The one-year rate two years from now will have to be a rate such that after earning 12.5% for two years, you will end up with an average return over three years of 10%. The answer *has* to be less than 10%, right? A spot rate can't be negative, and B is the only choice less than 10%. If you want to do the calculation, it is:

$$\frac{(1+S_3)^3}{(1+S_2)^2} - 1 = 2y1y; \quad \frac{(1+0.10)^3}{(1+0.125)^2} - 1 = 2y1y; \quad 2y1y = 5.17\%$$

This question is an example of how taking a few seconds and applying some big picture understanding can actually save you some time. Also, if you did the calculation, you could use the preceding logic to check yourself.

2.   An annual-pay three-year note with an 8% coupon has a yield to maturity of 8%. An analyst's pricing model forecasts that if the benchmark yield curve shifts up by 50 basis points, the bond's price will decrease to 98.75, and if the benchmark curve shifts down by 50 basis points, the bond's price will increase to 100.25. The bond's effective convexity is *closest* to:
    A. −400.
    B. 30.
    C. 240.

The correct answer is A. At first glance, this looks like a calculation that requires the formula for effective convexity. But step back for a moment and look at the information given. With an 8% coupon and an 8% yield to maturity, the bond's price equals par value. For equal-sized changes in the benchmark curve, the estimated price increase is less than the estimated price decrease. This is opposite what we would expect for a bond that has positive convexity. This bond must have negative convexity and choice A is the only answer that is negative.

If you prefer, you can do the calculation:

$$\text{effective convexity} = \frac{V_- + V_+ - 2V_0}{(\Delta \text{curve})^2 \, V_0} = \frac{100.25 + 98.75 - 2(100)}{(0.005)^2 (100)} = -400$$

Essential Exam Strategies

Indirect or Confusing Wording

Despite what you might hear from other candidates, we honestly don't think CFA Institute purposely writes confusing questions. It is more likely that a particular question is trying to approach a concept from an unusual perspective. That is a good way to test your grasp of a concept, but sometimes the wording makes it difficult to figure out what is being tested. If you get confused by a question, think it through but don't waste too much time on it. Remember, you are probably not the only one scratching your head.

"Distractor" Answers That Are True But Not Correct

These are answer choices that seem like good answers for any of several reasons:

- They might be true, but not appropriate answers (or at least not the best answer).
- They might be consistent with irrelevant information provided in the question.
- They might include "buzzwords" or common misconceptions about a concept.

Be very careful with these types of distractors because they may make sense even though they are wrong. They may also make you think you could defend them as an answer choice. You might think, "Well, they want me to answer 'A,' but I think 'B' is okay and I can argue the point with anyone." Think again—you will never get to argue the point. Instead, select the *best* answer that is true all of the time and applies in every case, not the one you think could work.

Answer Choices That Can Be Eliminated

We have stressed the importance of reading every answer choice before making your selection. This strategy will help you avoid missing a better answer. Similarly, when you are struggling with a question, eliminate the worst answer to narrow your choices and improve your odds of earning some points.

INDEX

A

ability to bear risk 194
absolute advantage 82
absolute risk objectives 194
absorption approach 88
accelerated depreciation method 106
accounting equation 91
accounting profit 55
accounting return on equity 211
accounts 94
accounts payable 114
accounts receivable 114
accrual accounting 96
accrual method 102
accrued expenses 96
accrued revenue 96
accumulated other comprehensive income 117
action lag 81
active investment strategy 206
additional paid-in capital 94
addition rule 21
adjustable-rate mortgage 243
adjusted trial balance 96
adverse opinion 92
affirmative covenants 227
agency bonds 233
agency RMBS 244
aggregate demand curve 71
aggressive accounting 151
allocational efficiency 203
alternative hypothesis 34
alternative investments 278
alternative markets 197
alternative trading systems (ATS) 199
American depository receipts (ADRs) 210
American options 262

amortization 105, 107
amortizing structure 228
angel investing stage 282
annuity 9
antidilutive securities 109
arbitrage opportunity 263
arc elasticity of demand 51
arithmetic mean 14
ascending price (English) auction 47
ask price 201
ask size 201
asset-backed securities 198
asset-based models 219
assets 90, 94
audit reports 92
auto loan ABS 246
available-for-sale securities 116
average age 139
average cost method 106
average cost pricing 67
average revenue 56

B

backfill bias 279
backup lines of credit 233
backwardation 284
balance of payments 85
balance sheet 90, 112
balloon payment 228, 243
bank 176
bank discount yield 13
banker's acceptances 173
barriers to developing a single set of standards 98
barter transaction 104
base currency 86
basic accounting equation 95
basic EPS 109
basis point 250

Index

©2015 Kaplan, Inc.

Z

Notes